# RELIGIOUS FREEDOM, REI ~ DISCRIMINATION AND T

This book considers the extent to which
workplace, with particular reference to th
nation provided by the Employment Equa                      ჟulations
2003. It establishes a principled basis for dete.              ჟpe of religious
freedom at work, and considers the interacti          ᎥᎥ of religion with the
right not to be discriminated against on grounc      religion.

Discrimination on grounds of religion and belief within the workplace raises
many complex and contested issues, not least because of the multi-faceted nature
of religious discrimination. Discrimination can occur where secular employers
refuse to employ or accommodate religious employees, as well as where religious
groups refuse to employ those of a different religion, or those of the same religion
whose interpretation or practice of the faith differs. Adding to the complexity is
the fact that freedom of religion is protected as a fundamental human right which
may be enjoyed by both religious individuals and religious groups. Although it is
not an absolute right, its importance to individuals means that religious freedom
may warrant a degree of protection in the work context.

The book begins with a study of the basis for protecting religious freedom and
considers the extent to which that right should be exercised in the specialised context of the workplace. It takes a comparative approach, considering the position in
other common law jurisdictions (the USA and Canada), and within the European
Union. It locates the debate surrounding these issues within a philosophical and
theoretical framework in which the importance of freedom of religion, and its role
within the workplace, is fully debated.

# Religious Freedom, Religious Discrimination and the Workplace

Lucy Vickers

·H A R T·
PUBLISHING

OXFORD AND PORTLAND, OREGON
2008

Published in North America (US and Canada) by
Hart Publishing
c/o International Specialized Book Services
920 NE 58th Avenue, Suite 300
Portland, OR 97213-3786
USA
Tel: +1 503 287 3093 or toll-free: (1) 800 944 6190
Fax: +1 503 280 8832
E-mail: orders@isbs.com
Website: http://www.isbs.com

Hart Publishing, 16C Worcester Place, OX1 2JW
Telephone: +44 (0)1865 517530 Fax: +44 (0)1865 510710
E-mail: mail@hartpub.co.uk
Website: http://www.hartpub.co.uk

British Library Cataloguing in Publication Data
Data Available

ISBN: 978-1-84113-687-5

Typeset by Hope Services, Abingdon
Printed and bound in Great Britain by
TJ International Ltd, Padstow, Cornwall

To my parents, Henry and Mary Blyth

# Acknowledgements

The research for this book was carried out whilst on research leave funded by the Arts and Humanities Research Council. I would like to thank the AHRC for their support, and Oxford Brookes University for providing matched funding to enable me to take sabbatical leave to complete this book. I would also like to thank the fellows of Lincoln College, Oxford for their hospitality and use of their SCR and library during my sabbatical year. Many individuals—friends, family and colleagues—have discussed the issues raised in the book with me, and have helped me to shape my ideas, in particular Professor Peter Edge and Chara Bakalis both of Oxford Brookes University, and Professor Chris McCrudden, of Lincoln College, Oxford. My thanks to you all. Thanks also go to Professor Terry Dworkin (Indiana University), Professor Peter Bowal (University of Calgary), Associate Professor Carolyn Evans (University of Melbourne) and Pauline Roberts (Cardiff) who read drafts of chapters and gave invaluable feedback.

# Contents

# Table of Cases

# Table of Legislation

## UK Statutes

## UK Statutory Instruments

## National Legislation

# 1

# Religious Discrimination and Religious Freedom at Work

## I Introduction

Freedom of religion is well established as a fundamental human right in international and domestic law. Yet the extent to which that freedom should be enjoyed in the context of the workplace is not so well established in the UK.[1] Although legislation protecting against religious discrimination was introduced at the end of 2003,[2] the interaction of the non-discrimination regulations with broader issues of religious freedom is not clear. The concepts of religious freedom and religious discrimination are clearly closely related: freedom of religion will be fettered if its exercise leads to discrimination at work.[3] Yet the right to religious freedom is not absolute, and limits placed on religious freedom in the context of work can be justified when necessary to protect the rights of others. There will be times when religious freedom may exist in the world outside, but may be legitimately restricted at work. The purpose of this book is to examine the interaction of the rules on religious discrimination with the right to religious freedom and to contribute to the debate over the proper limits on religious freedom in the workplace.[4]

The aim of recent non-discrimination legislation would appear to be to protect the civil liberties as well as the social and economic rights of members of different religious groups. It was introduced to comply with an EC Directive on equality at work,[5] in turn founded on Article 13, added to the EC Treaty in 1997, which provided powers for the EU to combat discrimination on grounds of sex, race, religion, disability age and sexual orientation. Viewed in the context of other equality and non-discrimination rights, the religious discrimination regulations can be seen to form part of a comprehensive system to address social and

---

[1] Protection was introduced in Northern Ireland in the Fair Employment Acts 1976 and 1989, and replaced by the Fair Employment and Treatment (Northern Ireland) Order 1998.

[2] The Employment Equality (Religion and Belief) Regulations 2003.

[3] The relationship is discussed in more detail in chapter three.

[4] The focus of what follows is on the regulation of religious interests in the employment relationship. It does not consider religious discrimination in the provision of goods and services, as prohibited by the Equality Act 2006.

[5] Directive 2000/78/EC establishing a general framework for equal treatment in employment and occupation [2000] OJ L303/16 (the Employment Equality Directive).

economic disadvantage, where such disadvantage is linked to membership of particular groups.[6] Viewed from this perspective, the right to religious freedom at work is most likely to bring to mind images of employees from religious minorities being protected against direct discrimination caused by prejudice on the part of employers. It will also protect against more indirect forms of discrimination, for example, where employers unreasonably refuse to adapt uniforms to be compatible with religious dress codes, or refuse to adapt working time to allow time off for major religious festivals. The religious discrimination regulations would also fill gaps in the protection against race discrimination, whereby discrimination against Sikhs and Jews was prohibited,[7] but discrimination against Muslims was not.[8]

However, the fuller picture of what non-discrimination on religious grounds may entail is more complex. This is largely because of the multi-dimensional nature of religious discrimination: religious individuals may not only be victims of discrimination, but may also discriminate against others. For example, religious groups may want to employ priests or other key workers, or may run a social or commercial enterprise in order to raise funds or as an element of their mission. They may want to keep themselves separate from non-members and may discriminate against others in order to do so. Moreover, discrimination may occur between individuals of different religions or between those of the same faith, but whose level of commitment or interpretation of the faith differs. Thus prohibiting discrimination on grounds of religion in order to reduce economic disadvantage experienced by religious minorities introduces a range of further questions regarding the scope of religious freedom which should be enjoyed by religious employers.

A further reason for complexity in determining the correct parameters of religious freedom at work is that there are many different types of workplace. What is appropriate for a small religious employer may not be appropriate in a larger secular workplace, and may differ again with respect to public sector employment. Even within the public sector there may be diversity in terms of what is appropriate, as the border line between the public sector and the private sector is not always clear.[9] The fact that some publicly funded services are delivered through bodies which are religious in nature adds to the complexity here. For example, religious schools can be state funded and yet remain religious foundations, and religious groups are involved in delivery of a range of other services such as adoption services, and services for young people, which are either directly or indirectly funded by the state.[10] The range of different types of employment in which religious

---

[6] For a full discussion of the European policy regarding the Directive see M Bell, *Anti-Discrimination Law and the European Union* (Oxford, OUP, 2002).

[7] This is because it amounted to discrimination on grounds of ethnic group: *Mandla v Lee* [1983] 2 AC 548, *Seide v Gillette* [1980] IRLR 427.

[8] *Tariq v Young* Case 247738/88. Muslims can come from a range of ethnic groups.

[9] See ch 3 and D Oliver, 'Common Values in Public and Private Law and the Public/Private Divide' [1997] *PL* 630.

[10] See the work of the Catholic Children's Society. See also the work of the Children's Society providing support for children and young people at risk and which receives funding in part from central government (Annual Report 2005–6, The Children's Society).

freedom may be exercised is thus very wide, and means that it is difficult to determine a simple answer to the question of how religion should be treated at work. However, finding an answer will become increasingly necessary as the government seeks to increase the involvement of faith based organisations in the provision of public services.[11]

Complexity also arises from the fact that as well as protecting the positive rights of religious individuals and groups, the right to religious freedom may have a negative dimension. It may also encompass a right not to believe, and indeed a right to be free from religion or religious influence. Thus the interests of workers who do not wish to be subjected to the beliefs of a religious group or individual also need to be taken into account. Add to this the fact that there are many different religions and also different groups within those religions, and that the very definition of religion is contested, and it is clear that determining the proper scope for religious discrimination protection and religious freedom at work is not a straightforward task.

Before considering the ways in which the law might respond to the range of difficulties which emerge when considering the proper scope of religious freedom in the workplace, it is important to identify some of the problems religious individuals experience in terms of employment, as well as some of the conflicts that may arise if religious freedom is to be protected at work.

## II  Religion in the UK

According to the 2001 census,[12] Christianity is the religion of 72 per cent of the population, although other data suggests that a much smaller percentage of the population are regular church goers.[13] Fifteen per cent of the population declared themselves to have no religion, but this group is likely to be much larger if one adds in those who give Christianity as their religion for the purposes of the census, but whose identity with the faith is largely nominal. In terms of religious grouping, five per cent of the population belong to a non-Christian religion: the largest group is Muslim (3% of the population, but 52% of the non-Christian population), followed by Hindus (1%) Sikhs (0.6%) Jews (0.5%), Buddhists (0.3%) and finally other religions such as Spiritualists, Pagans, Jain, Wicca, Rastafarian, Bahá'í, and Zoroastrian where the percentages are very small.

---

[11] See, for example, Press Release, 11 January 2007, from The Department for Work and Pensions, in which the Minister for Employment and Welfare Reform, Jim Murphy, said he wants to see a greater role for faith-based groups in UK welfare delivery.

[12] See Office of National Statistics, Focus on Religion, available at <http://www.statistics.gov.uk/focuson/religion> (accessed 5 July 2007).

[13] In a poll published in *The Guardian* (London, 23 December 2006) only 33% of those questioned described themselves as 'a religious person'.

Although eight per cent refused to answer the question on religion, and it is clear that the number of Christians is far lower in terms of those with an active religious involvement, the number of religious adherents remains high, and the range of beliefs is wide. Even within Christianity, the numbers attending religious services once a month are high. Data for the Church of England suggests that 1.7 million people take part in a Church of England service each month, and data for the Catholic Church estimates the number of Catholics as around four million, with weekly Mass attendance at just under one million.[14] With respect to the minority religions, the numbers of adherents identified in the 2001 Census were in the thousands.[15]

Within the religious groupings, a number of subgroups exist. Taking the example of Christianity, huge variations within the religion exist. Not only is there the divide between Protestant, Catholic and Orthodox churches, but even within the Protestant church there are Anglican, Baptist, Methodist, and numerous other denominations. Within the groupings, some would not classify the others as truly Christian denominations. Thus the potential exists for discrimination between religions and within them.

Of course, even among those declaring a religious affiliation, levels of commitment will vary enormously from the nominally religious to the 'obdurate believer'.[16] For some, belief is central to their sense of identity: it will determine many if not most aspects of their lives, and they will not yield their religious beliefs or practices to other interests. Others may identify themselves as believers, and may even attend religious services or ceremonies, but their beliefs may not be particularly strong, and religion may not be the primary focus for their sense of identity. For such individuals, conflicts between religious belief and the needs of the workplace may be minor or non-existent. For example, where a conflict arises between a work dress code and religious tradition, some may be happy to ignore the religious tradition in order to accommodate an employer's demands. Similarly, many Christians will not believe that they are forbidden to work on a Sunday. Of those who do, some will refuse to work, while others may decide that they are prepared to work nonetheless, or at least are prepared to work on occasion. Clearly 'obdurate believers' are likely to have more difficulty in reconciling religion and work than those with more yielding views. The same may be said with respect to non-belief. Many lack their own religious beliefs but are happy to accept manifestations of belief by others. Others may be classified as 'obdurate unbelievers', who object to being subjected to others' demonstrations of belief. Such individuals may not be happy to work in an environment where religious symbols are present, or where religious dress is worn by staff.

[14] Statistics available on the website for the Catholic Church of England and Wales <http://www.catholic-ew.org.uk> (accessed 1 February 2007 and the Church of England website <http://www.cofe.anglican.org> (accessed 1 February 2007).
[15] Spiritualists (32,000), Pagans (31,000), Jain (15,000), Wicca (7,000), Rastafarian (5,000), Bahá'í (5,000) and Zoroastrian (4,000).
[16] The phrase comes from A Bradney, 'Faced by Faith' in D Oliver *et al* (eds), *Faith in Law* (Oxford, Hart Publishing, 2000).

To an extent, then, declared religious affiliation or non-affiliation may not tell us much about the effect of religious belief on the workplace because, although susceptible to general classification, the effects of religious belief or its absence are highly personal.

## III  Experience of Discrimination

According to data from the National Statistics Office, employment patterns vary according to religion. For example, in 2004, Jewish, Muslim and Buddhist people were most likely to be self-employed,[17] and some religious groups were disproportionately represented in particular industries, such as Muslim men working in distribution, hotel and restaurant industries, and Jewish men being more likely than men from any other group to work in the banking, finance and insurance industry.[18] Of course, data relating to employment patterns and education of itself may not provide evidence of discrimination in employment, but the uneven distribution of religious groups across employment sectors at the very least is not suggestive of employment being discrimination-free.

A similarly uneven distribution as between religious groups can be seen in relation to educational attainment. In 2004 the religious group with the lowest level of qualifications was Muslims and they were also the least likely to have degrees or equivalent qualifications. After Muslims, Sikhs were the next most likely to have no qualifications, followed by Buddhists, Christians and Hindus. Jews were the least likely to have no qualifications. For those obtaining degree level education, Jews (44%), Buddhists (30%) and Hindus (29%) were the most likely to have a degree. Those without a religion were more likely to have a degree (22%) than Sikhs (20%) and Christians (16%).[19] Although not directly related to employment, levels of educational achievement are closely linked to access to and success within employment, and so inequality in education levels is likely to lead to differences in career prospects.

[17] One third of Jewish people were self-employed, and one fifth of Muslims and Buddhists, compared with one in ten of the rest of the population: Office of National Statistics Focus on Religion, available at <http://www.statistics.gov.uk/focuson/religion> (accessed 5 July 2007).

[18] 37% of Muslim men in employment were working in the distribution, hotel and restaurant industries compared with 17% of Christian men and no more than 27% of men in any other group. More than one in seven Muslim and Sikh men worked in the transport and communication sectors compared with less than one in ten from any other religious group. Jewish men were more likely than men from any other religion to work in the banking, finance and insurance industry: (Office of National Statistics Focus on Religion, available at <http://www.statistics.gov.uk/focuson/religion> (accessed 5 July 2007).

[19] In 2004 a third of Muslims of working age in Great Britain had no qualifications, the highest proportion for any religious group. They were also the least likely to have degrees or equivalent qualifications (12%): Office of National Statistics, Focus on Religion, available at <http://www.statistics.gov.uk/focuson/religion> (accessed 5 July 2007).

The statistical suggestion of the presence of discrimination in the workplace is complemented by other evidence of workplace discrimination. In a study commissioned by the Home Office and published in 2001,[20] discrimination was found both on grounds of religious status, such as refusal to employ people because of their religious beliefs, and on grounds of religious practice, such as refusal to accept a religious dress code. Employment was found to be one of the areas of life where religious individuals were most likely to experience unfair treatment.[21] Discrimination was marginally more frequent in the private than the public sector although the difference was not large. Fewer incidents of discrimination were reported in the voluntary sector. Incidents of unfair treatment were reported by all religious groups including Christians, but Muslims reported a consistently higher level of unfair treatment, both in terms of the number of individuals reporting incidents and the number reporting incidents as frequent rather than occasional.

Unfair treatment was identified in the behaviour of managers and colleagues as well as in the policies and practices of employers. Examples of discriminatory practices include being required to work on Saturdays or Sundays, being subjected to dress restrictions, suffering reduced promotion prospects and experiencing disrespectful attitudes towards religious customs. One example given in the Home Office report is of a Muslim woman who believed she was unsuccessful in a job application because she refused to shake hands with the interviewer at the end of the interview. Other examples include a Muslim woman who felt she was judged negatively because she would not drink alcohol at work social occasions; a Sikh woman who was moved from her work in a bakery for wearing a bangle, even though it tested negative for bacteria; and Muslim women treated less favourably for wearing headscarves.

The concerns raised in the Home Office study are reflected in the early case law under the Employment Equality (Religion and Belief) Regulations, with cases involving requirements to work on Saturdays or Sundays,[22] and disputes over dress[23] and grooming codes.[24] One particularly high profile case involved the

---

[20] P Weller *et al, Religious Discrimination in England and Wales*, Home Office Research Study No 220, February 2001.

[21] The other areas identified as being most likely to give rise to experiences of unfairness were education and the media.

[22] See *James v MSC Cruises* 12 April 2006, case 2203173/05. Reported in *Equal Opportunities Review* No 157, October 2007. A member of the Seventh-day Adventist Church was dismissed for refusing to work on a Saturday, but the Tribunal held that there was no indirect discrimination as the requirement to work on Saturday was justifiable on business grounds. See also *Williams-Drabble v Pathway Care Solutions Ltd* 11 January 2005, case 2601718/04 reported in *Equal Opportunities Review* No 141, May 2005 where a refusal to change a rota requiring Sunday working was indirect discrimination under the Regulations.

[23] See *Ferri v Key Languages Ltd* 9 August 2004, case 2302172/04, *Equal Opportunities Review* No 136, December 2004. The case involved the wearing of overtly religious jewellery. The case turned on other matters, but the Tribunal suggested that adverse inferences may be drawn in a discrimination case from an instruction to remove religious jewellery.

[24] See *Mohmed v West Coast Trains Ltd* UKEAT/0682/05, which involved an instruction to a customer services assistant to trim his beard. Mr Mohmed wished to retain his beard for religious reasons. The claim of religious discrimination was rejected.

dismissal of a member of teaching support staff for refusing to remove a veil (which covered her face while leaving her eyes visible), when providing bilingual language support in the class room.[25] The EAT decided that the refusal to allow the member of staff to teach while wearing the veil did not amount to indirect religious discrimination. It acknowledged the religious interests of the teaching assistant, but held that the restriction on wearing the veil was proportionate in order to uphold the interests of the children in receiving the best instruction possible. In reaching its decision, the school had undertaken an investigation and had observed that teaching was more effective when the face was uncovered. This also accorded with the advice available from the local authority's education service that face coverings were inappropriate for teaching because they prevented children from catching non-verbal signals from the teacher's face. The school had not therefore acted on the basis of subjective assumptions in reaching its conclusion, and had taken seriously the assistant's religious interests. Possible ways to accommodate the request to wear the veil had been investigated, but none had proved practical. The case does seem to turn on its particular facts and cannot be taken as a precedent on whether schools or other employers can restrict the wearing of the headscarf. What it illustrates, however, is an acceptance that dress codes such as restrictions on the wearing of the veil or headscarf will involve indirect discrimination, unless the restriction can be justified as being a proportionate means of achieving a legitimate aim.

In research undertaken by ACAS about the use of the Regulations, the concerns raised are similar again to those brought up by early case law and predicted as a result of the Home Office study. Around half of the religion and belief cases dealt with by ACAS have been brought by Muslims, with the rest split between Christians, Jews, Hindus, Sikhs and those describing themselves as 'non-Catholic' bringing cases against Catholic schools. In many cases, individuals have been dismissed after having made requests to their employers to have their religious needs accommodated. Claims have raised a fairly wide range of concerns. Many cases have involved bullying and harassment, with behaviour from managers including verbal abuse, giving individuals impossible deadlines, subjecting claimants to increased scrutiny, denying access to training, refusing holiday requests, and disputes over dress codes. Another common cause of disputes has been the practice of religious employers recruiting or promoting only those who share the organisation's beliefs, with a number of cases involving recruitment or promotion in Catholic schools.[26]

---

[25] *Azmi v Kirklees Metropolitan Council* [2007] ICR 1154. The case involved a claim for direct and indirect discrimination, harassment and victimisation. Ms Azmi was successful only in the victimisation claim as a result of the handling of the claim by the local authority. The case is discussed further below at p 164.

[26] B Savage, 'Sexual orientation and religion or belief discrimination in the workplace' (ACAS, London, 2007, ref 01/07), and A Denvir *et al*, 'The experiences of sexual orientation and religion or belief discrimination employment tribunal claimants' (ACAS, London, 2007, ref 02/07).

# IV  Tackling Religious Discrimination

The examples outlined in the reports and cases discussed above make clear that the experience of religious discrimination in the workplace is a reality for many people. However, moving from identifying the presence of a problem to determining the best way to tackle it is never easy. In the case of religious discrimination, particular difficulties arise because of the fact that any rights created to protect the religious freedom of individuals in their working lives will also apply to those of no religion. Any protection against religious discrimination will also apply equally to religious employers who are restricted in their freedom to discriminate in favour of religious staff. As a result of the restrictions which non-discrimination protection imposes on the freedom of religious bodies to choose staff who share their religion, some religious groups voiced fierce opposition to the non-discrimination protection, even though they might have been thought to have been the intended beneficiaries of the protection.[27]

The reason for the opposition was two-fold. First was a concern that religious bodies will not be able to staff their organisations with fellow believers. Although exceptions apply where being of a particular religion is genuinely necessary for the job, some religious bodies have felt that the exemptions are too narrow. A second concern is that the preference of religious bodies for fellow believers may result in other forms of discrimination, such as discrimination on grounds of sexual orientation, protection against which was introduced at the same time as the religious discrimination regulations. Both these concerns arise from the inherent conflict that can arise between eradicating less favourable treatment on grounds of religion and protection for religious freedom in a broader sense. Whilst these concepts are inherently linked, they can also be seen to be in tension.[28]

## Conflicts Arising from the Exercise of Religious Freedom at Work

The first area of conflict between non-discrimination rights and the right to religious freedom concerns the exception to the non-discrimination rules for religious bodies, to enable them to appoint religious staff to undertake work of a religious nature. If the exception is too broad, and any employer can require staff to be of a particular religion because it deems the employment to be religious, this would clearly create a large lacuna in the protection available. It would be particularly difficult where employers are in sectors, such as education, where a significant proportion of employers are religious in nature. To allow church schools to require all staff to be Christian, for example, could significantly reduce the

---

[27] For example, see the briefing of the Christian Institute, *European Threat to Religious Freedom* (London, The Christian Institute, 2001).

[28] See further discussion at p 43.

employment prospects of non-Christian teachers.[29] However, restricting any exception to those who carry out an explicitly religious role at work means that religious groups may have to employ those who do not share their beliefs. This restricts the freedom of religious groups to employ fellow believers. Such restrictions do not operate for other types of organisation, who can demand loyalty to the employer's ethos from all staff without being subject to legal scrutiny in the same way. For example, a development agency can quite legitimately require all staff to be committed to the aims of the agency, without breaching any discrimination rules. However, a requirement for a religious commitment imposed on all staff in a religious organisation may be too extensive to come within the scope of the exception for religious employment provided in the non-discrimination regulations.[30]

This conflict, however, can be exaggerated. The UK Religion and Belief Regulations do allow for religious requirements to be imposed in order to maintain the religious ethos of a religious employer. These must be proportionate, a concept discussed in detail in later chapters, and this effectively leaves the question of whether it is appropriate to impose such a requirement open for determination by a tribunal, taking into account the particular features of the job and the organisation. Perhaps a more valid concern, however, is that uncertainty over whether a particular job is covered by the exception will lead to religious employers erring on the side of caution and opening up jobs to those of different beliefs which may not, strictly, need to be opened up. In this way it may be that the religious freedom of groups to employ or work with those of the same religion is chilled rather than specifically legally limited, as employers impose more far-reaching limits on themselves than those which are required by the law. However, although valid, concerns about the consequences of incorrect understandings of the law are of a different order to concerns about the correct ambit of the law, and it is the latter which is under consideration here.

Another area of serious contention is the difficulty caused where rights to religious freedom conflict with other rights such as rights to equality on grounds of sexual orientation, or rights to be free from religion. Taking sexual orientation equality first, there is a clear conflict between religious freedom and non-discrimination on grounds of sexual orientation with regard to certain religious groups. Some (but not all) Christians, Jews and Muslims are hostile to homosexuality on religious grounds, believing it to be forbidden. They will be unwilling to employ homosexual staff, to work with homosexual staff, or to offer services to homosexual clients. These different types of sexual orientation discrimination will cause different difficulties to organisations. Religious employers may refuse to employ people because they are gay. This may be on grounds of sexual orientation, or on the ground of religion, for example, if they believe that the individual cannot be in good standing with the religion if they live in a homosexual relationship.

---

[29] See discussion at pp 168–173.
[30] See discussion at pp 135–137.

The difficulties are not limited to religious employers. Secular employers will need to decide how to deal with religious individuals who will not provide services to gay clients, or who have religious objections to working closely with gay staff. For example, a social worker could refuse to assess a gay couple who are seeking to adopt. Or a religious employee may express a preference not to share an office with a gay member of staff. Such staff could argue that their religious beliefs are not being respected if their views are not taken into account. On the other hand, accommodation of such views will involve sexual orientation discrimination.

Other difficulties can arise in terms of conflict between the rights of religious and non-religious employees. Some staff may wish to work in a religiously neutral atmosphere. It is impossible to reconcile their interests with those of religious staff who wish to manifest their religious affiliation in the way they dress or behave at work. If an employer does not let an employee wear religious dress at work, this may be indirectly discriminatory on grounds of religion, unless it can be justified, for example on grounds of protecting the interests of those who want to work in a neutral atmosphere. Similarly, if an employer does not let an employee offer services to the public in religious dress this may indirectly discriminate against the employee on grounds of religion, unless it can be justified in the name of those who want neutral service provision. It is not at all clear how such conflicts should be resolved: one individual's religious preference may offset another individual's secular preferences.

## Resolving the Conflict in the Workplace

The conflicts identified above involve a range of individual and group rights, based on religious interests and on equality rights. The context in which this conflict is played out is the workplace, a forum in which rights are rarely enjoyed in absolute terms. For example, the right to freedom of religion can, arguably, be protected by the freedom of an individual not to enter a particular workplace. Put plainly, while an individual may have a clear right to freedom of religion, he or she does not have a clear right to exercise that freedom at work. However, to restrict religious freedom to the world outside work is to restrict religious freedom to a significant extent and would certainly harm the economic and social interests of religious individuals. Finding some compromise whereby religious individuals can work, where to do so does not disproportionately interfere with the rights of others, must be the aim of any legal regulation of the issue.

Finding such a compromise is the aim of much of what follows. The third chapter considers why religion should be protected in the workplace at all. It suggests that protection is justified on the basis that it helps to uphold fundamental interests in equality, autonomy and human dignity, but that protection may be limited where proportionate, taking into account other conflicting rights. The chapter also examines the concept of proportionality and how it should be determined in the context of the workplace. It seeks to identify a range of factors of relevance when deciding the proper scope for protection, and to develop a model for deter-mining proportionality in the context of religion and work. This model is then used as a measure of the adequacy of the legal protection available for religious interests at work. The fourth chapter assesses human rights standards on religious freedom as they may apply at work, with reference to the jurisprudence of the European Convention on Human Rights, and the Human Rights Act 1998. Subsequent chapters consider the current workplace protection in the UK against discrimination on grounds of religion and belief, and compares this protection with that available elsewhere in the European Union, in the United States and in Canada. Before turning to consider these issues, however, a fundamental issue of definition must be addressed: what is meant by religion and belief? It is not intended to provide a comprehensive review of the question here, but a working definition needs to be produced for the purposes of the discussion in the rest of what follows, and this is the subject of the next chapter.

# 2

## Seeking a Definition of Religion and Belief

Before looking at the reasons for protecting religion at work, the preliminary question of how to define religion needs to be considered. The question of what constitutes a religion is the subject of much debate which is well rehearsed elsewhere,[1] and an exhaustive examination of the question will not be undertaken here. It is important, however, to begin with some attempt to define one of the main terms to be used throughout what follows.

## I  What is 'Religion'?

Although there are many recognised religions in the world, simple attempts to define the term 'religion' almost immediately run into difficulty. A belief in God, which may unite Judaism, Islam and Christianity, is clearly insufficient, as some religions such as Hinduism are polytheistic. A move to 'belief in God or gods' immediately comes up against the fact that Buddhism does not include belief in a 'god'. And yet these are recognised as major world religions, and they will have been within the contemplation of those who drafted the various international documents protecting the right to freedom of religion. The difficulties are compounded once one considers less well known religions such as various pagan traditions, and the rise in new religions whose traditions and beliefs may be undocumented and totally unfamiliar to the general population. And what of the 'religion' adhered to by only a handful or even only one person? Moreover, the

---

[1] For the debate in the USA on the definition of religion, see: 'Toward a Constitutional Definition of Religion' (1978) 91 *Harv LR* 1056; K Greenawalt, 'Religion as a Concept in Constitutional Law' (1984) 72 *California LR* 753; G Freeman III, 'The Misguided Search for the Constitutional Definition of Religion' (1983) 71 *Georgetown LJ* 1519; D N Feofanov, 'Definition of Religion: An Immodest Proposal' (1994) 23 *Hofstra LR* 309; R R French, 'From Yoder to Yoda: Models of Traditional, Modern and Post Modern Religion in U.S. Constitutional Law' (1979) *Arizona LR* 41; B Clements, 'Defining "Religion" in the First Amendment: A functional approach' (1989) 74 *Cornell L R* 352; R O Frame, 'Belief in a Non-Material Reality—A Proposed First Amendment Definition of Religion' (1992) *Univ of Illinois LR* 819; J Choper, 'Definition of "Religion" in the First Amendment' (1982) *Univ of Illinois LR* 579; M McConnell, 'The Origins and Historical Understanding of Free Exercise of Religions' (1990) 103 *Harvard LR* 1409. See also: W Sadurski, 'On Legal Definitions of Religion' (1989) 63 *Australia LJ* 834; and C G Hall, ' "Aggiornamento" Reflections upon the Contemporary Legal Concept of Religion' (1997) *Cambrian LR* 7.

question arises as to whether other belief systems, such as veganism, pacifism or communism, are protected, and whether their protection is predicated in them being classified in some way as analogous to religion. What is significant about the court decisions which have dealt with such questions is the marked reluctance of courts to get involved in creating an all-encompassing definition.

Indeed, the major international human rights documents do not give any detail on what is meant by religion. Under the ECHR, the protection extends to 'religion or belief', thus avoiding the need to identify exactly what constitutes religion, in contrast to other forms of belief. Nonetheless, to qualify for protection, the European Court has required that beliefs 'attain a certain level of cogency, seriousness cohesion and importance'.[2] Similarly, the UDHR avoids a definitive statement about what constitutes religion, in favour of broader terminology, which includes theistic, non-theistic and atheistic beliefs.[3]

It has been suggested that, in the case of the ECHR, the failure to produce a clear definition of terms was deliberate, given lack of agreement at the time of drafting, in particular over whether atheism should be included as a religion or belief.[4] Yet, the lack of definition does not appear to have hampered the Court and Commission on Human Rights from reaching decisions in cases regarding atheism,[5] Druidism,[6] Divine Light Zentrum,[7] Scientology,[8] Krishna Consciousness,[9] pacifism,[10] and veganism.[11]

It can be argued that the lack of a clear definition has some advantages.[12] In the first place, in many cases, the question of whether beliefs are religious in nature or not does not need to be answered precisely, as the case can be disposed of on other grounds. Indeed, when one considers the ECHR case law, it is clear that at times cases have been disposed of on other grounds, without addressing in depth whether the belief system in question was 'religious'. Where a ruling is required, if there is no set definition, there is no danger of courts being prevented from finding that a belief system is religious because of an outdated or under-inclusive definition. Courts are then in less danger of discriminating against newly established religions or those of minority groups. Without a set definition, courts can determine on the facts before them whether the beliefs should be protected, and

[2] *X, Y and Z v UK* (1982) 31 D&R 50, and *Campbell and Cosans v UK* (1982) 4 EHRR 293.
[3] See 'General Comment No 22 (48) on Article 18 UDHR by the UN Human Rights Committee' (1994) 15 *Human Rights LJ* 233, para 2.
[4] C Evans, *Freedom of Religion under the European Convention on Human Rights* (Oxford, OUP, 2001) 51; and C Evans, 'Religious Freedom in European Human Rights Law' in M Janis and C Evans (eds), *Religion and International Law* (The Hague, Martinus Nijhoff, 1999 and 2004) 389.
[5] *Angelini v Sweden* (1988) 10 EHRR 123 (Eur. Comm. HR).
[6] *Chappel v UK* (1988) 10 EHRR 510 (Eur. Comm. HR), *Pendragon v UK* (1998) EHRR CD 179.
[7] *Swami Omkaramamda and the Divine light Zentrum v Switzerland* (1981) 25 D&R 105 (Eur Comm HR).
[8] *X and the Church of Scientology v Sweden* (1976) 16 D&R 68.
[9] *ISKCON v UK* (1994) 76A D&R 90.
[10] *Arrowsmith v UK* (1978) 19 D&R 5.
[11] *H v UK* (1993) 16 EHRR CD 44.
[12] See W Sadurski, 'On Legal Definitions of Religion' (1989) 63 *Australia LJ* 834.

they can adapt the definition to the circumstances, and take into account modern developments in our understanding of religion.

A further reason for taking the view that no definition is needed is the fact that neither the European Convention on Human Rights, nor the Employment Equality (Religion and Belief) Regulations, restrict protection only to 'religion'. The ECHR refers to 'religion or belief' and the Regulations cover 'religion or philosophical belief'.[13] This means that the exact dividing line between religious and non-religious beliefs does not need to be drawn, and beliefs such as humanism and atheism will be covered. Despite their clear non-religious content, it is clear that these beliefs are intended to be protected, and yet equally clear that other non-religious views, such as political views, are not. Thus the coverage of belief as well as religion does not avoid the difficulty of definition—it just shifts location. The divide is located between 'religious or philosophical beliefs' which are subject to special protection, and other beliefs which are not. In order to determine on which side belief systems such as 'transcendental mediation' or 'veganism' should fall, one must still determine what is meant by the core terms 'religion' and 'philosophical belief'.

Tempting as it may be to avoid definition, to do so altogether leaves courts acting in a vacuum, and without any principles to guide them. It becomes difficult to predict how a court will make its assessment, and impossible to challenge any individual decision. Moreover, minority religions are particularly likely to be left unprotected.[14] A working definition of religion is therefore required, in order to provide a principled basis for deciding cases, and to help determine when a philosophical belief will qualify for protection. Any definition needs to be broad enough to be able to respond to new religions, but also clear enough to be applied to individual cases.[15] A full and lively academic debate exists surrounding the 'proper' definition of religion, a debate which can only be touched on here, in order to explain the definition which will be used in what follows.

The literature on the subject suggests three approaches to the definition of religion. First is a content-based definition, concerned with identifying the core content of beliefs which makes them religious in nature. Second is an attempt to reason by analogy with those religions which are universally recognised. The idea is to produce a list of key indicators of religion, against which to test those that are less well known. The final approach is to look at the purpose of protecting religion, and to work towards a purposive definition.

---

[13] Amended from 'similar philosophical belief' by s 77 Equality Act 2006.
[14] See 'Toward a Constitutional Definition of Religion' (1978) 91 *Harv LR* 1056.
[15] See P Cumper, 'Freedom of Thought, Conscience and Belief' in D Harris and S Joseph (eds), *The International Covenant on Civil and Political Rights and the United Kingdom* (Oxford, Clarendon Press, 1995) 359.

## Content-based Definitions

The simplest way to define a religion is to set out a series of beliefs which any religion will contain. The approach is seen in some of the early cases in the UK in which religions are defined as relating to a belief in God or some other supreme being. Clearly such a theistic definition is inadequate, as it fails to reflect a wide range of spiritualities which do not rely on the concept of an external 'supreme being'. Nonetheless, more inclusive definitions may be possible. One suggestion, based on the writing of Paul Tillich,[16] is that religion relates to a person's 'ultimate concern'. The idea is that, if we look deep enough, we all have concerns which are 'ultimate', in that they are absolute, unconditional and unqualified. These 'ultimate concerns' give meaning and orientation to our lives. In effect, everyone has a 'religion' so defined. Clearly the test is subjective; pretty much any belief can suffice as long as it is 'ultimate' for the believer, but this may be an advantage. Objective tests of religion run the danger of failing to protect minority or new religions because of their failure to meet 'objective' standards designed by the 'majority'.[17] A definition based on 'ultimate concern' is capable of including less well established religions, as well as philosophical movements such as humanism or atheism which do not have traditional religious roots.

However, the very inclusiveness of the definition is also its weakness. The suggestion that everyone has an 'ultimate concern' may be true, but by classifying all such views as 'religious' it leaves no space for those who identify themselves as a-religious. Moreover, the definition seems very subjective, and somewhat opaque, with no principled way to distinguish between, for example, an 'ultimate concern' with the music of Elvis and an 'ultimate concern' with the tenets of Islam.[18]

Although to define religion as an 'ultimate concern' may not be the answer, there have been many other suggestions of alternative content-based definitions. For example, Choper[19] has defined religion as concerning beliefs which have 'extra-temporal' consequences. Such a definition may help explain why religious adherents may make choices that seem totally irrational to the non-believer: a decision to refuse life saving medical treatment is not irrational if understood as a means of avoiding eternal damnation. The definition also provides a reason for the protection of religion: failure to obey religious rules has, in the view of the religious person, consequences beyond those which are visible and can be experienced in this world. Requiring someone to act in a way that they believe will have negative consequences which can last for eternity involves a serious injury to their well-being, which is difficult to equate with any disbenefit understood in secular terms. However, although the concept of 'extra-temporal consequences' may prove useful in understanding some religious activity, as a determinant of whether a belief

---

[16] P Tillich, *Dynamics of Faith* (New York, Harper & Row, 1958).

[17] See 'Toward a Constitutional Definition of Religion' (1978) 91 *Harv LR* 1056.

[18] T Macklem, 'Reason and Religion' in P Oliver *et al* (eds), *Faith in Law: Essays in Legal Theory* (Oxford, Hart Publishing, 2000) 79.

[19] J Choper, 'Definition of "Religion" in the First Amendment' (1982) *Univ of Illinois LR* 579.

system is religious or not it risks being under-inclusive: any belief system which does not include a belief in some sort of after-life will be excluded.[20]

A broader content-based definition is suggested by Feofanov[21]: religion is 'a manifestly non-rational (i.e. faith based) belief concerning the alleged nature of the universe, sincerely held'.[22] The definition does not require any particular organisational form or structure for a belief to be religious, but relies largely on non-rationality as the distinguishing feature of religion. The non-rationality of beliefs may provide the reason for protecting the beliefs, but it is not the non-rational nature of the beliefs alone which is the determining feature of religion under this definition. The writer points out that the non-rational beliefs must be about the nature of the universe, questions relating to our place in the universe and the meaning of our lives and deaths. '[N]on-rational beliefs about tomorrow's weather' should not, without more, be defined as religious. The definition suggested by Feofanov is attractive as it seems to be capable of explaining the difference between an 'ultimate concern' with Elvis, and an 'ultimate concern' with Islam.

However, the difficulty with definitions based on the content of the belief system is that they risk being under-inclusive, and in some cases potentially over-inclusive too. On the one hand, the definition can be too detailed, with the consequence that it is unable to develop and respond to developments in religious and philosophical thinking. It can also be based on very orthodox understandings of religion. On the other hand, definitions that are broad enough to encompass a full range of religions that exist or may exist in future become too opaque and meaningless: as with refusing to define at all, we are given no real principled basis for determining the content of religious beliefs. As a result of these difficulties, an alternative approach has been suggested: defining religion by analogy with those religions which are universally recognised as religions.

## Defining Religion by Analogy[23]

Defining religion by analogy with those religions that are well recognised may be an attractive approach. The idea here draws on the approach outlined by H L A Hart in *The Concept of Law*,[24] that most terms have a 'penumbra of uncertainty' surrounding the outer parameters of the meaning of the term; the extent of the penumbra can be determined by reasoning by analogy with the core meaning. For example, in discussing whether international law is really law, Hart compares it with municipal law, to see whether it shares its features. No one feature is sufficient

[20] For further criticism of Choper's approach see B Clements, 'Defining "Religion" in the First Amendment: A functional approach' (1989) 74 *Cornell LR* 352.

[21] DN Feofanov, 'Definition of Religion: An Immodest Proposal' (1994) 23 *Hofstra LR* 309.

[22] *Ibid* at 385.

[23] See, in particular, K Greenawalt, 'Religion as a Concept in Constitutional Law' (1984) 72 *California LR* 753; and G Freeman III, 'The Misguided Search for the Constitutional Definition of Religion' (1983) 71 *Georgetown LJ* 1519.

[24] H L A Hart, *The Concept of Law* (Oxford, Clarendon Press, 1961).

of itself to determine whether a system is 'legal', but if the two systems share enough important features then international law can be said to be legal in the same way as municipal law. A similar approach is used by Wittgenstein[25] to show that 'games' have no common shared feature, but that they share a family of resemblances. Such an approach to defining 'religion' overcomes the difficulties identified above, whereby each definition can be undermined by pointing to a set of 'religious' views which do not seem to match the definition. Instead, a number of criteria are given which are neither necessary nor sufficient in themselves to define religion but which, if they are present in sufficient quantity, can indicate that a belief system is religious, even though another religion may share none of the same criteria.

A range of criteria have been identified that indicate that a belief system is religious, largely drawing on the features of well established major world religions. Criteria include[26]: a belief in God or a supreme being; a comprehensive view of the world and human purposes; a belief in an after-life; communication with 'God' via worship and prayer; a particular perspective on moral obligations derived from a moral code or from a conception of God's nature; practices involving repentance and forgiveness of sins; 'religious' feelings of awe, guilt and adoration; the use of sacred texts; and organisation to facilitate the corporate aspects of religious practice and to promote and perpetuate beliefs and practices. A further criterion identified in one major US case which suggests definition by analogy is that

> the test of belief . . . is whether a given belief that is sincere and meaningful occupies a place in the life of its possessor parallel to that filled by orthodox belief in God.[27]

The idea is that many of these criteria are present in the 'core' religions that are well accepted as religions. However those who advocate the approach[28] are clear that no single feature is determinative: should one or more be missing, the belief system can still be a religion. So polytheist or atheist beliefs may still be religious, as would beliefs which do not link a claim to transcendental reality to a particular moral practice. Less well known 'religions' can be tested against the list. If they share sufficient characteristics with what we can agree to be religions, then we can classify them as religions too.

This approach has several advantages over the content-based definitions of religion, largely due to its flexibility. It is not prescriptive, and is capable of adapting over time to reflect developing understandings of religion. However, it has been criticised on a number of grounds. First, on the basis that it runs the danger of encouraging a view that some religions are superior to others.[29] The parallels

---

[25] L Wittgenstein, *Philosophical Investigations* (Oxford, Basil Blackwell, 1953).

[26] See K Greenawalt, 'Religion as a Concept in Constitutional Law' (1984) 72 *California LR* 753.

[27] *US v Seegar* 380 US 163 (1965).

[28] K Greenawalt, 'Religion as a Concept in Constitutional Law' (1984) 72 *California LR* 753; and C G Hall, ' "Aggiornamento" Reflections upon the Contemporary Legal Concept of Religion' (1997) *Cambrian LR* 7.

[29] See T Macklem, 'Reason and Religion' in P Oliver *et al* (eds), *Faith in Law: Esays in Legal Theory* (Oxford, Hart Publishing, 2000) 79.

between the list and mainstream understandings of Christianity are clear. It may not be appropriate, for example, for Scientologists to have to show similarities and analogies with Christianity, Islam and Hinduism before being classified as 'religious'. The other criticism is that reasoning by analogy is inherently opaque and vague. Analogies can be strong or weak, and it is not clear how strong the analogy has to be between a well-established religion and a less well known set of beliefs, before the set of beliefs can be classified as 'religious'. Does the analogy have to be clear, or is a loose analogy sufficient?[30]

Something of a compromise between the content-based definitions and those which suggest reasoning by analogy was suggested in the decision of the Australian High Court in their ruling on Scientology.[31] In *The Church of the New Faith v The Commission of Pay-roll Tax (Victoria)*[32] Wilson and Deane JJ stated that no single characteristic is determinative, but that the following criteria were helpful in characterising beliefs as religious: a belief that reality extends beyond that which is capable of perception by the senses; that the ideas relate to man's nature and place in the universe and his relation to things supernatural; that the ideas are accepted by adherents as requiring or encouraging them to observe particular standards or codes of conduct, or to participate in specific practices having supernatural significance; that adherents constitute an identifiable group (even if loosely knit); and that adherents themselves see the ideas as religious.[33]

This shorter list of criteria is similar to some of the content-based definitions. However, the list is not definitive, and the beliefs do not need to match all the criteria to be classified as religious. To this extent, then, the approach resembles the analogy approach, and has the consequent advantages of flexibility. However, the aim is not to classify beliefs as religious because of their resemblance to mainstream religions, and so to that extent it escapes the problem of suggesting that some religions are superior to others. Moreover, the fact that the list exists, albeit not in a definitive form, means that the 'definition' is not too vague or uncertain to be capable of meaningful use. A definition of religion based on criteria such as those set out in *The Church of the New Faith* seems to provide a workable basis upon which to consider the questions which are the subject of this work. Although it does not provide a definitive test of when a set of beliefs comprises a religion, it does begin to provide an answer to the question of when beliefs are religious.

However, the remaining difficulty with the list approach is that it does not explain the reason for including the particular criteria. If one reasons by analogy one has reason for the inclusion of some criteria over others: beliefs are religious because they are like known religions. Even though the hierarchy inherent in the approach may be distasteful, there is a rationale for the inclusion of the criteria. Without such

---

[30] See D N Feofanov, 'Definition of Religion: An Immodest Proposal' (1994) 23 *Hofstra LR* 309; B Clements, 'Defining "Religion" in the First Amendment: A functional approach' (1989) 74 *Cornell LR* 352.

[31] *The Church of the New Faith v The Commission of Pay-roll Tax (Victoria)* [1982–3] 154 CLR 120.

[32] [1982–3] 154 CLR 120.

[33] *Per* Wilson and Deane JJ, 174.

a rationale, it is not clear how courts, as a matter of principle, should decide how belief systems which meet some but not all the criteria should be classified.

For example, a dedication to football may meet several of the criteria, but few would suggest it should be counted as a religion. A passionate football fan may engage in associated rituals (weekly match attendance) and find a significant level of personal fulfilment from them. He may wear certain forms of dress (replica kit) and associate with others with the same views to discuss the game, and may sing songs associated with a love of football. Football could therefore meet, loosely, some of the listed criteria: the 'ideas' are accepted by adherents as requiring or encouraging them to observe codes of conduct; and 'adherents' constitute an identifiable group (even if loosely knit), and some may claim an analogy with religious observance. Clearly, the list is only partially met, and in particular football does not entail a belief that reality extends beyond that which is capable of perception by the senses. But the Australian Court held that no single characteristic is determinative, and football does seem to meet some of the criteria, albeit to a limited degree. As with the analogy approach, it is not clear how loosely one can meet the criteria before reaching a threshold of 'religion'. Whilst helpful, the list therefore needs something more if it is to provide any sense of certainty and cohesion. To find a more complete definition, then, we must look at why the criteria are included, and this entails a purposive approach.

## The Purposive Approach to Definition

If we can identify why we need to protect certain belief systems, then it may help to create more certainty, in particular because it will provide a rationale for including the criteria by which we define religion.

The reasons for protecting religion through the legal system will be considered in more detail in following chapters, but will be briefly summarised here in order to provide a general purpose for protecting religion that can aid the definition of terms. One reason may be that, historically, religion has been protected as a political and pragmatic response to religious conflict. A second reason relates to religion as an expression of personal autonomy and identity; or alternatively as an expression of group identity. In either case, religious freedom can be viewed as part of a general cultural diversity which as a plural, liberal society we choose to celebrate and affirm. However, if this is the only purpose for protecting religion, there is no principled reason to distinguish between 'religious belief' and other beliefs such as a passionate belief in the importance of football or a dedication to English country dancing.

Macklem, in 'Faith as a Secular Value',[34] addresses the question of why religion is protected, and produces an answer that may help provide a rationale for including particular criteria within the defining list. His argument is complex but the basic thesis is that it is the fact that religious views are based on faith, rather than

---

[34] (2000) 45 *McGill LJ* 1.

reason, that gives rise to the need to protect them. Religious views are not suscep-tible to reasoned judgment, and therefore cannot be changed by recourse to rea-son. Yet despite their irrational nature, the views can be said to have a secular value, and therefore to be worthy of protection via a rational legal system. Their value lies in the fact that these faith views also enable their holders to come to terms with matters that are unknowable, and beyond reason, matters such as the nature and purpose of life. By helping people come to terms with the unknowable, faith can help increase the well-being of believers. Although some people deal with the unknowable issues of life by recourse to reason, some do so by faith. The value of religion, in Macklem's view, then, is its ability to help those individuals to deal with the unknowable in life, and thereby increase their sense of well-being. This value is not dependent on the question of whether the view of the unknowable is itself correct, nor is it dependent on whether the religion actually increases well being: the capacity to increase well-being is sufficient.

The key issues in Macklem's version of the value of religious belief are that the views are faith-based, and therefore not susceptible to reason; and yet those views are of value because of the role they play in individual lives. The difficulty for those with such beliefs is that the beliefs are not rational, and so cannot be tested accord-ing to the usual rules of the legal system, a system which is based purely on ratio-nal argument. Thus, when set against a rational set of beliefs, the 'religious' will lose. Unless those views have a value, the fact that they will lose is of no matter, hence the importance of being able to place value on 'religious' belief. Clearly it is not all 'irrational' beliefs that need protection: the belief in the importance of view-ing a weekly football match is, after all, irrational. However, those beliefs which enable individuals to deal with the unknowable in life are of some objective value to the secular world, but their irrational nature makes them vulnerable to being disregarded by the rational legal system.[35] Thus, the function and purpose of protection of religious beliefs within the legal system is that protection enables non-rational views about the nature of the world, views that have an effect on some individuals' ability to make sense of the world, to be protected via an other-wise rational system. Other irrational views, for example, about the importance of football or country dancing, do not qualify for the same protection.

Such an approach views the importance of religion as based in its role in fulfill-ing individual dignity and autonomy. In sum, the argument is that some people's understanding of the world and concept of the good is based on non-rational foundations. Yet protection of individuals' autonomy in choosing and following their own concept of the good is fundamental to the concept of dignity, equality and autonomy on which human rights protection is based.[36]

Clearly, a purposive definition of religion runs the danger of circularity. If we redefine the purpose of religion to be 'protecting beliefs of significant importance

---

[35] This point is also made in P W Edge, *Legal Responses to Religious Difference* (The Hague, Kluwer Law International, 2002) ch 1.
[36] See fuller discussion in ch 3.

to an individual's sense of identity' we may be able to define 'religion' to include football and country dancing. However, looking for a meaningful purpose for protection, and using this to provide a rationale for determining which characteristics to use to define religion, does create a more complete definition than that provided by either purpose or a list of criteria alone. The definition offered here draws on both the list of criteria suggested in the *Church of the New Faith* case and the purpose of protecting religion provided by Macklem.

Religion, then, can be taken to include a belief that reality extends beyond that which is capable of perception by the senses. To be 'religious' the belief system must also have some relation to man's nature and place in the universe and his relation to things supernatural: it must have something to say to adherents about their place and function in the world. Religious beliefs should require or encourage adherents to observe particular behavioural standards or codes of conduct, and may include specific practices having supernatural significance, such as rites of worship. Finally, adherents constitute an identifiable group and see the ideas as religious. Although no individual criterion is determinative of the issue, using Macklem's explanation of why religion is important it would seem that the first two criteria are the most important. It is the belief in some form of external reality, and the belief that this has some link to man's place in the world, that is most important in helping adherents make sense of the unknowable, and it is thus these elements that are the most important. Whether an adherent claims 'religious' identity may be less important. Thus, football and country dancing fail to meet the threshold to be termed a religion because, despite loosely meeting some criteria, they do not meet the core criteria (a belief in an external reality and a belief that it has some link to man's place in the world), which give religion its value.

## II Defining Belief

The fact that protection under both Article 9 ECHR and the Employment Equality (Religion and Belief) Regulations 2003 is not limited to religion only means that some of the difficulties of definition can be overcome fairly easily. Any borderline religion is likely to be defined as a belief instead, qualifying it for protection in any event.

It would seem that although beliefs clearly do not need to be religious in nature to be protected, there is still some limit on the types of belief to be covered. After all, to be included in the definition of belief in this context brings with it rights to respect for those beliefs from others. As Malcolm Evans points out: '[n]o system could countenance the right of anyone to believe anything and to be able to act accordingly'.[37]

Given that the term 'belief' or 'philosophical belief' would encompass religious beliefs in any event, it would seem that the inclusion of the term 'religion' in the

---

[37] M Evans, 'Religious Liberty and Non-Discrimination' in T Loenen and P Rodrigues (eds), *Non-Discrimination Law: Comparative Perspectives* (The Hague, Kluwer Law International, 1999) 131.

protections provided by the ECHR, the Equality Directive and the Employment Equality (Religion and Belief) Regulations 2003 places some boundaries around the meaning of 'belief'.[38] This suggests that although beliefs do not have to be religious, the outer boundaries of what is protected may be determined in some way by analogy with the term 'religion'.[39]

Indeed, Regulation 2(1) of the Employment Equality (Religion and Belief) Regulations was originally drafted to define 'religion or belief' as 'any religion, religious belief, or similar philosophical belief'. To be defined as 'similar' to religion was viewed as offensive to some humanists and atheists,[40] and the definition was amended by the Equality Act 2006 to remove the term 'similar'.

The use of the term 'belief' or 'philosophical belief' means that belief systems which are specifically non-religious, such as humanism, atheism and agnosticism, are clearly intended to be covered, without needing to broaden the meaning of 'religion' to encompass them. Yet the purposive approach to defining religion may still be useful in determining the correct parameters to the meaning of 'belief' in this context. The explanatory notes to the original version used the 'analogy' approach in drawing the parameters of what constitutes a 'similar philosophical belief',[41] stating that effectively 'the belief should occupy a place in the person's life parallel to that filled by the God/Gods of those holding a particular religious belief'. On this analysis it is clear that humanism and atheism are covered, whereas a devotion to football is not. It is probable that the same conclusion will be reached even with the term 'similar' removed.[42] This limitation on the scope of protected beliefs is reflected in the ECtHR case law, which provides that in order to qualify for protection beliefs do not need to be religious but must 'attain a certain level of cogency, seriousness, cohesion and importance'.[43]

Similar restrictions on the meaning of the term 'belief' are reflected in the legislation of some member states which have implemented the Equality Directive. For example, the explanatory notes to the Austrian implementing legislation state:

> The term 'belief' is tightly connected with the term 'religion' . . . Belief is a system of interpretation consisting of personal convictions concerning the basic structure,

---

[38] This would follow the rule of statutory interpretation that suggests that where wide words follow words with a more restricted meaning, the wider words are interpreted as meaning things that are *ejusdem generis* (of the same genus or class) as the more restricted words.

[39] See the comments of Baroness Scotland at *Hansard* HL vol 673 col 1109 (13 July 2005) 'the term "philosophical belief" will take its meaning from the context in which it appears; that is, as part of the legislation relating to discrimination on the grounds of religion or belief'.

[40] Comments on the Draft Employment Equality (Religion or Belief) Regulations 2003, British Humanist Association, January 2003. See also the comments of Lord Wedderburn in the debate on the Regulations, *Hansard* HL vol 649 col 788 (17 June 2003). Out of interest, having identified himself as having beliefs which were specifically not 'similar' to religion, he went on to swear 'If [the minister] does not fail in the courts on the sexual orientation regulations, *by heaven*, he will one day on these regulations' (emphasis added).

[41] DTI Explanatory Notes for the Employment Equality (Religion and Belief) Regulations, para 13.

[42] See the comments of Baroness Scotland at *Hansard* HL vol 673 col 1109 (13 July 2005): 'in drafting Part 2, it was felt that the word "similar" added nothing and was, therefore, redundant'.

[43] *X, Y and Z v UK* (1982) 31 D&R 50, and *Campbell and Cosans v UK* (1982) 4 EHRR 293.

modality and functions of the world; it is not a scientific system. As far as beliefs claim completeness, they include perceptions of humanity, views of life, and morals.[44]

In the Netherlands the term *levensovertuiging* (philosophy of life) is used in place of *overtuiging* (belief) in order to place limitations on the type of belief that can be covered. The term 'philosophy of life' requires a coherent set of ideas about fundamental aspects of human existence, and includes broad philosophies such as humanism, but does not extend to more general views about society.

The approach used in Austria and the Netherlands, and the definition in the UK legislation of belief as a 'philosophical belief', suggests that belief should not extend to 'single-issue' beliefs. Although, the protection of the ECHR has been extended in some cases to beliefs which are, arguably, 'single issues', such as pacifism[45] and veganism,[46] at times the consideration given to the question of definition was scant, and the cases were decided on other grounds. It might not be the case, therefore, that single issue beliefs should be protected under the term 'religion and belief'.

# III  Towards a Definition of Religion and Belief

For the purposes of what follows, religion and belief can be taken to include beliefs which are necessary to the dignity and integrity of the individual.[47] They should relate to man's place in the world, be important in helping the believer make sense of the unknowable, and be a means through which the individual develops a sense of the good. Defined in this way, protection of religion and belief is not limited to those belief systems that have already been defined and protected in the past, and is open to development as human thought develops. It thus attempts to avoid the dangers of too tight a definition which may be under-inclusive. However, it should be clear from the definition that protection is only available to those beliefs which are sufficiently serious to the individual to affect his or her sense of identity and understanding of the world.

After all, the legal protection available to religion and belief extends beyond tolerance of differences in opinion. It involves a form of obligation on individuals, who are required, at the very least, to set aside personal preference to avoid discrimination against those of different beliefs, and at times more significantly to take positive steps to accommodate religious practices. If this is to be required of people, there must be clear and cogent reasons. These reasons are explored in the next chapter.

---

[44] Explanatory notes of the amended Equal Treatment Act, Country Report Austria, European Network of Legal Experts in the non-discrimination field (Human European Consultancy, Migration Policy Group, 2006).

[45] *Arrowsmith v UK* (1978) 19 D&R 5.

[46] *H v UK* (1993) 16 EHRR CD 44.

[47] See Hepple and Choudhury, *Tackling religious discrimination: practical implications for policy makers and legislators* Home Office Research Study 221 (London, Home Office, 2001), who point out that Article 13, which provides the basis of the Employment Equality Directive, should be interpreted in the light of Article 1 EU Charter of Fundamental Rights, which states that 'the dignity of the person must be respected and protected'.

# 3

## Protecting Religion at Work

## I Introduction

The Employment Equality (Religion and Belief) Regulations 2003 add to the growing range of protection that has been made available to the employee over the last forty years. The work relationship, traditionally viewed as a private contractual arrangement between master and servant, has been transformed into a highly regulated relationship, in which the worker is protected on many fronts. Statutory protection[1] and developments in the common law[2] have increased the duties which are imposed on employers to protect their employees' interests. Moreover, under the Human Rights Act 1998 public employers must respect the human rights of their employees and, although not explicitly provided for in the Act, the protection probably extends indirectly to private sector workplaces.[3] The range of legal protection available to employees thus suggests that the workplace can no longer be viewed purely as a private forum governed by contract: it can be argued that the employment relationship is becoming increasingly constitutionalised, and is a place in which workers' personal rights are granted a measure of respect.

Despite these developments in the employment relationship, it remains the case that neither freedom from discrimination, nor freedom of religion per se, is an absolute right, and at times they may have to give way to other competing interests, particularly when exercised in the context of work. The main aim of employers is the running of efficient and profitable businesses; and employees give up a degree of autonomy when they enter the workplace, in return for a wage. At times the interests of the employer will not be compatible with full protection for all the rights the employee might enjoy in the world outside work.

Moreover, not only are the religious interests that arise at work not absolute in nature, but there are also other good reasons to argue for their restriction. In

---

[1] Eg, the Sex Discrimination Act 1975, Race Relations Act 1976, Employment Equality (Sexual Orientation) Regulations 2003, Employment Equality (Age) Regulations 2006, Disability Discrimination Act 1995, Trade Union and Labour Relations (Consolidation) Act 1992, Working Time Regulations (1998) SI 1998 No 1833, The Maternity and Parental Leave etc Regulations (1999) SI 1999 No 3312, National Minimum Wage Act 1998.

[2] *Malik v BCCI SA* [1997] IRLR 462, *Woods v WM Car Services (Peterborough) Ltd* [1981] IRLR 347.

[3] For a full discussion of how the Human Rights Act 1998 can be applied in public and private workplaces, see ch 4, and L Vickers, *Freedom of Expression and Employment* (Oxford, OUP, 2002) ch 3.

particular, religious groups often do not recognise other fundamental rights and freedoms, such as rights to be treated equally on grounds of gender, sexual orientation or other grounds. Within the context of work, protecting religious interests may also impose financial costs on employers. It is thus important to determine the extent to which religious interests should be protected or accommodated when they conflict with other interests which are also protected in the work context. In effect, the question which arises is whether it is ever acceptable to privilege religious rights over other rights, such as equality-based rights, or the commercial interests of employers, by requiring the protection or accommodation of religious interests in the work sphere. Can religious employees expect that their religious interests will be accommodated at work where to do so imposes some cost on others?

As with other conflicts, such as that between privacy and free speech, a resolution may be found by engaging in a balancing exercise, with rights or interests weighed against each other to decide which should prevail. The legal terminology used is one of protecting or accommodating religion where it is proportionate or reasonable to do so, but in practice the meaning of such indeterminate phrases will involve a degree of balancing of interests or values.[4] In order to make any sense of the process of balancing rights, we need to have some idea of why the various interests and values are engaged, so that we can judge their metaphorical weight. If the reasons for protection are merely that religion has traditionally been viewed as important in our culture, this may not weigh too heavily when set against equality rights based on essential human dignity. If, however, religious rights too are protected as a result of a link with autonomy and dignity, they may weigh more equally when set against similarly justified interests.

Thus it is necessary to establish whether it is acceptable for the state, via the legal system, to protect religious interests at all, and in particular when they conflict with other interests. This will be considered in two parts: first, the arguments for and against protection of freedom of religion; second, whether and to what extent that protection should operate at work. A framework of protection can then be created, to enable the debate on the proper scope of the protection for religion within the workplace to take place in a coherent manner. Before turning to consider the question of why religion should be protected at work, two preliminary issues will be discussed: one regarding why religion is subject to its own protection and a second issue relating to terminology.

## Particular Protection for Religion?

The first preliminary question is whether freedom of religion should be the subject of specialised protection, or whether it can be adequately protected using other rights such as the right to privacy, the right to freedom of association and the

---

[4] For a discussion of various approaches to interpreting what is 'proportionate' see J Rivers, 'Proportionality and Variable Intensity of Review' (2006) 65(1) *CLJ* 174.

right to freedom of expression. This is because it is arguable that freedom of religion is just a specialised sub-species of these other human rights, and requires no additional protection beyond that available to them.[5] Indeed, it is true that a good deal of the practical protection provided to freedom of religion could be provided by use of these other rights. Much religious practice and ritual could be protected by the right to free expression, public worship could be protected by freedom of association, and the right to privacy could be used to protect against any overly invasive requirements to disclose religious affiliation.

Yet protection based on the particular right to freedom of religion is more extensive than that based on more general protection for free expression and association. It protects the *forum internum* as well as the *forum externum*, so it is more than just expression, but linked to freedom of thought, belief and conscience, even if the view is not expressed. Freedom of expression is protected because of its causal connection with upholding autonomy, and because it can aid the discovery of the truth. Freedom of religion is not protected because it helps discover the truth, and there is no need for the thoughts to be communicated to achieve protection. This suggests that the protection is based on something beyond the right to freedom of expression.

The right to privacy also fails to capture the full nature of freedom of religion. The right to discuss religion and share ideas is protected, separating the right from that engaged by the concept of privacy. If religious freedom were to be based on privacy interests, it might seem acceptable to limit protection to the private sphere. Yet religious expression is often of a public nature. Similarly the right to freedom of association does not capture what it is that is occurring when religious people meet for worship or other rituals, in terms of the significance of the 'content' of any meeting as helping to define its importance.

Thus although the right to freedom of religion could be broken up into parts, and separately protected via the protection provided by other human rights, the scope of the protection is only comprehensible once it is seen as a whole. Moreover, it is clear that freedom of religion is protected as a separate fundamental right in all the major human rights documents.[6] The right not to be discriminated against on grounds of religion is also present in many lists of grounds of equality.[7] The acceptance of the need to provide protection for religious rights and interests is almost universal.

However, the scope of protection in the work context is dependent on an understanding of why it warrants protection at all. Once we have a reason to protect religion, we can start to understand what 'weight' religious interests have when balanced against other rights with which they may be colliding. The issue is highly complex, draws in debates about the nature of all human rights, and is the subject of its own full literature, which is not replicated here. Instead, in the following

---

[5] See J Nickel, 'Who Needs Freedom of Religion?' (2005) *Univ Colorado LR* 941.

[6] For example, Art 18 Universal Declaration on Human Rights, Art 18 ICCPR, Art 9 ECHR.

[7] For example, Art 14 ECHR, Art 13 Treaty of Rome, Art 21 EU Charter of Fundamental Rights, and also the constitutions of South Africa, Canada, the USA and India.

sections several reasons for and against protecting religious interests are given. Conclusions are then drawn about the extent to which religious interests should be given protection within the legal system in general before turning to the specific question of the extent to which religion should be protected in the workplace.

## Terminology: Rights or Interests?

The second preliminary issue relates to terminology. The context in which the issue of religion is discussed here is the workplace, a sphere that from the start involves non-absolute rights: to restrict rights at work does not involve absolute restrictions on those freedoms, just a restriction on their protection in the context of work. As a result, to discuss the issue in terms of rights may be unhelpful. The law governing the employment relationship creates a number of employment rights, such as rights not to be unfairly dismissed, a right to be informed of the main terms and conditions of employment and so on. These are legally enforceable rights of great importance in the context of employment law, and reflect human rights values of dignity and respect to individuals which apply in the workplace as well as outside. However, rights not to be unfairly dismissed, or to a minimum term of notice, remain employment rights, and are not human rights as traditionally understood. The difficulty when considering the issue of religious rights at work is that the language of freedom of religion and human rights mixes with the language of employment rights.

There are two dangers if this takes place. First, if the employment rights relating to religion are invested with the power of the language of human rights, their importance or strength may become inflated. The corollary of inflating the importance of workplace rights is a corresponding deflation in the power of the language of human rights, as the terminology of rights is devalued by over-exposure. To say that an employee has a right to reasonable notice before dismissal is not to say that there is a breach of human rights if that employment right is not upheld. If we use 'human rights' terminology too readily, rights become merely aspirational. Rather than demanding that they be realised as a matter of urgency, we can become inured to the idea that the protection of rights is just something we would, ideally, wish to achieve, and that failure can be adequately compensated financially. If we become too accustomed to such a limited view of 'rights', we run the danger of accepting a reduced level of protection for those rights which are recognised to be fundamental in international law.[8]

The second danger is that by using the same language to discuss freedom of religion generally and freedom of religion at work, the fact that the workplace is a limited sphere is forgotten. The fact that the workplace is only one part of individuals' lives (albeit, as argued below, a very important one) should not be ignored. Where conflicts arise between different rights, such as gender equality rights and rights to

---

[8] See C Douzinas, *The End of Human Rights: Critical Legal Thought at the Turn of the Century* (Oxford, Hart Publishing, 2000).

religious freedom, it should not be forgotten that none of the rights is being discussed in absolute terms, but only in the context of work. Suggested compromises between conflicting rights may be appropriate in the work context, without necessarily implying that they are appropriate in a more general sense.

In order to avoid confusion, or the inflation of terminology, the term 'religious interests' is used in what follows, when referring to the right to freedom of religion in the work context. This is to avoid the suggestion that the right exists in an absolute sense, reflecting the fact that the rights are operating in the limited sphere of the workplace. It should be noted that the fact that rights terminology is not used should not be taken to undermine the importance of the interests discussed. Instead, it will be argued below that freedom of religion is a value or interest that is of sufficient significance that it warrants a significant level of protection at work, and that reasonable accommodation of religion within the workplace should take its place as one of the employment rights enjoyed by workers.

Protection for religion in the work context can potentially include an obligation not to discriminate against employees on grounds of religion and belief, and an obligation on the employer to accommodate the religious practice of the employee, where to do so involves some cost to the employer. The need for accommodation reflects the fact that religious practice or observance, as well as belief itself, is protected, and religious practice can only really be protected by a process of accommodation.[9] At times, protection of religious interests may take the form of allowing an employer to discriminate against others, and in such cases this will be clear from the language used. Although currently it is only the right not to be discriminated against which is protected in the domestic legal sphere,[10] for the purposes of this chapter, and in order to assess the underlying rationale for these legal rights, both the terms 'protection' and 'accommodation' of religion will be used to describe different modes of protection. Later chapters will discuss in more detail the best form for any legal protection that should be provided for religious interests at work.

## II  Why Protect Religious Interests?

In many cases, the protection of religious interests will not involve any cost to others, and there is clearly little difficulty in upholding rights to religious freedom

---

[9]  See C Jolls, 'Anti-discrimination and Accommodation' (2001) 115 *Harvard LR* 642, who argues that 'accommodation' of difference forms part of the concept of discrimination. This view is consistent with the interpretation of equality in *Thlimmenos v Greece* (2001) 31 EHRR 15 which held that failure to treat different people differently is as unjust as failure to treat similarly people who are the same. This suggests that the concept of accommodation is implicit in the concept of indirect discrimination. For the contrary view, see M Kelman, 'Market Discrimination and Groups' (2001) 53 *Stanford LR* 833. L Waddington and A Hendricks, 'The Expanding Concept of Employment Discrimination in Europe: From Direct and Indirect Discrimination to Reasonable Accommodation Discrimination' (2002) 18/3 *IJCLLIR* 403 consider that reasonable accommodation should be treated as a form of discrimination *sui generis*.

[10]  This illustrates the overlap between human rights and employment rights.

where to do so involves no conflict with other protected interests. For example, protection of the right of staff merely to hold religious views is unlikely to conflict with the rights of others. More complex is to determine the reasons for protecting religious interests when they give rise to some form of conflict, for example where the manifestation of religious views interferes with other rights.

There are several ways in which religious interests can conflict with other legitimate interests. First is the fact that many religions do not recognise fundamental rights and freedoms, such as rights not to be discriminated against on grounds of birth, status, gender, sexual orientation or other grounds. It is therefore arguable that a society that values equality and dignity should not protect or accommodate the views of those who do not share those fundamental values.[11]

A second conflict which arises when protecting religious interests is caused by the inherent collision between the interests of religious people and the interests of those outside the religious group. In effect, freedom of religion can be understood to have both a positive aspect, which protects the interests of the religious individual or group, and a negative aspect, which protects individuals from having the religious views of others imposed upon them.[12] Clearly some forms of protection for the positive aspect of religious freedom risk conflicting with protection for its negative aspect.

A third difficulty is that protection for religious interests is unlikely to proceed on the basis that the state endorses one religious viewpoint as, exclusively, correct. A range of religious beliefs are protected, even though in some cases they claim to have an ultimate and exclusive understanding of the truth, making them mutually incompatible.[13] Given that the state is not in a position to determine which, if any, religions or beliefs are true or false, legal protection will not be based on the view that the belief is possessed of an exclusive version of the truth. The protection must therefore be based on something other than the argument that the religious belief is exclusively true. If religious claims are not protected on the basis of their exclusive truth,[14] then it is arguable that the costs of protecting religious interests should not be imposed on others.

A fourth reason for denying protection for religious interests is the argument that religious affiliation is a chosen characteristic: given that the religious person has chosen to belong to a religion, his rights should yield when set against the rights of others based on non-chosen characteristics. For example, it is arguable that if one is to balance a religious person's right to discriminate against women

---

[11] See M Nussbaum, 'A plea for difficulty' in S M Okin (J Cohen, M Howard and M C Nussbaum, eds), *Is Multiculturalism Bad for Women?* (Princeton University Press, Princeton, 1999) and B Barry, *Culture and Equality* (Cambridge, Polity Press, 2001) for the view that cultural rights should not be protected at the expense of the equality rights of others.

[12] See *Kokkinakis v Greece* [1993] 17 EHRR 397 where the Court confirmed that improper proselytism can interfere with the freedom of conscience of others.

[13] This can apply to atheism as much as to theist or other religious beliefs. The belief that there is no god is incompatible with traditional religious belief.

[14] If the international community were to come to the view that in fact one religion was 'true' the implications for public life would be enormous!

against the woman's rights not to suffer discrimination, the balance will come down in favour of the woman's rights because gender is not a chosen characteristic, and religion is. The idea is that the religious person can change religions if he or she wishes to, or at least choose to change his or her level of practical commitment to those beliefs, in order to avoid the resulting disadvantage. In contrast, the woman cannot change her gender. This argument has been used to explain why a hierarchy exists within discrimination law between the protection available for gender and race equality and that available for religion.[15]

However, there are strong reasons to reject a limitation of the protection for religion based on the idea that religious belief is chosen. In the first place, the question of whether it is a chosen characteristic is highly contested. A high percentage of religious adherents stay in the religious groups into which they were born, suggesting little mobility between religious groups. Ultimately, whether religion is chosen, and, if so, whether it should be termed a 'fundamental choice', is an intractable question, and is unlikely to solve the difficulty over the scope of any protection available for religious interests.[16] Furthermore, regardless of whether or not religion is a chosen personal characteristic, it is clearly closely related to an individual's concept of identity and self-respect, and the cost to the individual of renouncing religious affiliation should not be underestimated.[17]

These various reasons may suggest that protection for religious interests should be limited. However, before reaching such a conclusion we need to turn to consider the strength of the reasons in favour of protecting religion, to see if they are strong enough to warrant protection, especially when to do so imposes some level of cost on others. In particular, we need to see whether there are any reasons that are strong enough to balance against the first argument, that religion should not be protected at the expense of other equality rights.

Several justifications for protecting religious interests are set out below. The initial justifications are fairly weak, and are likely to give way in any competition with other interests. The final reason, based on autonomy and dignity, is stronger, but provides equal justification for the protection of other interests such as equality on grounds of gender and sexuality, which may conflict with religious interests. This final justification for protection of religion, therefore, does not necessarily create a case for religion to trump other interests: it merely suggests a reason why religion should be protected alongside them. The extent of the religious interest, when in competition with other interests, is then explored further in the specific context of the workplace.

---

[15] D Schiek, 'A New Framework on Equal Treatment of Persons in EC Law' (2002) 8 *European LJ* 290, and M Bell and L Waddington, 'Reflecting on inequalities in European equality law' (2003) 28 *EL Rev* 349.

[16] See further discussion below at pp 39–40.

[17] See P W Edge, 'Religious rights and choice under the European Convention on Human Rights' [2000] 3 *Web JCLI*, and R Wintemute, *Sexual Orientation and Human Rights* (Oxford, OUP, 1985).

## Religious Reasons

Many of the earliest writers on human rights argue for their protection on a religious basis: humans are made in the image of God, they are all equal, and are entitled to the basic human rights protection due to this status. However, many
religions also accept religious explanations for gross breaches of human rights, as
well as accepting serious inequalities between people, either by believing that God
ordains inequality, or that some people are not equally human (for example,
women or slaves).[18]

Apart from the potential for some rather startling conclusions about basic
equality that remain compatible with religious thinking,[19] the obvious difficulty
with such religiously based explanations for human rights protection is that the
reasoning is self-serving. It is not acceptable to base a rational system of protection
for religious freedom and equality on reasoning that is predicated on the truth of
the religious viewpoint. For example, legal protection for human rights can be
based on a Christian view that God created all men in his image. Indeed such reasoning can and has led to significant protection for rights,[20] as well as the less
enlightened thinking referred to above. However, the reasoning gives no basis for
non-Christians to respect human rights.

As discussed above, protection for different religions cannot proceed on the
basis that one religious view reflects absolute truth. Thus, if protection is to be
afforded to religious interests in general, rather than to the interests of one particular religion, it must be based on reasoning that can be accepted by a range of
parties, religious and not, rather than just adherents of one religion. A secular
explanation is therefore needed for why religious interests should be protected,
one that is not dependent on acceptance of any particular religious world view.[21]
That secular explanation should not be based on an assumption that religious view
points are wrong, as to do so would, in effect, privilege atheism, itself a particular
world view. Instead, reasons must be sought that are not reliant on the acceptance
of any particular religious views, but which rely on reasons that can be agreed by
all people, regardless of whether they personally hold religious views. To use
Rawls' terminology, the reasons given for protecting religious interests should be
susceptible to 'public reason', that is, based on arguments that are accessible to all
reasonable citizens.[22] The basis for protecting religion can therefore not relate to
the truth or otherwise of the particular belief, for 'if there are truths about religious

[18]  eg, Ephesians 5 vv 22–23, Colossians 3 v 22.
[19]  See for example the verse in the popular children's hymn *All Things Bright and Beautiful* by
C F Alexander, usually omitted from modern hymnbooks: 'The rich man in his castle, The poor man
at his gate, He made them, high or lowly, And ordered their estate'.
[20]  For example, it provided a religious motivation for the movement for the abolition of slavery.
Galatians 3 v 28: 'There is neither Jew nor Greek, there is neither bond nor free, there is neither male
nor female: for ye are all one in Christ Jesus' (King James Version, 1611).
[21]  See D Myerson, *Rights Limited: Freedom of Expression, Religion and the South African Constitution*
(Cape Town, Juta, 1997).
[22]  J Rawls, *Political Liberalism* (New York, Columbia University Press, 1993).

matters, they are not truths that can be publicly demonstrated'.[23] The case for the protection of religious interests is, instead, better made using reasoning which is not dependent on religious belief.[24]

## Conflict Resolution and Social Inclusion

An obvious 'public' reason for protecting religious interests is as a response to the conflict so often caused by religious difference. This can be seen in the writing of Locke,[25] who argued for religious tolerance as a response to centuries of war and atrocities inflicted in the name of religion. More recently we can see a commitment to religious equality as a response to religious conflict, for example in the constitution of India,[26] and with the introduction of religious equality legislation in Northern Ireland.[27] Clearly equality between religions is likely to be a fundamental safeguard of any peace accord which follows a religious conflict. Religious freedom is then granted as part of a peace-keeping methodology.

In effect, both sides in any conflict are given space to practice their religion, not as a result of any objective belief in its value, but as a form of compromise between otherwise warring factions. In a conflict involving other interests a compromise might also involve some sort of equal recognition of rights. For example, a conflict over a right of way might well be settled by allowing both parties a level of access. No moral judgment need be made about the value of the right of way. A guarantee of freedom of religion as part of a peace deal thus carries with it no tacit acceptance that religion is of value. It just represents an acceptance by all parties of a need to settle the dispute. In effect, the parties adopt a *modus vivendi* which does not involve any acceptance of the validity of the other side's viewpoint.[28]

An alternative version of this view, which applies to all states (and not just 'post-conflict' societies), is that protecting religious interests within society helps to prevent alienation of minorities. Thus is it not full scale civil war that is prevented, but more generalised social unrest within societies. Where minorities suffer religious discrimination, this is likely to lead to conflict within society. Social exclusion from education, or from participation in the political or economic life of the country, will lead to conflict and unrest, even if this is not demonstrated in violence. In practice individuals will not always surrender their religious interests

---

[23] D Myerson, *Rights Limited: Freedom of Expression, Religion and the South African Constitution* (Cape Town, Juta, 1997) 18.

[24] Of course, one might query whether the concepts of dignity or autonomy suggested below as a rational basis for the protection of religion are any more 'neutral' than the religious reasons rejected here. However, a full discussion of such a debate is beyond the scope of this chapter.

[25] *A Letter Concerning Toleration* (1698).

[26] Arts 25–28 Constitution of India.

[27] Introduced by the Fair Employment (Northern Ireland) Act 1976, and since amended.

[28] J Rawls, *Political Liberalism* (New York, Columbia University Press, 1993) 148. He contrasts mere *modus vivendi* unfavourably with the creation of an 'overlapping consensus' in which all parties, although holding different comprehensive world views, can share opinions on how to order the fundamentals of political life.

in order to participate fully in society, and so it is necessary to provide some protection for these interests so that some of the social ills caused by non-participation are avoided. In effect, tolerance of different religious interests can be viewed purely pragmatically as a useful tool for preventing the social disintegration that can follow the exclusion of minorities. Applied in the context of work, religious interests should be protected in order to enable religious minorities to have access to the financial and social benefits of work, thereby increasing social inclusion of minority groups.

The role of religious freedom as a method of enhancing social inclusion, and avoiding conflict, social unrest or social exclusion is thus well established, and of significant pragmatic value. However, it provides little reason to protect religion in the absence of disputes or conflict. For example, conflict resolution and social inclusion reasoning fails to explain why we should protect mainstream religions, such as Christianity in the UK, whose adherents do not appear to be under threat of alienation from society. Nor does it provide a reason to protect minority religious groups that do not face exclusion and pose no immediate threat of social unrest. Moreover, such utilitarian reasoning provides no reason for preventing the avoidance of social conflict by other means, such as by suppressing an unpopular minority.

A further limitation on the use of conflict resolution as a reason to protect religion in the context of work is that it carries no commitment to the idea that religion has any inherent value. It merely recognises that the religious beliefs are highly valued by the parties, and elicit high levels of emotion and devotion. Given that religion, under this theory, has no independent value, it would give way very readily when confronted by any other value or interest that has its own independent value, such as business interests, or other equality interests.

## 'Aesthetics'

There is no doubt that religion is hugely important to individual religious people. It provides a rich source of personal and group identity, and is immensely varied. From this it can be argued that religious freedom should be protected on the basis that it helps sustain diversity in our world. It adds to the variety of cultural practices and traditions which can be seen among different nations and peoples, and preserves a level of choice of cultural practice for future generations. Maintaining diversity can have benefits linked to individual autonomy and identity, as explored below. However, in some accounts, the benefits of maintaining diversity amount, in effect, to the view that religion should be protected because it is aesthetically pleasing[29]: different religions have value because they reflect a variety of practices which have developed through our history, akin to cultural or artistic practices. The difficulty with such an argument is that although this may justify giving some

---

[29] On this argument, see B Parekh, *Rethinking Multiculturalism* (Basingstoke, Palgrave, 2000) 165 *ff.*

weight to religious interests, the weight would be small.[30] Thus the protection of different religions can be justified on aesthetic grounds, in the same way as we might protect other cultural practices, for example by providing funding for teaching art forms such as ballet or classical music. But we need a stronger moral basis for the protection of religion if it is to prevail in any conflict with other interests. Reasoning based on aesthetics also fails to match the significant level of protection available to freedom of religion in human rights documents, which suggests that religion deserves greater protection than freedom of cultural expression.[31]

## Social Cohesion

Other pragmatic reasons for protection of religion exist. One example can be viewed as a weaker version of the argument based on conflict resolution, and is the view that religion helps create social cohesion and helps many people to live moral lives. Religious groups can also serve as useful social units, enabling their members to participate in social and political life. Moreover, some religious groups provide services for their members, such as education, social and health care. Religious groups therefore serve a valuable social function, and can be generators of social capital.

Again this may well be so, but it does not give any moral basis for protecting religions when their teaching conflicts with the general socially accepted mores. Some religious practices may work to undermine social cohesion, and may undermine others' attempts to provide social or health care. For example, a religious school may wish to offer education only to members of the religious group; or religious parents may deny their children routine immunisations. To argue for protection for the rights of groups to act in such a way, based on the idea that religion helps maintain social cohesion, is problematic. Similarly, there is no reason, based on the need for social cohesion, to allow protection for those whose beliefs conflict with fundamental beliefs of the society. For example, it is difficult to argue, on social cohesion grounds, for the protection of an individual who holds the religious belief that it is wrong for married women to work. Indeed, the problem with basing protection for religious interests on the need for social cohesion is that many of the conflicts between religion and other rights arise precisely because of a lack of shared morals or values in society.

None of the reasons set out so far provides sufficient reason to protect religion if it comes into conflict with other rights. A religion that is protected for aesthetic reasons will only be protected as long as no greater interest arises and, presumably, as long as it remains 'aesthetically pleasing': we would not argue for the mainte-

---

[30] *Ibid*, 166.
[31] For example, religious freedom, viewed as a civil and political right, is protected under the ECHR, and is directly enforceable against the state. If religious freedom is protected as a social, economic and cultural right, the protection will not be directly enforceable.

nance of female inequality for reasons of diversity, and maintaining tradition. Similarly, reasons based on social cohesion only work for as long as the religion is working to maintain cohesion. Minority religions which do not comply with the general traditions of a society would require no protection on such a basis.

Thus, if religious interests are to be protected even where they conflict with other interests, we need to find an alternative reason for doing so. If we cannot find such a reason, other than for aesthetic or conflict resolution reasons, then there is no call for protection of religious interests in contexts such as the workplace. Religious interests should only be protected if a religiously neutral but morally justified reason can be found.

One religiously neutral reason for providing protection can be based on an alternative version of the social cohesion argument above. The failure of some religious groups to agree with the morals or values of mainstream society can lead them to retreat into isolated groups, risking social exclusion. Protecting the religious views of such minority groups will enable those groups to avoid exclusion. Facilitating social inclusion for groups who otherwise may risk exclusion provides perhaps the strongest secular reason for providing for the protection of religious groups even where to do so imposes a cost on others. However, that reason alone may not be enough to override other interests which may conflict with the protection of religious freedom. Moreover, it only works where the religion in question is a minority religion, and where its members risk social exclusion if they are not protected. Protection based on this ground alone is likely to lead to differing levels of protection for different religious groups, causing additional problems of coherence within the protective system.

A justification for protecting religious difference, that itself does not distinguish between religions can, instead, be found in the concepts of dignity and autonomy.

## Autonomy and Dignity

A more robust justification for protecting freedom of religion as well as equality rights can be found in the wide debate within liberal political theory on the nature of human rights and their provenance. Although early works of political theory were based on religious understandings of the nature of humankind and its importance to God, since the Enlightenment there has been a search for a human rights theory which is not predicated on the existence of God.[32] The search and its findings remain highly contested, but despite this there remains a degree of consistency among writers on the importance of the autonomy and dignity of human beings. On the basis of these moral first principles, a framework for protection for human rights can be built, among them a right to religious freedom.

The basic foundational concept is the Kantian idea that humans should be treated as ends rather than means. They all have an essential dignity, which sets them apart

---

[32] For an overview of the history of this thought see J M Kelly, *A Short History of Western Legal Theory* (Oxford, OUP, 1992).

from non-humans and makes them uniquely valuable.[33] Dignity is not a natural, empirical, characteristic of human beings, but is a status conferred by humans on themselves, to set them apart from other species.[34] It involves a moral judgment that humans are of intrinsic, incomparable and indelible worth, independent of their abilities or accomplishments.[35] Though this setting apart of humankind is sometimes explained in religious terms (for example, Christianity teaches that God created man in his image),[36] it is also a concept shared by non-religious people on the basis that humans enjoy a unique capacity for higher level consciousness and thought. Humans have moral power, and a capacity to develop a conception of the good.[37] With or without a religious explanation, the idea that human beings can expect others to respect the dignity inherent in their humanity is one that has been agreed virtually universally, perhaps most famously in the Universal Declaration of Human Rights: 'All human beings are born free and equal in dignity and rights'.[38]

Identifying any substantive content for a 'right to dignity' is problematic, not least because many people subsist without enjoying such a right, and it is not clear what such a right should contain.[39] But the same is not the case for the acceptance of dignity as a value the legal system should seek to enhance. The idea that humans should respect each other's dignity, and that society should work to uphold and enhance the dignity of its members, provides useful first principles when seeking guidance on why the legal system should protect certain interests. The concept also requires a level of respect for individuals' identity, enabling them to have a secure sense of themselves as individual and as part of a community.[40]

This concept of dignity would seem to encompass at least two other elements. First is the idea of equality between humans.[41] Humans may not be equal in their abilities and attributes, but they are equal in their humanity and moral worth. There is an objective good in upholding their equality, and in attempting to create a society in which all can flourish. Second is the concept of individual dignity, which comprises the notion of autonomy, that human beings should be able to develop their own ideas of the good and exercise control over their lives.[42]

Dworkin[43] argues that, by virtue of being human, all people share a fundamental right to equal concern and respect. Although he justifies his commitment to

---

[33] E Kant, *The Moral Law: Kant's Groundwork of the Metaphysics of Morals* (H J Paton, trans) (London, Hutchinson, 1963).

[34] B Parekh, *Rethinking Multiculturalism* (Basingstoke, Palgrave, 2000) 130 *ff.*

[35] D Réaume, 'Discrimination and Dignity' (2003) 63 *Louisiana LR* 645, 675.

[36] Creationists may understand the creation story in a literal sense. Others understand it more figuratively, to explain the unique relationship between God and man.

[37] See J Rawls, *A Theory of Justice* (Oxford, OUP, 1999, revised edition).

[38] Art 1. Dignity also features in the preamble to the United Nations Charter, and the preambles of the ICCPR and the ICESCR.

[39] See Moon and Allen, 'Dignity Discourse In Discrimination Law: A Better Route To Equality' (2006) *EHRLR* 610.

[40] D Réaume, 'Discrimination and Dignity' (2003) 63 *Louisiana LR* 645, 675.

[41] B Parekh, *Rethinking Multiculturalism* (Basingstoke, Palgrave, 2000) 132.

[42] J Rawls, *A Theory of Justice* (Oxford, OUP, 1999, revised edition).

[43] See R Dworkin, *Taking Rights Seriously* (London, Duckworth Press, 1977) and *A Matter of Principle* (Cambridge Mass, Harvard University Press, 1985).

human rights by using equality rather than autonomy as the foundational concept, the conclusion remains that human beings have rights by virtue of some essential quality inherent in being human. Some would argue that we have a right to equality because of our autonomy; others that we have a right to autonomy because of our essential equality. Even if there is no agreement as to which is the foundational concept, they are deeply interlinked, and there is agreement that a commitment to providing protection for human rights can be based on the concepts of equality, dignity and autonomy.[44] Terms such as the dignity and the equal moral worth of humanity are, of course, somewhat imprecise. However, as acknowledged by Raz, this imprecision is 'but a reflection of the incommensurabilities with which life abounds'.[45]

The basis for endowing humans with dignity and autonomy was their capacity for high level consciousness or conscience, independent thought and the potential to develop an individual concept of the good.[46] Humans also possess the capacity to develop a sense of personal identity and the notion of equality will mean that it is important to preserve the self-respect and sense of self-worth of individuals. These aspects of dignity interrelate: one's sense of identity can help to shape one's concept of the good; and the concept of the good feeds into the individual's sense of identity.[47] This is not to say that the concept of dignity requires that individuals should never suffer a sense of embarrassment or shame,[48] but that they should not be made to feel to be inferior at a more fundamental level: they should be sure of their essential equality and dignity as human beings, and have a sense of self-worth.[49]

The need for identity and self-worth, arising from basic human dignity and autonomy, leads to the view that for individuals to flourish they need to enjoy the freedom to choose their own concept of good. In order for that choice to be meaningful, it is essential to protect freedom of conscience and thought, including the freedom to choose, or to change, religion. Even if one believes that the secular rather than the religious view of life is correct, respect is due to the religious view because otherwise one fails to respect the choices religious people have made about their view of the good.[50]

There is no doubt that, given freedom of choice, there will develop a range of understandings of what a concept of the good might contain. Protecting freedom of conscience will involve protecting a wide range of beliefs, including the beliefs of those whose conscience and sense of personal identity are religious in character.

---

[44] For a much fuller explanation of these ideas, see D Feldman, 'Human Dignity as a Legal Value' [1999] *PL* 682.

[45] J Raz, *The Morality of Freedom* (Oxford, OUP, 1986) 409.

[46] J Rawls, *A Theory of Justice* (Oxford, OUP, 1999, revised edition).

[47] See D Réaume 'Discrimination and Dignity' (2003) 63 *Louisiana LR* 645, 675.

[48] See D Feldman, 'Human Dignity as a Legal Value' [1999] *PL* 682.

[49] Rawls identifies self-respect as a 'primary good'. *A Theory of Justice* (Oxford, OUP, 1999, revised edition).

[50] M Nussbaum, 'A plea for difficulty' in S M Okin (J Cohen, M Howard and M C Nussbaum, eds), *Is Multiculturalism Bad for Women?* (Princeton University Press, Princeton, 1999).

Some find their sense of identity and worth in their beliefs about their relationship with a supreme being; others' sense of identity may be more rationally based and may have no religious aspect. Many will want to ask questions about their nature and place in the universe. Indeed, Nussbaum argues that an ability to 'search for meaning of life in one's own way is a central element of a life that is fully human'.[51] For some, a sense of the religious enables them to make other important choices necessary for the autonomous life.[52]

A case for respecting a range of different concepts of the good can be made on the basis of equality: if all humans are equal, and we know that they will have different, but valuable, conceptions of the good, their different conceptions will deserve equal respect.[53] For religious individuals, religion is in important source of identity. A personal sense of identity is closely connected with self-respect and self-worth and is a valuable aspect of autonomy. Hence, enabling an individual to maintain a sense of identity is a valid method of upholding individual self-respect and dignity. For the majority to impose its values on a religious group, or to force a minority group to conform to the views of the majority, involves the imposition on the group of an alternative concept of good, and undermines the autonomy and dignity of the minority group.[54] A reduced level of autonomy in this regard leads to a failure properly to treat members of the minority group as the moral equals of the majority.

The case for protecting religious interests could equally be based on the notion of autonomy: maintenance of a full range of beliefs about the contents of the good life is a necessary precondition to full respect for human autonomy. If a person is to experience the freedom to chose that is inherent in an understanding of autonomy, he requires the existence of a range of morally acceptable options to choose from. Thus the existence of a range of understandings of the content of the good life is vital for members of society to have adequate autonomy: for there can be no autonomous choosing if one lacks valid options to chose from. Thus 'valuing autonomy leads to the endorsement of moral pluralism'.[55]

One potential difficulty with basing protection of religious interests on the value of choice is that many religious people do not understand their religion to be a matter of personal choice[56]; they may instead feel chosen by their god, or they may view religious observance as an obligation or duty owed to their god, rather than as a chosen activity.[57] However, protection of religious interests does not have to presuppose that religious views are consciously chosen. The argument based on autonomy, dignity and equality includes the view that individual autonomy requires that one remain free to live according to one's conscience. If one believes that there is a

---

[51]  *Ibid.*

[52]  T Macklem, 'Faith as a Secular Value' (2000) 45 *McGill LJ* 1.

[53]  D Réaume, 'Discrimination and Dignity' (2003) 63 *Louisiana LR* 645, 678.

[54]  See B Parekh, *Rethinking Multiculturalism* (Basingstoke, Palgrave, 2000), who argues that cultural diversity should be protected because all cultures provide understandings of the good life.

[55]  J Raz, *The Morality of Freedom* (Oxford, OUP, 1986) 398 and see also 408.

[56]  See discussion at p 31 above.

[57]  See R Ahdar and I Leigh, *Religious Freedom in the Liberal State* (Oxford, OUP, 2005) 62.

god who requires one's devotion, respect for human autonomy requires protection of one's freedom to perform that devotion.[58] Whether the individual believes the devotion to be a chosen activity or not does not really change the argument. Providing some space, figuratively speaking, for an individual to perform religious devotions is part of the respect due to her as an autonomous, equal member of the human race. The question of whether religion is chosen or not does not materially change the case for its protection. It remains clear that infringing freedom of conscience will undermine the ability of the individual to live the autonomous life, in terms of either 'choosing' a concept of good or acting on the principles and values identified by one's conscience as those by which to live.[59]

One might argue that protecting religious interests for the reasons set out above runs the danger of protecting any belief that is important to someone, on the basis of respect for the inherent human dignity of the belief holder; or that any hobby which becomes an important part of an individual's sense of identity should be protected. Indeed, one of the difficulties in basing human rights protection on the concepts of autonomy and dignity is that the concepts are so wide-ranging that virtually any interest can be classed as a right worth protecting.[60] However, although it may not be polite to pour scorn on a matter that another holds dear, if one is to protect practices or beliefs on grounds of dignity, it is only those which feed into an individual's ability to make sense of the world, and through which they develop a sense of the good, that require protection. Thus a person's interest in being allowed to participate in, for example, country dancing because of its importance to them as a form of artistic expression will not require the same level of protection as a belief relating to the existence of a supreme being. It is therefore not every interest that will warrant protection in the name of respect for autonomy and dignity.[61]

The argument set out above leads to the conclusion that religious freedom is an important aspect of the individual autonomy and self-respect due to all people as a result of their humanity. If we accept that all humans are equal, we need to give equal concern and respect to the different world views that they develop. Of course, this reasoning applies to many other aspects of individual identity. To demonstrate that respect for human equality and dignity involves respect for religious world views is not to suggest that this aspect of human identity should take precedence over any other, such as gender, sexuality or race.[62] It is merely to demonstrate that religious interests are valid interests that need consideration alongside other interests that flow equally from a concern for human dignity and equality.

[58] This will not, of course, be an absolute right. It may need to be balanced against other competing interests.
[59] 'One can see conscience as one of the fundamental aspects of human capacity, and interfering with freedom of conscience prevents people both from choosing a set of values by which to live and from giving effect to those values': D Feldman, 'Human Dignity as a Legal Value' [1999] PL 682, 696.
[60] See C Douzinas, *The End of Human Rights: Critical Legal Thought at the Turn of the Century* (Oxford, Hart Publishing, 2000) and the discussion at p 28 above.
[61] See discussion at pp 20–22.
[62] In the context in which the current work is set, these are the other main interests that arise from a concern with dignity, but it is not an exhaustive list.

## The Content of Religious Interests

In the jurisprudence of Article 9, religious interests are divided between the *forum internum* and the *forum externum*. The first refers to the right to have inner thoughts and beliefs, and the protection provided is absolute. However, this is likely to be of little import in the context of the workplace, as it only applies to the internal thoughts and beliefs of the individual, which are unlikely to be known to the employer. It is once religious beliefs are expressed or acted upon that difficulties are likely to occur, and such actions do not form part of the *forum internum*.

Acting on one's beliefs is protected under Article 9 in the form of a right to 'manifest . . . religion or belief, in worship, teaching, practice and observance' alone or with others. The right is not absolute, and can be restricted where proportionate to do so to safeguard the rights of others. It is the freedom to manifest religion which has the most potential to affect religious people in the workforce.[63] For example, a work uniform may interfere with a religious employee's right to manifest her religion. Similarly, the employee who requires time off for religious observance or who requires special dietary provision may claim to be manifesting religion.

An understanding of the content of religious rights based on a binary division between inner belief and manifestation of that belief may miss some of the additional aspects of religious belief and practice as experienced by religious individuals. Edge[64] divides religious rights into four categories: the right to a religious belief; the right to a religious identity; the right to be a member of a religious community; and the right to act on such belief, identity or membership. This categorisation usefully exposes the range of interests that a religious individual may have, and may help to define more clearly the range of behaviours or actions that may warrant protection. For example, the case law on the meaning of a manifestation of religion distinguishes between actions which are required by a religion, which warrant greater protection, and those which are merely motivated by a religion, which may be overridden more readily.[65] Understanding religious interests as including interests in expressing a religious identity may provide an additional explanation for why religiously motivated behaviour should be protected. An individual may believe a set of religious tenets; she may then have a choice about how to react to those beliefs, particularly where a specific response is not clearly mandated by the religion. For example, the decision to follow a religious dress code may be part of a desire to express a religious identity as much as an expression of the beliefs themselves. The additional categorisation of religious interests to include the recognition of matters of identity also reflects the role of religion in

---

[63] See ch 4 below for more detail on the meaning of manifestation of religion under Art 9 ECHR.

[64] 'Religious rights and choice under the European Convention on Human Rights' [2000] 3 Web JCLI.

[65] See discussion at pp 96–100 below. One of the practical difficulties of the distinction is that it can require courts to determine religious questions such as whether a particular practice is required by a religion or not.

upholding personal autonomy and identity, which was used above as the justification for protecting religious interests.

## Religious Interests and Group Rights

The categorisation of religious interests as including the right to belong to a community suggests that religious interests also contain a collective dimension, even though the recognition of religious interests presented above was cast in terms of individual rights, based on the principles of individual autonomy, dignity and equality. Indeed, the liberal basis of this line of reasoning is clear, and is based on a notion that human beings are individual and separate, with their own interests and moral rights. The right to freedom of religion is, on this view, a personal, individual interest. However, the concept of dignity, and the sense of identity which forms part of that, may demand some respect for community rights. This is because involvement in communities which share one's identity can be crucial to the development and enjoyment of a sense of identity and the experience of self-respect that goes with the valuing of that identity.[66]

Moreover, many religions contain a collective dimension in their practice. Groups of religious people may wish to have a religious leader, and may wish to be involved in collective acts of worship or other rites of religious observance. It is arguable that full religious autonomy for the individual will therefore need to include a group dimension.

There is some debate over whether religious interests should be understood to comprise an individual and a group dimension, which co-exist as separate but complementary aspects of religious freedom. If so, communal interests in religion would weigh equally with the individual interest.[67] However, the difficulty with this view is that if one recognises collective interests as having a separate independent existence, they could exist even in the absence of individuals standing behind the collective. It is not clear on what basis such group rights should be protected. The alternative view, taken here, is that collective rights are an important aspect of individual rights, but that they derive their value from individual interests. Full enjoyment of the individual interest in freedom of religion entails a measure of protection for the collective expression of that freedom, but collective rights gain their validity and value from the individuals who make up the collective.[68]

Although it may be a derivative interest, there is a clear collective dimension to religious freedom: comprehensive freedom of religion will require some pro-

---

[66] D Réaume, 'Discrimination and Dignity' (2003) 63 *Louisiana LR* 645, 678.

[67] See, on the failure of liberal views to take proper account of collective interests, B Parekh, *Rethinking Multiculturalism* (Basingstoke, Palgrave, 2000). See also R Ahdar and I Leigh, *Religious Freedom in the Liberal State* (Oxford, OUP, 2005) ch 2, and J Rivers, 'Religious Liberty as a Collective Right' in R O'Dair and A Lewis (eds), *Law and Religion* (Current Legal Issues, Vol 4, Oxford, OUP, 2001).

[68] J Raz, *The Morality of Freedom* (OUP, Oxford, 1986), 208. See also J Donnelly, *Universal Human Rights, Theory and Practice* (New York, Cornell University Press, 1989) 151 *ff.*

tection for the interests of associations of religious people. Enjoyment of religious freedom thus comprises rights to manifest and practice the religion, alone or with others, and rights to protection of one's religious identity by participation in group activity, freedom of choice of religious leader, and other collective rights.

## Freedom of Religion and Freedom from Religious Discrimination

Not everyone has a religious world view, but for those who do, it is an important aspect of their concept of self, and a significant part of their conception of the good. On the basis of the fundamental role religion plays in the lives of adherents, the case has been made for its protection as part of the respect that should be afforded to individual human dignity. Such an argument applies equally to all religious world views, as well as other philosophical beliefs relating to man's nature and place in the universe.[69] As personal autonomy and equality are so deeply interlinked it becomes clear that those with different views and values are entitled to equal concern and respect with regard to their religious outlooks. It is not tolerable for a society to allow differences in social and economic chances to be based on religious difference, as to do so is to deny equal worth to individuals. As noted above, it makes little practical difference whether the concern and respect is due to the essential equality of individuals, or whether the equality of individuals arises out of their essential dignity: in either case we can reach the position that different religious views should be tolerated, and that individuals should be treated equally in terms of concern and respect, without distinctions drawn on grounds of religion.[70]

The result of this line of argument is that freedom of religion and freedom from discrimination on grounds of religion are closely linked.[71] Freedom from religious discrimination is required because of the fundamental equality of human beings. It is unjust to allow inequalities in life prospects to arise as a result of an individual's religion. Respect for individuals' inherent dignity entails respect for their ability to come to their own conclusions about fundamental questions relating to the nature of life: to allow the exercise of this freedom to result in unjustified differences in life prospects infringes individual dignity. Freedom of conscience is a fundamental part of individual dignity and autonomy. That freedom will be fettered if its exercise leads to an unjustified reduction in life chances. Full and meaningful enjoyment of autonomy, equality and dignity therefore requires protection for both freedom from religious discrimination and freedom of religion.

---

[69] See discussion above at pp 13–24.

[70] J Donnelly, *Universal Human Rights, Theory and Practice* (New York, Cornell University Press, 1989).

[71] They are not the same concept, however. 'Non-discrimination is simply a tool that assists the realization of religious liberty; a means not an end': M Evans, 'Religious Liberty and Non-Discrimination' in T Loenen and P Rodrigues (eds), *Non-Discrimination Law: Comparative Perspectives* (The Hague, Kluwer Law International, 1999) 120.

## Conclusion

Arguments based on autonomy, dignity and equality give good grounds for providing protection for freedom of religion, freedom from religious discrimination, and some level of accommodation of religious practice. However, the basis for protecting religious interests is the same as that for protecting other rights, such as gender and sexual orientation equality, with which the religious interests may well conflict. The question of how to resolve the conflict between the right to religious freedom and equality on grounds of gender or sexuality is highly contested, and it is not proposed to attempt to resolve it fully here.[72] Instead, the issues are addressed in the particular context of the workplace. The difficulty here is that the right to freedom of religion is not absolute, and it may be argued that restricting its exercise at work is justified, where conflicts arise with the rights of others. It is therefore necessary to establish whether religious interests should be protected in the work environment; or whether it is adequate to limit the protection of religious interests to the world outside work.

# III  Protecting Religious Interests in the Work Context

Clearly, the right to religious freedom is not an absolute right. For example, in Article 9 ECHR it is accepted that restrictions on the manifestation of religion can be imposed where necessary to safeguard the rights of others. Moreover, it may be that the solution to the conflict between religion and other interests in the context of the workplace will be to rely on the fact that one does not have an enforceable right to a job. Hence any conflict between rights which occurs at work can be resolved by the religious individual resigning: religious freedom persists, and indeed is arguably protected by, the right to resign.[73] However, it will be argued below that such an approach fails to provide adequate protection for religious interests, given the strength of the argument in favour of their protection set out above.

---

[72] For some of the debate see: M Nussbaum, 'A plea for difficulty' in S M Okin (J Cohen, M Howard and M C Nussbaum, eds), *Is Multiculturalism Bad for Women?* (Princeton University Press, Princeton, 1999); B Parekh, *Rethinking Multiculturalism*, (Basingstoke, Palgrave, 2000); C Kukathas, 'Are There Any Cultural Rights?' (1992) 20 *Political Theory* 105; W Kymlicka, *Multicultural Citizenship* (Oxford, OUP, 1995); W Kymlicka, *Liberalism, Community and Culture* (Oxford, OUP, 1989); B Barry, *Culture and Equality* (Cambridge, Polity Press, 2001); P Kelly (ed), *Multiculturalism Reconsidered* (Cambridge, Polity Press, 2002); J Raz, *Ethics in the Public Domain* (Oxford, OUP, 1994) ch 8.

[73] See, for example, the approach of the ECHR in *Ahmad v UK* (1981) 4 EHRR 126 and *Stedman v UK* (1997) 23 EHRR CD168.

## Should Religious Interests be Protected at Work?

It has been proposed above that it is legitimate for society to provide some protection for religious interests without needing to resort to religious arguments. What has not been established is why this protection should extend to the workplace, given the undeniable fact that no one is forced to enter or remain in the workplace.

### The 'Right to Resign'

At its most basic, the employee's freedom of religion is protected through the employee's freedom to resign, if work and religion are incompatible. The relationship between employer and employee is voluntary, and if the employee has religious objections to complying with an employer's requirements, he or she can choose to not take up the employer's offer of employment. This freedom remains the ultimate protection for religious freedom.[74]

To take an extreme example, if a programme of 'religious instruction' were imposed upon staff who were forced to attend work, then there would clearly be a breach of religious freedom. In such circumstances, a right not to attend work would provide protection against the interference with the right to freedom of religion. The right not to work against one's will is well protected both within the interpretation of domestic labour law and in international human rights law. In domestic law it can be seen in the refusal of courts to require specific performance of employment contracts. Where employers leave their employment in breach of notice terms or other restrictive covenants, courts will not grant specific performance as a remedy to employers. Instead they opt for damages, or put employees on 'garden leave' rather than require employees to attend work unwillingly.[75]

Thus, freedom of religion at a basic level is protected by freedom to resign. Another illustration of the basic limits on religious freedom at work is that employers are never going to be required to accommodate every religious practice or belief at work: for example, a pacifist could not apply for a combatant role in the armed forces, refuse to take part in active service and then complain that she has been denied full freedom of religion. The right to religious freedom does not entail a right to be employed in the employment of the religious adherent's choice, or a right to demand that any religious practice be accommodated. Indeed, it is

---

[74] See A Bradney, *Religions, Rights and Laws* (Leicester, Leicester University Press, 1993), who suggests that the protection of religious interests in employment is relatively unproblematic, because the employee remains free to resign. See also R Epstein, *Equal Opportunity or More Opportunity? The good thing about discrimination* (Civitas, London, 2002) who argues that the freedom to resign is the best protector of employee interests, as the threat of resignation will cause employers to change their practices, or risk losing good staff and a good reputation. See also the counter-arguments by S Deakin in the same volume.

[75] There is no legally enforceable duty to work. The only sense in which such a duty exists is as part of the social security system, where some benefits are dependent on the recipient's willingness to try to find work, and to take suitable work that is available.

well established that religious observance does not have to be cost-free for the observer. The right to freedom of religion in Article 9 ECHR is not absolute. The freedom to practice religion, or to participate in religious observance, is only protected where it is proportionate to do so. This suggests that it is not an infringement of Article 9 to burden the practice of religion where it is proportionate to do so, for example by refusing to accommodate a religious practice which places too much of a cost on the employer.

It is clear, then, that in the final analysis protection for the religious interests of employees is provided by the right to resign. However, even though resigning may be the ultimate freedom, to limit protection to this somewhat drastic remedy may be to fail to provide adequate protection to religious interests. In order to determine the proper scope for the protection of religion in employment, it is worth considering the reasons for its protection in the context of work.

## The Case for Protection in the Workplace

It was established above that the right to freedom of religion is well founded and works to help sustain individual autonomy and dignity. To fail to provide any protection for the right in the work context is to fail to protect individual autonomy and dignity in a very important sphere of life. Clearly, the purpose of most workplaces is to engage in business and generate profit, not to create space for religious observance. It is certainly not suggested that workplaces should have as a primary concern the protection of religious interests, and yet employees spend a significant part of their lives at work and it is not feasible to expect them to leave their interests in autonomy and dignity behind when they enter the workplace.

It might be tempting to suggest that an answer to the conflict between work and religion is for religion to be confined to the private sphere of the home, with work forming part of the public sphere. However, requiring the separation of work and religion in this way is not a practicable option for many workers. Some individuals' work is religious in nature, so such separation is impossible; for others, who may work at home, making any separation is impracticable. Indeed, the difficulty of separating work from other parts of life is well recognised in the case law of the ECHR:

> it is not always possible to distinguish clearly which of an individual's activities form part of his professional or business life and which do not. Thus, especially in the case of a person exercising a liberal profession, his work in that context may form part and parcel of his life to such a degree that it becomes impossible to know in what capacity he is acting at a given moment of time.[76]

Special problems arise regarding religious practices which apply to individual's whole lives and which cannot easily be separated between the home and work spheres. Religious adherents often observe special behavioural codes of conduct, such as dress codes or practices of prayer. These practices have supernatural

---

[76] *Niemietz v Germany* (1992) 16 EHRR 7 para 29. See discussion at pp 89–91.

significance to the believer, and often apply at all times, rather than being restricted to a religious observance at a particular time of the day or week. Of course, some practices may be accommodated outside work; observance such as a requirement to pray each day may be observed without interfering with the work-place.[77] But the same is not true of other requirements. Religious dress codes may require a woman to have her head covered at all times when in public. Such a requirement cannot simply be dropped during working hours; indeed, it may be that work is the main forum in which the requirement arises, precisely because it is not a private space. To require the individual to reserve this type of religious observance to the world outside work amounts to a denial of the option to comply with the religious requirement. Whether it is acceptable to deny this option will be considered later; at this stage, it is sufficient to note that some religious requirements apply at all times, and cannot be limited to the non-work sphere.

Even for those who do not have specialised religious duties, there are sufficient objective benefits attached to working life that mean that religious interests should be given some degree of protection.

## Economic Benefits of Work

Work provides the main income stream for most people, enabling them to house, clothe and feed themselves and their dependants. For many, work also provides access to pension provision, sickness benefits, and a range of insurance services such as death-in-service payments. Paid maternity and paternity leave, tax credits for child care, and compensation for redundancy are also available for employees, with some employers providing substantial additional benefits such as subsidised housing, travel or health insurance. As well as the economic benefits provided directly by employers, there are other significant economic benefits of being in work, for example the fact that substantial sums of money can be borrowed on the promise of future earnings, providing those in work with the financial resources to buy their own homes. Those with independent financial means may also be able to achieve these economic benefits, but for the vast majority, paid work (whether as employee or self-employed) is the only way to access them. Access to such financial benefits also encourages social cohesion and helps to reduce social exclusion.[78]

## Non-Financial Benefits of Employment

Apart from the obvious and extensive economic benefits of work, there is significant support for the view that work brings other non-financial benefits. Work is related to concepts of responsibility and citizenship and is the medium through which many people gain self-respect and a sense of participation and inclusion in society.[79] Engaging in the workforce can promote engagement in wider civil society for

---

[77] Unless prayer is required so often and for so long that it is incompatible with completing a day's work.
[78] H Collins, 'Discrimination, Equality and Social Inclusion' (2003) 66 *MLR* 16.
[79] V Schultz, 'Life's Work' [2000] 100 *Colum LR* 1881.

otherwise marginalised groups. If minority groups are not encouraged to participate in civic life, their voice within the community will be far weaker, ensuring a continuance of their marginalisation.[80]

Moreover, many people invest psychologically in their work, and, depending on the job, it can also be an important signifier of social status. What one does as a job is one of the first pieces of information that people share when meeting, suggesting that it is an important part of many people's sense of identity.[81] However, although the importance of work as part of one's identity is significant, it should not be over emphasised. It was asserted above that religious interests should be protected on the basis that religious beliefs form an essential aspect of personal identity, fundamental enough to warrant significant protection, but that the same would not be said of other less important aspects of personal identity, such as a hobby. The sense of identity granted by employment is probably of similar weight in any proportionality test as that provided by participation in other activities outside work. It may be important to the individual, but is not so strong that it should outweigh other interests based on individual autonomy.

Not only is the sense of identity provided by work a weak interest, but it is evident that a sense of identity and the social status provided by work are not experienced by all workers. A more objective work-related benefit, therefore, is the psychological benefit of active participation in the workforce,[82] including a reduced level of depression, improved sense of well-being, and higher self-esteem. These benefits are enjoyed by all types of employee, not only those doing high status work which one might expect to carry such benefits.[83] The fact that these non-financial benefits are felt by all workers, not only those who gain traditional esteem or high financial reward, suggests that being in work does provide objective non-financial benefits. Yet it also suggests that it is not necessarily being in a particular job that brings these benefits: the benefits may be derived from any job. Proper treatment for religious observers will therefore not necessarily require that a particular person should be accommodated in a particular job, or in a job of his choosing.[84] However, if a failure to accommodate religion makes it very difficult for those of a particular religion to participate at all in the workforce, it will amount to a significant failure to protect those who hold the religious views in question.

Recognition of the importance of work in non-economic terms is clear within modern employment law, which increasingly requires respect for autonomy and dignity at work. The importance of the non-financial benefits of work, and its role

---

[80] See A Hirschman, *Exit, Voice and Loyalty* (Cambridge Mass, Harvard University Press, 1970), for the argument that groups that are traditionally discriminated against are particularly in need of a voice, as the other method of getting heard, exit, is not effective.

[81] K Karst, 'The Coming Crisis of Work In Constitutional Perspective' [1997] *Cornell LR* 523, 533 and V Schultz, 'Life's Work' [2000] 100 *Colum LR* 1881, 1891.

[82] For references see V Schultz, 'Life's Work' [2000] 100 *Colum LR* 1881, 1890.

[83] *Ibid*, 1892

[84] On the general difficulties of upholding a right to a job, see B Hepple, 'A Right to Work?' (1981) 10 *ILJ* 65.

in upholding individual identity and dignity, has been recognised in the recent development of the content of the employment contract and the creation of specific employment rights. The new 'family friendly' employment rights[85] can be viewed as a recognition of the importance of work to individuals, as well as being economically driven. Moreover, legislatively imposed requirements on employers to consult with employees on redundancies,[86] protection for the collective rights of employees,[87] and rights to union recognition[88] arguably reflect the idea that the workplace is more than merely a means to economic benefit for staff or employer. If economics were the only driver of employment legislation, many of these employment rights would not strictly be needed. The reason for protecting job security, and the imposition of workplace democracy, must be for reasons connected to the importance of work to the individual rather than merely the pure economic benefit of the employer. After all, dismissal of staff, and their replacement by others, causes no net loss of employment; and employees who are unfairly dismissed can receive compensation even if they immediately find employment elsewhere.

Developments in the duty of trust and confidence which is implied into employment contracts also reflect the increasing recognition of the non-financial significance of work to the worker.[89] For example, the duty of trust and confidence owed by the employer goes well beyond preserving employees' economic interests, to protect them from abuse or insult from their colleagues or others.[90] It also extends beyond the treatment of employees during working hours, and provides a duty to compensate where the employer's conduct has damaged the employee's future career prospects,[91] and a general duty to safeguard the employee's economic interests.[92] In *Johnson v Unisys*, the fact that the employment relationship must involve the observance of fundamental human rights was recognised.[93] It is thus well recognised by courts that work fulfils more than just an economic role in the lives of workers. This forms part of a general trend towards recognition of a right on the part of employees to dignity, respect and autonomy both at work and beyond.

---

[85] See, for example, Working Time Regulations (1998) SI 1998 No 1833, Maternity and Parental Leave etc Regulations (1999) SI 1999 No 3312, and Work and Families Act 2006.

[86] TULRCA 1992 s 188.

[87] TULRCA 1992.

[88] Employment Relations Acts 1999 and 2004 amending TULRCA 1992.

[89] For example, in *Gogay v Hertfordshire County Council* [2000] IRLR 703 there was breach of the term of mutual trust and confidence even though the suspension was with pay. The loss to the employee was therefore not merely economic.

[90] For example, see *Isle of Wight Tourist Board v Coombes* [1976] IRLRL 413, and *Moores v Bude-Statton Council* [2001] ICR 271 in which it is accepted that rudeness and abuse from someone at work can give grounds for a claim of breach of the terms of the employment contract.

[91] *Malik v BCCI* [1997] 3 All ER 1 and *Spring v Guardian Assurance plc* [1994] 3 All ER 129.

[92] *Scally v Southern Health and Social Services Board* [1992] 1 AC 294.

[93] [2001] UKHL 13, Lord Hoffman, at para 37.

## Protecting Religion for Equality Reasons

The reasons given above for protecting religious interests at work are based on the idea that employment is such an important aspect of life that to deny religious protection in that sphere is to create a significant infringement of religious freedom in practice. Denial of protection at work amounts to a significant reduction in religious freedom. An additional argument for protecting religion in the work context can be based on equality.

It has been argued above that work provides many benefits, both economic and psychological. The principle of equality demands that all people should have equal access to such benefits, and that life chances should not be dependent on holding a particular world view. Some people find it easy to access these benefits, because there is no incompatibility between their beliefs and employers' requirements. Such individuals will have an advantage over those whose religious beliefs make compliance difficult or impossible. The most obvious example of religious practices which may be easier or more difficult to reconcile with work is in days of rest and the requirement to attend work during the normal working week. For Christian workers in the UK, the weekly religious day of rest, together with the major religious holidays, coincide with the normal working week and working year.[94] This allows Christian workers to comply with religious observance while meeting most employers' requirements for work attendance. This is not the case for those of different faiths.

The resulting inequality in the ease with which groups can comply with employer demands in a way that is compatible with religious duties results in an inequality in access to the substantial benefits of employment, on grounds of religion. The argument from autonomy and dignity, used above to justify protecting religion, requires that religious belief should not determine access to benefits or cause differences in life chances. To argue that religious interests are protected by the right to resign is to ignore the inequalities of protection this provides.

The link between religious disadvantage and inequality is particularly stark where religious groups have suffered systematic disadvantage in the past. For these groups, access to work may represent the best way to avoid further social exclusion and economic disadvantage. Moreover, there is significant potential for religious inequality to intersect with other forms of inequality such as gender or race inequality, resulting in multiple discrimination for minority ethnic women from minority religious groups. Full equality therefore requires that access should be open to all and should not be dependent on religious affiliation.

The argument from equality suggests that it will not be possible to contend that the right to resign will provide sufficient guarantee for freedom of religion. The fact that some religious groups will need to exercise the option more often than

---

[94] This of course reflects the shaping of the 'normal' working calendar around the traditional Christian year, although the timing of Christmas probably reflects a much earlier accommodation by Christians of the traditions of pagan religions.

others means that the parallel right to equality is infringed, and leads to the conclusion that religious interests should be protected within the workplace.

Of course, the right to equality on grounds of religion is not absolute, and at times protection or accommodation may not be feasible. Yet the fundamental principle of equality demands that protection or accommodation be attempted, rather than leaving religious interests to be protected by the freedom to resign or withdraw from the workplace.

## Contracting Out

Even if one rejects the reality of the employee's freedom to resign in practice, weight can be added to the idea that religious interests are protected by the right to resign by the argument that those who accept employment have accepted a certain restriction on their autonomy. Workers sacrifice a good deal of their personal autonomy when coming to work: their employers will control how they spend their time, where they go, and what they say, with a consequent reduction in individual autonomy, for the duration of the working day. Thus it is arguable that the notion of autonomy cannot be used to argue for protection for religious interests at work: if so much individual autonomy has been given up on entering work, it is not clear why autonomy should demand protection of religious practice.

However, this argument misinterprets what is demanded by a respect for autonomy, as the term was used above to argue in favour of granting some level of protection for religious interests. The underlying autonomy and dignity of human beings demands a core level of respect for the person, which may include respect for their religious interests. This core respect is not undermined by a person doing as he is bid and complying with his employer's instructions in order to fulfil the needs of the business, even though the individual is not a totally free agent when doing so. However, one cannot rely on the restriction on freedom inherent in being at work, rather than at leisure, to deny any protection for religious interests at work.

The reduction in autonomy that accompanies an agreement to accept an employer's instructions does not entail a consequent reduction in the extent to which an individual's core human dignity and autonomy should be respected at work.[95] It is thus not the case that entering the workplace involves an implicit acceptance that personal dignity and autonomy are limited within the workplace.

## Stepping Out of the Employment Relationship

One additional way to reconcile the competing interests at stake in cases where religious interests clash with other interests is to protect religious individuals, but not within the traditional employment relationship. For example, a religious

---

[95] In fact, it has been suggested by Collins that much of the legal protection for employees at work can be understood to be based on the need to protect the dignity and autonomy of employees in the workplace. H Collins, *Justice in Dismissal* (Oxford, Clarendon Press, 1992) 16.

group who wished only to employ men might be refused protection: any woman who was refused employment could then claim against the employer. The resulting conflict of rights could be resolved by accommodating the needs of the religious employer and allowing such an employment policy, or by refusing to accommodate and granting the woman a remedy against the employer. An alternative might be to allow the religious group to opt out of the employment relationship altogether. That way they would not be subject to the non-discrimination rules that apply to the relationship. The difficulty here is that there may be significant consequences for other areas of employment law of widening the range of quasi-employment relationships. The definition of the term 'employee' for the purposes of the ascription of employment rights is developing very fast. As courts determine the types of contractual arrangement to which employment or worker status should be afforded, so employers seem to draft contracts in order to avoid the creation of such a status in their workers.[96] To create a sub-group of workers to whom usual workplace rights do not apply could be a dangerous option. Any alternative non-employment status could be exploited by other employers to deny protection to vulnerable workers.[97] It is thus better to seek the correct level of protection for religious interests within the employment relationship, than to achieve the same end by excluding religious organisations from the relationship altogether.

## And Yet . . . The Residual Protection of the 'Right to Resign'

There are many good reasons to protect religion at work within the employment relationship. The reasons are based on the importance of religion, the importance of work, and the equality interest in distributing the benefits of employment without discrimination on religious grounds. They also reflect the failure to respect core dignity if workers are allowed to contract out of protection. Yet, despite all these reasons to protect religious interests at work, in the final analysis the right to resign does provide the ultimate protection: if the employee finds it impossible to reconcile religious practices or beliefs with her work-based obligations, she is free to leave.

The fact that religious freedom can be protected through a freedom to resign, but that other rights may also be so protected, pervades any assessment of how to resolve any conflict of rights which arises in the context of the workplace. Any assessment of the level of protection that should be afforded to religious interests must be carried out in the light of this residual protection. However, the arguments above regarding the importance of work and the importance of religion mean that resignation should remain the residual protection where accommoda-

---

[96] For full discussion of the development of the law on the definition of employment, and the implications of the changes, see M Freedland, *The Personal Employment Contract* (Oxford, OUP, 2003).

[97] For example, the question of whether there is mutuality of obligation between workers and employers to provide and undertake work may be determinative of the question of employment status, leading employers to draft contracts with no such mutuality, even though in practice work is offered and personal service is expected and performed.

tion of the religious interest is inappropriate, rather than the starting point for the provision of protection.

## Conclusion

Religious belief has crucial significance for individual identity, linked as it is with beliefs about man's nature and place in the universe. Given the gravity of the issues involved in the lives of adherents, they should not have to relinquish their practices too lightly. However, important as they are, religious interests are not absolute. It is accepted that in some circumstances burdens may need to be placed on religious practice, and that at times the rights of others will prevail over religious interests.

However, the non-absolute nature of the rights as exercised in work cuts both ways. The rights with which religious interests may collide, if they are rights being exercised at work, are equally subject to the residual protection of resignation. If a worker is unhappy with the accommodation offered to a religious employee she also enjoys the freedom to resign. Moreover, it is well established that there is no clear right to work in a particular job.[98] In effect, the right to resign ensures that neither religious rights nor the other rights enjoy automatic precedence.

The importance of employment as a benefit to which all should have equal access means that respect for religious interests should be provided in the work context, along with respect for other rights. The importance of the benefits offered by working suggest that to deny the opportunity to some to take up those benefits because of their religious beliefs would be to significantly diminish their dignity.[99]

It is not argued here that religious interests should take priority, merely that they should not be ignored. They should take their place alongside other interests as worthy of some protection at work. Where the protection of religion gives rise to conflict with other interests, the additional and complex question arises of how much protection should be granted, and how the conflicting interests should be reconciled. As suggested at the start of the chapter, the method generally used for reconciling competing legal rights is to engage in a balancing exercise, in order to determine whether it is proportionate to uphold religious interests over other interests, or vice versa. What follows is an examination of the various interests and issues that need to be considered in order for the proportionality of any legal response to be assessed.

[98]  The European Charter of Fundamental Rights Art 15 provides that everyone has a right to engage in work and to pursue a freely chosen or accepted occupation. However, this does not extend to providing a right to a particular job.

[99]  D Réaume, 'Discrimination and Dignity' (2003) 63 *Louisiana LR* 645, 688.

# IV The Proportionality Equation: Religion and the Workplace

The case has been made above for providing a measure of protection for religious interests at work. However, it has also been recognised that religious interests can conflict with other interests within the workplace, such as the economic freedom of the employer, and the equality and other interests of fellow employees. If both sets of interests are to be given adequate protection, then a fair balance needs to be struck between them. In some cases, the competing rights will be irreconcilable, and all that can be hoped for is for the competing interests to be held in some sort of equilibrium. The most common method of finding an equilibrium as between different interests is to restrict interests only as far as it proportionate to do so, in the light of the other competing interests.

Proportionality is a mathematical term, which implies that the correct balance can be calculated with a degree of precision. But when using it in the legal context, one is measuring incommensurable interests, and mathematical precision is impossible. Although the use of proportionality aims to introduce an element of objectivity into the analysis, it is inevitable that value judgments will be made as to the relative importance of the different interests.[100] Nonetheless, in the absence of a better analogy, the concepts of balance and proportionality are used by courts to determine conflicting interests. They enable a structured approach to be taken to balancing fundamental rights against each other, and will be adopted here.

In assessing whether it is proportionate to protect religious interests, one assesses whether the accommodation required serves a legitimate aim and whether there is a proportionate relationship between the means used and the aim one is trying realise, given the existence of competing interests. This involves considering whether the aim can be realised using alternative means which impinge less on other interests. The strength of the argument in favour of protection of religious interests at work demonstrates that their protection serves a legitimate aim. Whether or not accommodation should be required in any particular case will thus depend on whether it is proportionate to do so, bearing in mind the relative strength of the competing interests in question, and whether the aim can be realised in a way that reduces the adverse impact on those other interests.

The determination of proportionality will depend on the assessment of a complex range of factors. It is not proposed to establish with precision here what

---

[100] For a discussion of the theoretical difficulties inherent in any balancing exercise of this type, see L Vickers, *Freedom of Speech and Employment* (Oxford, OUP, 2002) ch 2. See also J Rivers 'Proportionality and Variable Intensity of Review' (2006) 65(1) *CLJ* 174, who argues that the values are not truly incommensurable: 'few would view with indifference a massive loss of liberty for a marginal gain in national security' (at p 201). He argues instead that the difficulty is that the balancing of rights can only be carried out in a crude manner. Further support for the use of proportionality as a method for resolving conflicts between rights can be found in D Beatty, *The Ultimate Rule of Law* (Oxford, OUP, 2004).

the outcome will be in any given case. Instead, a range of the factors that should influence the determination of whether it is proportionate to accommodate religious interests at work will be considered, on the basis that the more detailed the consideration given to the question, and the more complete the range of factors considered, the more objective the determination of the question can be. Given the incommensurable nature of the interests being considered, precision and pure objectivity are not achievable, but a reflective and detailed consideration of relevant factors may lead to outcomes which can be more readily justified to those on either side of any conflict.

The first issue in the proportionality equation is to assess the relative strength of the competing interests. The strength of the interest in protecting religious interests within the workplace was discussed earlier in the chapter. The second issue is to consider the range of interests with which such interests may compete in the workplace, such as employers' financial interests and the equality interests of other employees. These interests, considered below, will interact with each other, and may act singly or cumulatively to suggest that protection should be limited. Finally, a range of additional contextual factors will be considered which may have an effect on the determination of whether it is proportionate to require protection. Issues in this category include the type of employer, as well as background issues such as whether the workplace is viewed as a public or a private space.

## Competing Rights

### The Equality Rights of Others

The most obvious interests with which religion is likely to compete are the equality rights of others. For example, an employee who has religious objections to working on an equal basis with women would need to be able to show that his religious interests outweighed the interests of gender equality if he is to succeed in having his religious views protected. Similarly, a religious employer who was unhappy about employing a gay man would need to show that his religious interests should prevail against the equality interests involved.

Given that the basis for protecting religious interests in employment is the need to protect human autonomy and dignity in the practically important sphere of the workplace, it is unlikely that religious interests will often prevail over other equality interests, similarly based on dignity and autonomy. The interests in equality on grounds of gender and race are generally recognised to be the most powerful equality interests, and are granted greater legal protection than other grounds.[101] Some[102] have justified this on the ground that biological differences and ascriptive

---

[101]  M Bell and L Waddington, 'Reflecting on inequalities in European equality law' (2003) 28 *EL Rev* 349; M Bell and L Waddingon, 'More Equal Than Others: Distinguishing European Equality Directives' (2001) 38 *CML Rev* 587.

[102]  For example, D Schiek, 'A New Framework on Equal Treatment of Persons in EC Law' (2002) 8 *European LJ* 290.

differences (sex, age, ethnicity) should be granted greater protection. Others[103] point to differences in the socio-political context in which the discrimination occurs, and the differing levels of historical disadvantage, and of social exclusion. These factors suggest that, as a general rule, race and gender equality interests will take precedence over competing religious interests, and such a position would reflect the current legal and political compact.

However, the strength of the case for protecting religious interests, together with the fact that the interests are not being protected at large but in the more restricted context of the workplace, means that there may be times when religious interests should be accommodated, even when to do so involves infringing some other equality right. In effect, it may be the case that in some circumstances the factors discussed below combine in such a way that it is proportionate to accommodate religion even though to do so involves giving precedence to religious over other equality interests.

## The Negative Aspect of Freedom of Religion and the Protection of Religious Interests

As noted above, tension exists in the protection of religious interests as a result of the extension of the protection to many forms of religion and belief. Those who have a particular religious belief are protected equally with those who have either a different belief or none. The double-sided nature of the protection, protecting belief and absence of belief, creates an inherent conflict. For example, to give full protection to the rights of believers to practise their religion in public places entails an infringement of the rights of non-believers to enjoy those same public places free from the influence of religion. In assessing whether it is proportionate to protect religious interests in any situation, then, it will be necessary to consider in the balance both the interests of the religious group or individual, and the interests of those who wish to remain free from the influence of religion.

## Rights to Privacy, Freedom of Speech and Freedom of Association

The argument was made above that the workplace is a sufficiently important part of life for religious interests to be protected there. If this is true for religious interests, then the same must be true for other fundamental human rights such as rights to privacy, freedom of speech and freedom of association.[104] At times, the employee may enjoy a right to privacy, which will need to be balanced against an employer's need to know information regarding religious affiliation. For example, where a religious employer has a genuine occupational requirement that an employee be of a particular religion, the invasion of privacy entailed in establishing that the employee complies with the requirement is likely to be proportionate.

---

[103] eg, C McCrudden 'Thinking about the discrimination directives' (2005) 1 *European Anti-Discrimination Law Review* 17.

[104] Protected under Arts 8, 10 and 11 ECHR respectively.

If there is no genuine occupational requirement to be of the religion, the invasion of privacy may be viewed as disproportionate, depending on other circumstances. Clashes between religious interests and freedom of speech may also occur, particularly with regard to the protection against religious harassment at work. The freedom to debate religious doctrine may need to be balanced against the need to protect the dignity of religious workers. Again, the proportionality of any restriction will need to be considered in the light of many other factors, such as whether the harassing speech was directed at the victim.[105]

Freedom of association is another right with which religious interests interact. The interest in being free from religious discrimination may come into conflict with the rights to freedom of association of groups who need to engage employees to serve the group's needs. For example, to require that a group must employ someone who disagrees with their beliefs, in order to avoid infringing discrimination rules may, arguably, interfere with the right to freedom of association of the group. However, such an interference may be proportionate if it is viewed as necessary to uphold the religious interests of those involved.

In each case, the interaction of the competing interests must be taken into account in assessing the proportionality of any suggested protection of religious interests. Moreover, as with religious interests, the interests in privacy, freedom of expression and freedom of association are not absolute rights, and the proportionality equation will need to be assessed in the light of the freedom to resign, which remains the residual protection for all fundamental rights in the context of the workplace.

## Economic Efficiency

The employer will have a number of interests to be taken into account when assessing the proportionality of any protection of religious interests, including the interest in the good management and efficient running of the enterprise. Good management and efficiency enables the employer to maximise profits, as well as serving the more general public interest. A strong economy and good levels of employment are dependent on the existence of profitable businesses, which rely on a certain level of employer freedom to manage the business free from too many external constraints.[106]

It will no doubt be the case that that protecting religious interests at work will involve the employer in financial costs in some cases. For example, allowing staff time off for religious observance increases the length of time that those staff are economically inactive. Even if time off is awarded without pay, this may still reduce the capacity for employers to use plant to maximum efficiency or generate

---

[105] See further discussion below at pp 145–152.

[106] For more on where the balance between employee protection and employer freedom should lie see R Epstein, 'In defense of the contract at will' (1984) 51 *U of Chicago LR* 947 and R Epstein, *Equal Opportunity or More Opportunity? The good thing about discrimination* (London, Civitas, 2002) and the reply by S Deakin in the same volume.

profit at the same rate as they are able where no time is awarded for such activity. Economic loss for the employer can also have an adverse effect on other workers, especially if it is at such a level as to risk the viability of the business. Other forms of accommodation may also be unrealistic given the need to respect the rights of other employees at work. For example, a religious employee who needed to work in a single sex environment may not be able to be accommodated without significant interference with the interests of other workers.

The need for employers to be able to run viable businesses is clearly a factor to be considered when assessing the proportionality of any protection for religious interests. It is arguable that protecting the autonomy and dignity of staff at work will lead staff to feel more valued, leading to the recruitment of better staff, higher motivation, and ultimately higher profits. However, this may not always be the case, and it is inevitable that at times protection of religious interests will lead the employer to incur costs, for example, because of the need to employ extra staff to cover religious leave; or because of a loss of custom if religious interests are accommodated.[107] Where the profitability of an enterprise would be reduced if religious interests were to be protected, this may tilt any balance against the protection. However, the employer's interest in enjoying the fruits of the business is clearly not an absolute interest. A large number of employment rights in the UK restrict the right of the employer to put profit before the rights of others, such as restrictions on working time,[108] unfair dismissal[109] and the need to safeguard health and safety.[110]

Of course, not all employers run in order to make a profit. The public sector does not operate with a primary brief to make profit. Instead, its primary purpose is the delivery of the various services it provides, although financial efficiency may be required of it in order to achieve this. As well as the public sector, there exists a large sector of not-for-profit organisations, whose aim may not be to improve economic efficiency, but to provide a service, but who are nonetheless required to use the employment relationship to regulate the relationship between the organisation and those that work for it. For example, a religious group which has as its aim the propagation of a religious message may need to utilise the employment relationship to regulate its relationship between workers and the organisation. The economic interests of such organisations are unlikely to be as significant in the analysis of the proportionality of any restriction on religion as the economic interests of for-profit organisations.

Although not an absolute interest, then, the need for an employer to run an economically viable business is a clear interest that needs to be taken into account in assessing the proportionality of any protection of religious interests.

---

[107] For example, an employer could argue that customers may prefer not to be served by staff wearing religious dress.
[108] Working Time Regulations 1998 (as amended).
[109] s 98 ERA 1996.
[110] The Health and Safety at Work Act 1974.

## Employer Autonomy and Reputation

An additional factor to take into account in assessing proportionality is that the employer, as well as the employee, may be entitled to some respect for autonomy. Both the European and US legal systems recognise that companies as well as individuals can enjoy the right to freedom of expression.[111] In some cases, protection of employees' religious interests could clash with the right of the employer to portray the image to the public that it would wish. For example, an employer that wishes to project a secular image may not wish its employees to attend work in religious dress.

However, the need to uphold employer autonomy will not always prevail over religious interests of staff. Corporations who act as employers will not find fulfilment through self-expression, as a human right. If there are no other factors at stake, the human interest in upholding autonomy and dignity should prevail over the rights of a corporation. However, where other interests are also of relevance, such as economic interests, then the balance may be more fine.

It was argued above that the individual right to religious freedom involves a degree of protection for collective religious rights.[112] The right of a religious group to enjoy a level of autonomy is reflected in the protection for freedom of religion which extends to a right to manifest religion alone or in community with others.[113] This means that religious groups should enjoy some of the protection afforded to individual religious interests.

A respect for group autonomy should mean that religious groups are enabled to enter employment relationships, in order better to organise or facilitate religious activity. In some cases, religious groups may want to appoint someone to act as a teacher, or as a full-time religious official. In other cases, the religious group may want to appoint other staff, for example catering or administrative staff, to improve the group's ability to fulfil its manifestation or practice of religion. For example, a church which spreads its message to young people by running a youth group may wish to employ a group leader. If there are a large number of groups, it may need a leader's co-ordinator, and, of course, work with young people may be only part of the outreach work the group engages in. It is not difficult to see how a large organisation will generate its own bureaucracy and administrative systems, which will need staffing.

In other cases, religious individuals may wish to work with others of the same religious persuasion, grouping together to supply goods and services without any specific religious link. For example, a group of Christians may wish to run a café or a group of Muslims may wish to open a book shop. In these cases, the employment is not the result of the need for support for religious activity, but is a secular activity, carried out by a religious group. In these cases, the link with freedom of religion is less direct, although it is still present. In some cases the activity may

[111] *First National Bank of Boston v Bellotti* 435 US 765 (1978).
[112] See discussion at pp 42–43 above.
[113] Art 9 ECHR.

reflect a personal preference by the employer to work with co-religionists. In others, the view of the employer may be that the activity can be the forum for some type of religious outreach; it may provide opportunities for proselytism. In each case, the activity is motivated by religion, and although not directly involved in the manifestation of belief, it is the result of the outworking of religious commitment.

Full respect for autonomy involves the recognition that religious groups have an interest in being able to act as employers, as part of the respect due to group autonomy and dignity. As with the other interests discussed here, this is not absolute, and needs to be weighed against other interests. In assessing the extent of the religious employers' interest in autonomy the extent of the link between the activity engaged in and the manifestation of religion is important. Where a group acts as the employer of a religious person who officiates at religious ceremonies, the employee is playing a key role in the group's manifestation of religion and the autonomy of the religious group should be accorded great weight when set against other interests.[114] Where the activity is only motivated by religion, rather than being an outworking of religious practice, then the weight accorded to the employer's autonomy may be less.

## An Interest in Being in Work

There is no legally enforceable right to work,[115] but the importance of work to the individual, for both financial and non-financial reasons, was highlighted above. The argument was made that individuals gain such benefits from work that they should not be unreasonably denied the opportunity to participate in the workplace on grounds of religion. Thus the case was made for accommodating religious interests within the workplace.

The interest in having a job is clearly not absolute. However, it can provide a significant component of individual autonomy. If an individual is excluded from employment because his religion cannot be accommodated, this will be a relevant factor to take into account when assessing where the balance should lie between clashing interests.

The extent of exclusion from work can vary: because of religion, a person may be denied access to a particular job which she would like; she may be denied access to a particular profession; or she may be denied access to the workforce altogether. Clearly total exclusion will be more serious, and more difficult to justify, than exclusion merely from the particular job for which the religious person applied.

If a religious person is unable to take up a job because she cannot meet its requirements, but remains free to take other jobs, there will only be a minor infringement of her interests, as she remains free to take up other work. For example, a Christian might be unwilling to work for a shop which requires its staff to work on Sundays. The individual remains free to work for other shops, or in

[114] See, for example, *Hasan and Chaush v Bulgaria* (2002) 34 EHRR 55 at para 62; and *Serif v Greece* (2001) 31 EHRR 20.
[115] B Hepple, 'A Right to Work?' (1981) 10 *ILJ* 65.

another occupation, and so her interest in working is not significantly reduced. Similarly, a refusal to allow staff in a café in a large town to wear headscarves would limit the choice of job for a Muslim woman who wears a headscarf, and wishes to work at that café. However, she may still be able to work in a different café. Thus her job opportunities are diminished, but only marginally so.

Of course, accommodation of particular days of work, or the wearing of head-scarves, may be very simple for the employer. In such a case it may still be proportionate to require accommodation because of the ease with which the employer can achieve this, set against the infringement of freedom of the employee of any denial.

If the employer is a small employer, with no possibility of rearranging shifts, or if there are strong reasons for imposing the uniform rule, then it may not be proportionate to require accommodation: the economic or other interests of the employer may then outweigh the interests of the employee. In contrast, if all shop workers are expected to work on Sundays, then the Christian who wants to work in the retail sector may find it hard to work in the particular area of work she wishes to. This is a more serious infringement of her interest in having a job, as she is excluded from a particular sector of employment. Similarly, if a large employer such as the NHS were to ban the wearing of headscarves, this would severely limit the freedom to choose a career for many Muslim women. The interests served by such a restriction would need to be very strong if they were to counteract the interests of Muslim women in being able to choose a career as a health professional.

In some cases, a religious requirement may be very difficult to accommodate, because it may in turn involve the employer in infringing others' rights. For example, an employee might refuse to work with women on religious grounds. It is likely to be proportionate for a secular employer to refuse to accommodate such an employee, not least because to do so could amount to indirect discrimination against women. The equality rights of women in the same employment would be infringed by acceding to any such request, and these interests in dignity and respect would outweigh the rights of the individual religious employee.

However, the same might not be the case if the employer shared the religious view. Allowing a religious employer to accommodate such a request would infringe the rights of others and would amount to indirect discrimination against women.[116] However, depending on the circumstances, it is possible for this to be justified as proportionate. One factor to consider is whether the religious employee can be employed elsewhere in the absence of the accommodation. In practice, most employers would not accommodate such a request, and so if a person cannot be employed by a co-religionist, he may find it difficult to be employed at all. This amounts to a significant infringement of his interests because of the importance of work to individual dignity and autonomy. If the effect of a failure to accommodate is that an employee becomes virtually unemployable, then any

---

[116] The employer may not refuse to employ women, but a workplace where such requests are accommodated is likely to be a difficult place for women to work, and so they will be at a disadvantage in comparison to men.

countervailing interests will need to be extremely strong if they are to outweigh the effective denial to the employee of a chance to work at all.

Of course, the interest in working applies to both the religious employee and the female employee who will thereby be disadvantaged. If the employer is of a size or a nature that means that the woman is denied access to employment, or to a particular type of employment, then accommodation of the religious requirement is unlikely to be proportionate. For example, if a major local employer had a religious ethos, which accepted that men may wish to work separately from women, the resulting gender discrimination would be unlikely to be proportionate, because it would reduce the chances of women to work in the area. If, however, the employer were a small employer, and plenty of other job opportunities were available to women, such a practice could possibly be proportionate, if it were necessary to enable the religious minority to work at all, and depending on the interaction of the other factors that are relevant to the proportionality equation. This is not because of the size of the employer per se, but because of the effect of any denial of employment on the individual's general employment prospects.

## The Right to be Free from Offence

One further competing right which should be considered when assessing the proportionality of protecting religion at work is the right to be free from offence.[117] The concept of dignity, with which autonomy and equality are so closely related, is infringed where an individual is subjected to offence or abuse. To insult or offend another on the basis of their religion, gender, sexual orientation or any other personal characteristic is to devalue the other person and treat them as of less worth. A practice cannot be said to be harmless if it involves a reduction in the dignity accorded to an individual. Even if there is no direct victim, the tolerance of such behaviour can be said to be harmful as it implies a lack of respect for individual dignity. The importance of the interests in not being offended is recognised in the inclusion of anti-harassment measures in the equality legislation: harassment on grounds of religion, gender, sexual orientation, disability and race are all prohibited on the basis that such behaviour infringes individual dignity.

However, it may be that the wrong of causing offence is one that has to be tolerated, at least to some extent, if we are to provide sufficient space to all to follow their conception of the good. Clearly, requiring an individual to tolerate being offended will only be acceptable when it is proportionate. Thus, in assessing whether it is acceptable to allow an individual to cause offence, the range of factors discussed above will also need to be assessed. The aim of this section is to assess the weight that should be given to the right not to be offended so that it can be properly taken into account in assessing the proportionality of any proposed exception to the general non-discrimination principle.

---

[117] See, generally, J Feinberg, *Offence to Others* (Oxford, OUP, 1985), looking at offence in the context of criminal law prohibitions on causing offence.

Offence may not only be caused by the presence of exceptions to the non-discrimination principle, but can also be caused in a variety of other ways that are of relevance here. Offence can be caused by harassment, behaviour that has the purpose or effect of violating dignity, or causing a hostile environment. In relation to the conflict between religion and other rights, harassment could occur if a religious worker were to cause offence to a co-worker by persistently telling her that her actions were sinful. Alternatively, allowing a male worker to refuse to work with women could create a hostile environment and cause offence to female workers. Where such behaviour is concerned, the interest in protecting the victim, based on her interest in maintaining dignity, is clear. The 'offender' may have some religious interests which are harmed by any restriction on his freedom of action, as the harassing behaviour may also entail the exercise of religious freedom. However, any such harm to the harasser's religious interests is likely to be proportionate given the legitimate aim of protecting the dignity interests of the 'victim'. Religious individuals may have a right to hold their beliefs, but they do not have a right to impose those views on others at work, not least because any 'victim' will find it difficult to avoid the offending behaviour, and the harasser does not have an absolute right to be in the workplace. If an employer allows an employee to treat another in a way that undermines her dignity, then the employer will have failed to provide adequate protection for the autonomy and dignity of its workers.

However, offence is not limited to that caused by direct harassment by an individual; it may be caused in other ways, and in some circumstances the interest in being free from offence may not be so strong. It may then be that the religious interests of the 'offender' can prevail over the interest of the victim in being free from offence. For example, if a religious employer is allowed to maintain an employment practice of only employing co-religionists (through use of a genuine occupational requirement) this could cause offence to those who are thereby refused a job, but would still be proportionate because of the religious interests of the group.

This becomes more problematic if individuals are denied the status of co-religionists because of their race, gender or sexuality. For example, a religious group which is intolerant of homosexuality could recruit only those of the same religion and it could be legal for such a requirement to be introduced, for example, because there is a genuine occupational requirement that the employee be of the particular religion. In such a case there may be no direct 'victim' to be offended: it is unlikely that a gay person will apply, because they are unlikely to belong to the requisite religious group. However, the denial of work to gay applicants could still cause offence in a more general sense: the dignity of gay and lesbian people is undermined by the tolerance of such behaviour within the legal system, through the acceptance of genuine occupational requirement exceptions, in such circumstances.

The question then arises of whether the fact that such practices are tolerated infringes dignity to such an extent that a genuine occupational requirement will be disproportionate in the circumstances. It is suggested below that although the harm should be recognised, it should not be accorded overriding weight in assessing proportionality. It may be that allowing such indirect harm to dignity is a price that has to be paid to enable groups with conflicting beliefs to live and work together.

The work of Feinberg in *Offence to Others*[118] may aid the analysis here. Feinberg considers a number of factors when assessing the level of harm involved in causing offence, including the seriousness of the offence balanced against the reasonableness of the offending conduct. Applied in the context of the workplace, rather than in the context of the criminal law, they suggest that the offence caused by the 'bare knowledge' of the existence of work practices which one finds offensive should not give grounds, of itself, to prohibit those practices. This is not to say that such practices should be allowed where other interests are harmed, merely that where the only harm is one of 'bare knowledge' it may not provide sufficient harm to justify prohibiting a practice.

In considering the seriousness of offence caused, Feinberg considers its magnitude in terms of its intensity, duration and extent. He also looks at questions such as whether it is possible to avoid the offence, or whether the victim has consented to be subject to it. In the work context these are difficult questions. Technically the employee who is a victim of more than single incidents of harassment may be able to resign,[119] but this freedom carries significant cost, and is not a very realistic option.[120] In the context of workplace harassment which is directed at a specific victim, the idea that a person consents to the harassment and is always free to leave will not carry much weight in assessing the seriousness of the offence. However, this may not be the case in the context of 'bare knowledge' offence. For example, a religious employer could require that staff be of the same religion, and the religion may teach that the employment of married women is wrong. In effect, requiring staff to share the religious view will mean that the employer will not employ married women. This impinges on the dignity of all married women, whether religious or not. However, the 'offence' is not directed at any particular woman, and those of the offended group are not forced to confront the offending behaviour. Thus, offence may exist, but it is less serious than that caused by direct harassment at work.

Balanced against the seriousness of the offence caused is the 'reasonableness' of the conduct which causes offence. Here Feinberg considers a number of issues[121]: the importance of the offending conduct to the actor; the social value of the behaviour; the value of freedom of expression; the presence of alternative opportunities

[118] J Feinberg, *Offence to Others* (Oxford, OUP, 1985).
[119] See discussion at p 45ff.
[120] On the debate surrounding the freedom to resign in the context of harassment, see E Volokh 'Freedom of Speech and Workplace Harassment' (1992) 39 *UCLA LR* 1791 and D Epstein, 'Can a "Dumb Ass Woman" Achieve Equality in the Workplace? Running the Gauntlet of Hostile Work Environment Harassing Speech' (1996) 84 *Georgetown LJ* 339, and L Vickers, 'Is All Harassment Equal? The Case of Religious Harassment' (2006) 65(3) *CLJ* 579.
[121] J Feinberg, *Offence to Others* (Oxford, OUP, 1985) 44.

for the conduct which might cause less offence to others; whether the conduct is motivated by malice or spite; and whether the conduct is to be expected in the locality.

Using the example of offence caused by bare knowledge that a religious employer's requirement that staff share the religion results in a failure to offer work to married women, these factors combine to suggest that offence caused should not, of itself, weigh particularly strongly in any assessment of proportionality, albeit that other factors may make the practice disproportionate. If the offending behaviour is the result of religious belief then it will be viewed as being of great importance to the actor, and the fact that religious freedom is protected within human rights law suggests that it is accorded social value: both of these factors weigh in favour of allowing the offending behaviour. The fact that the conduct is not directed at any individual and is not inspired by personal malice or spite similarly militates against the suggestion that the offence caused makes the practice disproportionate. In these circumstances, the balance between the seriousness of offence and the 'reasonableness' (in Feinberg's terms) of the offending behaviour is likely to come down in favour of allowing the offending behaviour to continue. This is because the behaviour is not directed at any particular person, relates only to 'bare knowledge' and can be avoided; and yet the behaviour is of great importance to the individual as an outworking of religious belief. Of course, there may be other factors which tip the balance against allowing the employment practice, for example, if married women are thereby significantly disadvantaged in the workplace because the employer is a major employer in the area.

The final factor suggested by Feinberg (whether the offensive behaviour can be expected and then avoided) is of more relevance in cases where an employee works for a religious employer and takes offence at some of the work practices. For example, a non-religious employee may find it offensive to be invited to pray by colleagues, or may find overtly religious conversations offensive. Here the conduct in question may be to be expected given the type of employer. If the employee has chosen to work for a religious employer, he or she cannot complain of offence when the employer acts in a religious manner.[122] The offending behaviour meets the standards of reasonableness set by Feinberg, suggesting that the balance should be struck in favour of allowing the behaviour to continue, even though the bare knowledge of the behaviour may cause offence to some. Again, if the employer is a major employer in the sector or in the area, then it is arguable that the employee has not really chosen freely to work in such an environment, and the religious practice may then be disproportionate overall.

Although it involves tolerating some level of offensive behaviour, such a compromise is essential if groups who disagree fundamentally on many issues are to co-exist in a plural democracy. It may well be that accommodating an employee

---

[122] Although this may also be subject to proportionality. For example, if it was not clear that religious activity would be expected at work at the start of the employment it may not be acceptable to impose such a requirement on non-religious staff.

who believes in women's inequality implicitly infringes the dignity of women. But it may correspondingly be argued by a religious employer that a refusal to allow accommodation of such views infringes the autonomy of the religious group, as it effectively prevents him from acting as an employer. Religiously motivated people should have the freedom to employ others, in order to fully exercise their freedom of religion, and their autonomy. It may therefore be proportionate to tolerate their employment policies, where there are no direct victims, even though their very existence may be offensive to some. For example, a religious group which is opposed to the employment of women could have a genuine occupational requirement to employ a co-religionist as a religious teacher. Women who share the faith will not want to work, and so there are no direct victims of the indirect discrimination involved. In contrast, where there are victims, for example, the employer is a large or monopoly employer and so the restriction on co-religionists has an impact on women's employment prospects, the level of offence caused may be one of the factors to take into account in assessing proportionality, albeit not necessarily the paramount interest.[123]

Such an approach would not create a licence to private employers simply to refuse to appoint people on religious grounds, as the right to be free from offence is only one factor in the proportionality equation. However, to return to the question of the weight to be afforded to the right not to be offended, it is suggested that 'bare knowledge' offence, caused by allowing genuine occupational requirements which may indirectly discriminate on other grounds, should not be given undue weight in the proportionality equation. It may be necessary to tolerate some level of 'bare knowledge' offence if groups who disagree fundamentally are to coexist.

## Contextual Issues

The factors discussed above should all be taken into account when assessing the proportionality of any protection of religious interests at work. In addition, the contextual issues discussed below should be considered, as they may have a bearing on the final outcome of any balancing of interests that is bound to occur when assessing proportionality.

The first contextual factor to consider is the type of employer. This involves the question of whether the employer is part of the public sector or the private sector, as well as a consideration of the special status of religious employers.

---

[123] See also L Cariolou, 'The right not to be offended by members of the British National Party' (2006) *ILJ* 415. The net effect of these rules may be that only small religious employers will be able to restrict employment to co-religionists, but this is not because of anything inherent in being a small employer, merely because of the range of factors considered in the proportionality equation such as the impact of any restriction on the employment prospects of those outside the religious group.

## The Public/Private Divide

The exact dividing line between public and private sector employers is acknowledged to be difficult to draw with any certainty.[124] The question has become increasingly complex in recent years after the privatisation of numerous public utilities, the contracting out of some parts of state-run enterprises such as cleaning and catering in hospitals to private contractors, and the move of parts of the public sector, such as individual prisons, to the private sector.[125] In the context of remedies such as judicial review, the division between the public and private sector is vital, as the status of the body determines whether the remedy is available at all. However, in the context of determining the proper scope of religious interests when in competition with other interests in the workplace, it may be best to understand the division as a continuum or spectrum rather than as a sharp dividing line.

The question of whether an employer is public or private sector could cause particular difficulties in the context of religion, as there are increasing moves to hand over the provision of public services to charitable or other private providers, some of which are religiously based.[126] Education provides a prime example of the provision of a public service by religiously based providers with a large proportion of state schools having the status of church schools. Here religious organisations provide services, funded by the state, which fulfil the fundamentally public obligations on the state to provide education for children. Other examples include charities involved in the delivery of public services, such as the provision of adaptations to the home for disabled people, of child welfare services and of health services, such as hospice care. In these cases, while the bodies themselves are not part of the public sector, they are clearly a long way along the continuum towards public status and away from purely private status.

## Public Sector Employers

Where the employer can be viewed as on the public end of the continuum, to the extent that they may fairly be said to represent the state, there may be additional factors at play, which call for particular types of protection for religious interests, whilst at the same time placing limits on the scope of the protection that is appropriate.

If the employer is viewed as representing the state, protection of religious interests should only occur where it accords with the aims and interests of the state. The

---

[124] D Oliver, 'Common Values in Public and Private Law and the Public/Private Divide' [1997] *PL* 630; G Morris, 'The Human Rights Act and the Public/Private Divide in Employment Law' [1998] *ILJ* 293; G Morris and S Fredman, 'Public or Private? State Employees and Judicial Review' (1991) 107 *LQR* 298; G Morris, 'Employment in Public Services: The Case for Special Treatment' (2000) 20 *OJLS* 167.

[125] See G Morris, 'The Human Rights Act and the Public/Private Divide in Employment Law' [1998] *ILJ* 293.

[126] See, for example, Press Release, 11 January 2007, from The Department for Work and Pensions, referred to on p 3.

state, if it is committed to a pluralist society, may wish to accommodate a range of religious practices, so that it can encourage equal participation in the workforce for a range of religious groups.[127] The state's interests here are in reducing social exclusion to certain groups by encouraging participation in employment. This prevents detriments caused by being excluded from the economic benefits of working. Equal participation at work also encourages social cohesion by including the minorities in mainstream society, and improving integration between social groups who make up the society.[128] It is also important for the state to reflect the full range of its citizenry in some jobs to reflect the inclusive nature of the society, sending the symbolic message to the rest of society that all citizens are equal and valued. Thus, ensuring that those from minority religions can participate in the armed services, or the police force, serves a legitimate aim of public policy.[129]

Moreover, many jobs or careers can only realistically be carried out in the context of state employment. Although there is a developing role for private medicine in the UK, the overwhelming majority of health-related careers operate in the context of the National Health Service. The same can be said for careers in education, where the vast majority of primary, secondary and tertiary education comprises state provision. Those choosing careers in health or education, or indeed social work, the armed forces, professions related to the criminal justice system, and many others have little choice but to be employed within the public sector. As discussed above, there is no doubt that staff in these sectors remain free to choose other forms of employment, and the proportionality question must be determined in the light of the residual right to resign. Nonetheless, the fact that whole sectors of employment could be barred to members of particular religions if no protection is allowed, is an important contextual factor to be taken into account in assessing the proportionality of any protection.

The various interests served by the protection of religious interests by public sector employers will vary according to the circumstances, such as the extent of the protection requested, and the strength of any competing interests. It may also vary according to the exact place on the public/private continuum the particular employer holds. The importance of having a cross-section of the population in terms of gender, ethnicity and religion may be stronger in an employment sector of symbolic importance such as the police and armed services, than in the case of a religious hospice providing care to patients, some of whom are funded by the state.

---

[127] See J Rawls, *A Theory of Justice* (Oxford, OUP, 1999, revised edition) 196, who argues that justice as fairness requires equal participation in the state.

[128] C Estlund, *Working together: How Workplace Bonds Strengthen a Diverse Democracy* (Oxford, OUP, 2003). See also M Kelman, 'Market Discrimination and Groups' (2001) 53 *Stanford LR* 833, 885.

[129] See further, P W Edge, 'Religious rights and choice under the European Convention on Human Rights' [2000] 3 *Web JCLI*, who cites the MacPherson Report's recommendation that those responsible for staffing 'should seek to ensure that the membership of police authorities reflect so far as is possible the cultural and ethnic mix of the communities which those authorities serve' (*The Stephen Lawrence Inquiry, Report of an Inquiry by Sir William Macpherson*, London, The Stationery Office, Cm 4262-I 1999 Recommendation 7). See also the discussion of the Police (Northern Ireland) Act 2000 at p 143.

However, the fact that a public sector employer represents the state may also work to create special limits on the extent to which religious interests can be protected, because of the equal interest the state has in upholding the dignity and equality of others on grounds of gender, race, sexuality and other grounds. Thus, although public sector employers may need to provide a level of protection to religious interests in order to uphold the public policy of promoting diversity and pluralism within the state, this will not extend to protecting religious interests at the expense of other equality interests to which the state is equally committed.

The public policy imperative of protecting the dignity of all members of society means that where religious interests conflict with other equality interests those equality interests will usually prevail, especially where the employer can be identified as on the public end of the public/private continuum. The right to freedom of religion may be sufficiently strong to warrant protection in the workplace, but the case for its protection is based on the same factors as the case for protection of equality on other grounds. The need to uphold dignity and autonomy leads to a need to protect the individual on a number of grounds, and does not give reason for one ground to trump another. The protection from discrimination on religious grounds does not give rise to grounds for overriding others' equality interests. It is therefore important that the state protects equality on grounds of gender, race and sexual orientation, for all the same reasons set out above, namely the symbolic importance of public sector employment as reflecting public policy, the dominance of the public sector in certain spheres of work such as health and education, and the need to encourage employment in all social groups so as to equalise access to economic benefits and to improve social cohesion. The assessment of the proportionality of any protection of religion should therefore take into account the status of the employer, and its place on the continuum between public and private employment, along with other interests such as the need to provide a high quality of service and to achieve a degree of economic efficiency. Those engaged in employment of a public nature should have their religious needs accommodated where possible, but only to the extent that to do so does not infringe other equality rights, in order to reflect the public policy of maintaining the dignity and equality of all groups in society.

## Private Sector Employers

In contrast, the private sector is not compelled to promote the state's social policy agenda, and may not have the same imperative to promote religious equality at work or to uphold other social policies within the workplace. Thus private employers may not need to provide the same level of protection for religious interests as public employers; but equally an employer which chooses to uphold religious interests may not have the same limit as public employers in terms of the extent to which they must also uphold other equality interests, at the expense of protecting those religious interests.[130]

---

[130] See discussion of autonomy of religious employers above at pp 59–60.

As with the public sector, the notion of private employment may also be understood as a continuum. One can draw distinctions between the levels to which enterprises engage with the public. For example, some employment relationships may resemble private family arrangements, such as employment of a nanny or domestic cleaner, or employment in a small family business. In some cases the parties might not in ordinary language understand themselves to be part of an employment relationship, but for the needs of employment law policy this classification is made.[131] Other enterprises engage to a greater degree with the public, and are more clearly within the category of employment with a more managerial relationship between employer and employee. One could go so far as to suggest that any body which provides services to the public, even though those services are not publicly funded, is somewhere along the continuum away from the purely private arrangement. An employer which wishes to engage with the general public in order to gain some benefit, such as access to the public market for the purpose of generating profits, is engaging with the public sphere to an extent, and could be required to conform to publicly accepted standards as regards the necessity to protect religion. This public level of protection is likely to involve some measure of accommodation to enable members of religious groups to achieve a degree of equality with other sections of the public, so as to reflect a basic level of protection for religious freedom. However, such employers would also be expected to limit religious accommodation where it is necessary to safeguard the equality rights of others. This argument can apply to religious ethos employers, where the religious group wishes to carry on a business, offering services to the public. They may have regard to the religious ethos in their recruitment policies, in order to respect the autonomy of the group, but this cannot be at the expense of the equality rights of others.

However, where the employment relationship is more truly private, as with the nanny or domestic cleaner, the requirements to protect religious or other interests may be lessened.[132] This may also apply to religious employers who are employing staff to serve the needs of the religious group, such as cleaning staff, or administrative staff, or employing a helper for a church toddler group. The extent to which such jobs can be viewed as religious in nature will depend on the details of the job description, and the religious beliefs of the parties involved. For example, some religious groups may require that certain services be carried out by co-religionists.[133] However, even where the work is not defined as religious in nature, the employment relationships in the case of those serving the needs of a religious employer are of a private nature, and do not involve any interaction with the pub-

---

[131] To interpret employment law not to apply to these essentially private arrangements would lead to different but equal difficulties in other areas of employment law. See above at pp 51–52.

[132] The point is also made by M Kelman, 'Market Discrimination and Groups' (2001) 53 *Stanford LR* 833, 849, that there may be less need for anti-discrimination rules with regard to employment relationships which are 'quasi-intimate' relationships.

[133] On the difficulty of determining the division between the religious private sphere and the secular private sphere, see R Wintemute, 'Religion vs Sexual Orientation' [2002] 1:2 *Journal of Law and Equality* 125.

lic market. Greater freedom may therefore be given to the religious group to act in accordance with their beliefs, even where to do so may indirectly interfere with other equality rights. In effect, the role of the state in requiring compliance with the socially accepted norms of behaviour is reduced where the relationship is such a private one.[134]

The treatment of religious interests within the employment relationship may therefore vary depending on where on this spectrum the employment fits, with more flexibility regarding the protection of religious interests being given to more private employment relationships. This may involve greater or lesser protection, depending on the employer's wishes, with religious ethos employers being given increased freedom to accommodate religion at the expense of other interests where the employment relationship is at the private end of the spectrum. The question of whether any particular protection or accommodation is proportionate should be assessed in the light of these contextual issues.

## Work as a Public or Private Space

There is an additional dimension to the question of whether employment is public or private in nature, and this is the question of whether the workplace itself should be seen as a public or private space. Although clearly the workplace is not private in the same way that the home is, work is not entirely a public space either. For example, individuals often enjoy close social friendships with colleagues, and may well socialise with them outside work. Indeed, a remarkable number of individuals meet their life partners at work. Courts have acknowledged the cross-over between work and leisure time in sexual harassment cases where after-work socialising has come within the remit of the employer's responsibility to protect staff against harassment. Examples from this case law of the cross-over between work as a public space and the private dimension of work are after-work drinks, work parties, or works family outings.[135] The private nature of the workplace is also reflected in workplaces which encourage staff to personalise their work spaces, by decorating them with pictures or photos, for example. Such practices demonstrate the hybrid nature of the workplace, formally a public space but experienced by many in practice as having a private dimension.

This private aspect of the workplace has been recognised in the case law of the ECHR. With respect to the right to privacy, it is recognised that individuals are entitled to a degree of respect for private life at work.[136] Moreover, in *Sidabras v Lithuania*,[137] the ECHR recognised that work can play an important role in one's 'private life', with a role in developing relationships with the outside world.

---

[134] It is plausible to achieve the same end by excluding such relationships from the definition of employment, but to do so would create further problems for vulnerable workers, and would be counter-productive. See discussion at pp 51–52 above.

[135] *Waters v Commissioner of Police of the Metropolis* [1997] IRLR 589, *Chief Constable of Lincolnshire Police v Stubbs* [1999] IRLR 91, *Sidhu v Aerospace Composite Technology* [2000] IRLR 602.

[136] *Halford v UK* (1997) 24 EHRR 523.

[137] App Nos 55480/00 and 59330/00, 27 July 2004.

It was also argued above that work plays an important role in creating individual identity and providing status. These may not be interests that prevail over other interests when considering the proportionality of protecting religious interests, but the assessment of proportionality should take into account that the workplace is not solely a public arena, but can also be regarded as having a private dimension.

One aspect of the private nature of the workplace is the role it can play in educating individuals about wider society. Not only is work an important forum in which individuals live out a large proportion of their lives, it is also an important space in which individuals can meet those they might not otherwise meet in other areas of their lives. For many, particularly those who live in religiously homogenous groups in their private lives, the workplace is the main forum for meeting those with differing views, and for sharing ideas. Estlund has gone as far as to argue that the workplace is a valuable forum for religious discourse.[138] Even though the facilitation of such discourse is clearly not the primary function of the workplace, it is clear that the workplace has the potential to act as a 'melting pot', where groups that might otherwise not mix actually engage with each other. As Schultz puts it, the workplace is 'one of the few arenas in which diverse groups of citizens can come together and develop respect for each other due to shared experience'.[139] Thus, encouraging religious groups to mix within the context of work can enable religious understanding and tolerance to be developed. Clearly, employers are not responsible for providing spaces for private socialising, nor for religious debate, and it is not suggested that they should be. Nor should employees be forced to mix socially with their work colleagues. However, any assessment of the proportionality of protecting religious interests at work should take into account the hybrid public and private nature of the workplace.

The fact that the workplace can be viewed as both a private and a public space has implications for the treatment of religious issues at work, particularly by religious ethos employers. Issues that may be viewed as wholly private, and therefore irrelevant to the employer in non-religious employment, may be of relevance to religious employers, and the recognition of a private dimension to the workplace means that they cannot be dismissed as irrelevant at work. For example, from a secular point of view, matters relating to the private lives of staff, as well as matters of personal and private morality, such as marital status and sexuality, should be irrelevant to the employer. However, religious employers can be intensely interested in issues of private morality as reflecting good religious standing and loyalty to the religion. Both employer and employee may view the employment as a forum for the exercise of religion as much as any other part of their lives. It is inevitable that matters of personal morality will be relevant to a religious employer who wishes to maintain a religious ethos: part of having a religious ethos at work is that

---

[138] C Estlund, 'Freedom of Speech in the Workplace and the Problem of Discriminatory Harassment' (1997) 75 *Tex LR* 687, and C Estlund, *Working together: How Workplace Bonds Strengthen a Diverse Democracy* (Oxford, OUP, 2003).

[139] V Schultz, 'Life's Work' [2000] 100 *Colum LR* 1881, 1885.

matters that to outsiders would be viewed as personal and private are shared. Where the employee has chosen to work for a religious employer, it may not be inappropriate for the employer to show interest in matters that in other contexts may be viewed as private.[140]

Of course, the extent to which secular employers have regard to personal morality is not a constant. Issues of private morality, such as honesty, may be relevant to the employer: it is accepted that an employer may dismiss for theft, rather than being required to put into place mechanisms to ensure that there will be no future incidents. Thus even with regard to secular employment matters of morality may be relevant, although the range of relevant issues may be greater with regard to religious employers. In considering the proportionality of an accommodation of religious interests, the fact that it is not always simple to create clear boundaries between a public workplace and the rest of life needs to be taken into account.

## Religious Manifestation or Religious Motivation

Under Article 9 ECHR a distinction is drawn between conduct which is motivated by religion and that which is a manifestation of the religion.[141] That which is merely motivated by religion is not a manifestation of religion, and so restrictions imposed by the employer on religiously motivated activity do not offend the ECHR. Although the distinction between the two can be difficult to draw at times,[142] a broad distinction may be relevant in determining the proportionality of any restriction on religious freedom. Where behaviour is mandated by the religion to which an employee adheres, any refusal to allow the behaviour will involve a greater infringement of religious interests than a refusal to accommodate religiously motivated behaviour.

To rule out employment protection for behaviours which are religiously motivated may be to provide too little protection for religious interests, not least because the distinction can be difficult to define with precision. However, taking account of the centrality of the belief to the religious individual may be of relevance for the determination of proportionality. Where a work practice prevents a religious person from observing key tenets of the religion it will be harder to justify any refusal to protect the religious interest, than where the practice interferes with a religious preference. For example, a key tenet of the religion may be a requirement to pray at certain times of day. To refuse time off for prayers will involve a more significant infringement of religious interests than either to fail to provide a comfortable space to pray (however desirable that may be), or to refuse time off for members of other religions who would like to form a prayer group, but who are not required by their religion to do so.

---

[140] See R Ehrenreich, 'Dignity and Discrimination: Toward a Pluralistic Understanding of Workplace Harassment' (1999) 88 *Georgetown LJ* 1, 27, who points out that the boundaries between public and private issues can be hard to draw in some harassment cases, where the judgment of whether behaviour is appropriate may be very context-specific.

[141] *Arrowsmith v UK* [1978] 3 EHRR 218.

[142] See discussion in ch 4 at pp 96–101.

Similarly, where religious interests collide with other interests, the centrality of the belief will be of relevance to the determination of proportionality. For example, where a religious group believes that religious rites can only be validly performed by men, that belief is so central to a core part of the religion that the gender equality interests of women will not prevail over the religious interests of the religious organisation. This is recognised in most human rights systems, where the freedom of religious groups to appoint their religious leaders is respected. However, where a preference for male staff applies other than in the appointment of those performing religious rites, then the equality interests of women will have more weight. In effect, the centrality of the belief to the religious belief system is of relevance to the determination of proportionality.[143]

## Organic or Functional View of the Religious Workplace

One particular difficulty that can arise with respect to religious employers is that the divide between work that is viewed as religious in nature and that which is not may be difficult to draw. Where employment is religious, it would seem proportionate to allow the imposition by the employer of religious requirements, if religious freedom is to be respected, even though to do so may infringe other equality rights. For example, a requirement that an employee should be an observant Muslim may indirectly discriminate against gays and lesbians, due to Islam's intolerance of homosexuality. It would seem clear that employment as a teacher of a religion, or as an officiator at religious ceremonies, is religious employment, and that religious requirements are appropriate even though they may infringe others' rights. Refusing to accept limits on the non-discrimination principle with respect to such religious functions would be a significant restriction on religious freedom.[144]

However, once one moves from the realm of religious practitioners, matters become more difficult, as the boundaries between work within the 'religious sphere' and the 'secular sphere' are less easy to draw. Some would claim that any work for a religious ethos employer is within the 'religious sphere' and that it is acceptable to impose strict religious requirements on such workers. Others would argue that once one leaves those who officiate at religious ceremonies to one side, other staff are outside the 'religious sphere' and religious restrictions should be limited to those that do not discriminate on any other ground. The question which arises here is the extent to which we allow the idea of the religious sphere to expand.[145]

---

[143] See B N Bagni, 'Discrimination in the Name of the Lord: A Critical Evaluation of Discrimination by Religious Organisations' (1979) 79 *Colum LR* 1514, who suggests an analytic framework based on concentric circles of spirituality and secularity: matters relating to the core, central circle, such as appointment of clergy should be insulated from state regulation.

[144] Moreover, as discussed above at pp 51–52, the alternative response, denial of employment status, causes as many problems as it solves.

[145] See R Wintemute, 'Religion vs Sexual Orientation' [2002] 1(2) *Journal of Law and Equality* 125.

The assessment of whether it is proportionate for religious employers to impose religious requirements on staff will depend on the range of factors discussed above, such as whether either party is denied access to the workforce. It will also depend on whether an organic or functional view is taken of the workplace.[146] The functional view is that the workplace exists to fulfil various functions, and each role should be considered with regard to that function. Thus the function of an officiator at a religious ceremony is to carry out religious observance, and it is necessary to comply with the religious rules if that observance is to be valid for the religious adherents. At the other end of the scale, the function of a cleaner of a church hall is to clean the building, and the religious beliefs of the individual worker have no impact on job performance. Again, there is a spectrum between these two extremes in which the religious nature of the functions is less clear cut. For example, it could be argued that an individual whose job is to teach the religion to young people, for example a church youth leader, need only have a good understanding of religious doctrine, without actually believing the truth of what he or she is teaching. However, most religious individuals would view it as essential that those who teach the religion to young people be active believers themselves.[147]

An alternative view of the workplace is more organic in nature, and recognises that some religious workers view work as a form of worship. For example, some Christians may view working for a Christian organisation as part of their Christian witness,[148] particularly if they work in a role which involves interaction with the public. Thus, some religious workers might argue that their work entails a manifestation of their belief, even though the work does not involve direct proselytism. If one takes an organic view of the workplace, viewing it a whole, one can see that a much greater range of jobs within the workplace should be viewed as religious in nature. A religious group may view every worker, from cleaner to religious teacher, as part of a team whose role is to witness to the truth of the religion. The idea that even the lowliest of workers can be fulfilling a religious function is well established in Christian teaching, and may resonate clearly with other religions too. If such a view is recognised by courts, it would enable religious groups to argue that a wide range of employment is religious in nature, although evidence may well be needed to show that religion permeates the particular workplace in practice.

## The Meaning of Equality

In assessing the proportionality of any response to religious discrimination regard should be had to the overall aim of discrimination law in promoting equality between different groups. The difficulty here is that equality has a variety of

---

[146] A Esau ' "Islands of Exclusivity": Religious Organizations and Employment Discrimination' (1993) 33 *Univ British Columbia LR* 719.

[147] This may not be the case in relation to the teaching of theology, or the teaching of religious education in schools, where not all religious experts are necessarily active believers.

[148] This point is developed in R Fahlbeck, '*Ora et Labora* on Freedom of Religion at the Work Place: A Stakeholder *cum* Balancing Factors Model' [2004] *IJCLLIR* 1.

meanings, and determining what 'promoting equality' might require is both complex and contested. Indeed, given the wide range of understandings of the meaning of equality, McCrudden has suggested that talk should now be of *equalities* rather than equality, in recognition that no single understanding of equality is complete.[149]

The most obvious meaning for equality is formal or symmetrical equality, which requires that like cases be treated alike, with a focus on the individual rather than groups. A broader approach to equality focuses on substantive equality in which equality of outcome and equality of opportunity are the focus rather than equal treatment. Such a substantive view of equality can take into account the relative disadvantage of some groups in contrast to others. Other models focus on the link between equality and individual dignity and identity, or on the facility for equality to act as a means of addressing social exclusion, by promoting participation and engaging in redistribution.[150] A further model of equality, from Fredman, identifies the need to allow all groups an equal set of alternatives from which they can pursue their own version of a good life.[151] From this she argues for the promotion of positive measures to allow all members of society access to the particular social goods. The idea is that equality does not need to include the 'same' treatment, but may instead involve different groups being able to pursue their version of the good life. Fredman also suggests that equality law should breach the cycle of disadvantage associated with 'out-groups'; promote respect for the equal dignity of all, redressing stigma, stereotyping, humiliation and violence because of membership of an out-group; affirm community identities; and facilitate full participation in society.

The vision of equality held by any tribunal or court will be an important contextual factor which is likely to influence the determination of proportionality. For example, if formal equality is the goal, courts are unlikely to view as disproportionate neutral requirements with which religious people have difficulty complying. Where Fredman's broader concept of equality is used, with promotion of participation as part of the vision of equality, outcomes could be quite different. Tribunals may want to encourage religious groups to engage in mainstream society by limiting the extent to which they can create religiously homogenous workplaces. Or they may take account of the role of religion in shaping cultural identity, and so allow minority groups the freedom to express their cultural identity at work. Such an approach results in a very nuanced approach to equality as the facts of different cases interact with the different factors.

Assessing proportionality in order to promote 'equality' is thus a very complex process, and requires an analysis of the interaction of different factors. In addition,

---

[149] C McCrudden, 'Thinking about the discrimination directives' (2005) 1 *European Anti-Discrimination Law Review* 17.

[150] See: C Barnard and B Hepple, 'Substantive Equality' (2000) 59 *CLJ* 562; H Collins 'Discrimination, Equality and Social Inclusion' (2003) 66 *MLR* 16 and C McCrudden 'Thinking about the discrimination directives' (2005) 1 *European Anti-Discrimination Law Review* 17.

[151] S Fredman, *The Future of Equality In Britain*, EOC, Working Paper Series No 5 (London, Equal Opportunities Commission, 2002) 11.

broader socio-economic issues will interact with pure equality issues to influence any outcome.

## Socio-Political Context

In assessing proportionality the socio-political context is also of significance where the view of equality is not purely formal. The importance of such factors as the historical disadvantage of the relevant groups, and the level of social exclusion or disadvantage currently experienced, should be taken into account in assessing whether it is proportionate to allow either religious freedom to be infringed or, indeed, whether other equality rights can be overridden in the name of religious freedom. Collins has argued[152] that discrimination law should serve the overall aim of social inclusion, and that this aim should help to determine the correct parameters of the law. Clearly this will not help resolve every contentious issue in this area, but helping increase social inclusion for groups that have suffered exclusion from society's goods in the past may help to resolve the clash between rights on a principled basis in some cases. For example, if it is acknowledged that Muslims have suffered disadvantage in access to the job market, it may be proportionate to require a greater level of protection for their religious practices than for religious groups for whom such disadvantage cannot be shown.[153] Thus the need to improve social inclusion for out-groups should be taken into account in assessing the proportionality of any religious requirement for a job.

However, factors such as historic disadvantage will not always point towards protection of religion, and what is proportionate could vary according to the religion in question: the Muslim community in Britain will have a different experience of disadvantage from the Anglican community. Where religious groups' employment practices discriminate against women, for example, historic disadvantage as a factor may cut both ways: it may favour protection of a minority religious group, as well as protection for women or lesbian and gay people who have also been subject to historic disadvantage. Where such contextual issues do not provide clear answers, the conflict will only be resolved with reference to the other factors discussed above. Thus, for example, although women have suffered disadvantage historically, this may not automatically outweigh the benefits of affirming community identities among disadvantaged communities who wish to employ only those of the same conservative religious traditions in their religious organisations.

## The Role of the State

One final factor which should be taken into account in difficult cases is the extent to which it is appropriate for the state to intervene to settle disputes. Where

---

[152] H Collins, 'Discrimination, Equality and Social Inclusion' (2003) 66 *MLR* 16.
[153] Such groups may be Christians, who as members of the majority religion may face less systemic disadvantage.

individual human rights interests are clearly infringed, it is right for the state, through the courts, to intervene to provide protection.[154] However, where the question of whether the rights are infringed or not is finely balanced, it may be worth considering whether it is proper for the state to intervene to uphold one set of interests over another, where to do so involves intervening in the conduct of what may be viewed as a type of private relationship. It is, arguably, not appropriate to expect legislative intervention in the regulation of the religious sphere. Of course, it might be argued that the employment relationship is public in nature, and so intervention is appropriate, but it is part of the argument of this chapter that employment has a private dimension so that the employment relationship is of a hybrid public-private nature.

Moreover, one of the reasons for providing protection for religious interests is the fact that protecting religious freedom can be a useful tool in preventing or overcoming religious conflict.[155] Although it was suggested above that this reason was insufficient alone to provide a rationale for the protection of religious interests at work, it remains of significance. Despite the existence of an established church within the UK, it is still arguable that the state should remain neutral in religious disputes. Courts may well be wary of intervening where to do so amounts to state regulation of religious matters. Again, whether or not state intervention will be appropriate will be determined by considering all the proportionality factors. The decision may depend on the centrality of the religious interest to the religious group, the extent to which the job involved is religious in essence and the extent to which any restriction interferes with the individual's ability to work, as well as the other factors discussed above.

# V Conclusion

It has been argued above that religious interests are sufficiently important to individual dignity and autonomy to warrant protection within the workplace. This is the product of the importance of the workplace as a forum for the exercise of fundamental rights combined with the importance of religious interests themselves. Equally important, however, are other rights based on dignity and autonomy, and rights to equality on a number of grounds such as gender, sexual orientation, race and disability. It is where these interests conflict that difficulties arise with regard to establishing the correct parameters for any protection for religion within the workplace.

It was not the aim of this chapter to reach conclusive answers on how to resolve such conflicts, as this would depend on the complex interplay of a wide range of factors. Instead, the aim was to consider the range of factors at stake in cases where

---

[154] *Young, James and Webster v UK* [1981] IRLR 408.
[155] See discussion above at pp 33–34.

religious matters arise at work, and to consider how those factors should be balanced in seeking proportionality in the treatment of conflicting interests. Those factors range across the personal interests of employees and colleagues, the business interests of the employer, and the religious interests of religious ethos employers, as well as wider contextual issues such as whether the employer forms part of the public or private sector, the extent to which the employer engages with public markets, whether the workplace can be viewed as a public or private space, and the socio-economic factors that are at work. Exactly how these factors interact will depend on the facts and the socio-economic context.

Within the employment context, any deliberations on proportionality must be carried out in the light of the fact that no-one has a right to a given job. This remains the basic answer when religious groups require excessive accommodation. The arguments for protection of religious interests are strong, but they do not require that an employer should have to make very costly adjustments to accommodate a religious employee. The employee's residual protection lies in his freedom to leave his job. Take the hypothetical example of an employee who wishes to work in public relations, whose core job involves 'meeting and greeting' clients, but who refuses, for religious reasons, to shake hands with women: this employee does not have a right to a job, and has no 'right' to work in this particular line of work. He remains free to exercise his freedom of religion outside work. It may therefore be acceptable for the employer to refuse to accommodate his religious practice.

However, the 'right to resign' argument will not always prevail. For example, a woman who wants to wear trousers at work for religious reasons, in a workplace where the uniform is a skirt, may need to be accommodated, unless there are very strong contra-indicators. Accommodation is unlikely to be costly to the employer, and a conclusion that her freedom of religion is protected by freedom to leave would seem inadequate, given the ease with which accommodation could be granted.

A particular problem is caused by religious ethos employers, and the question of whether it is ever proportionate to protect their religious interests at the expense of the equality interests of others. As a general rule, discrimination against others, even where motivated by religion, will not be proportionate. However, respect for autonomy may involve allowing some space for religious intolerance of others, albeit of a very limited kind. It may be that discriminatory religious groups should be allowed to retreat from mainstream society to create 'islands of exclusivity' from which they can exclude those with different views.[156] This allows adequate protection for religious freedom for individuals who hold these views, as they remain free to associate with those of the same religion. They also remain free to enter into employment relationships with others of the same faith, in order to regulate the provision of services within the group. Within this restricted sphere,

---

[156] A Esau, ' "Islands of Exclusivity": Religious Organizations and Employment Discrimination' (1993) 33 *Univ British Columbia LR* 719.

groups can operate in an exclusive manner, without being required to provide employment for those of other religions or lifestyles. Allowing religious groups to retreat in this manner provides sufficient protection for their religious interests, without causing much harm to other interests. Other interests may be infringed, but not to a significant extent. For example, a religious group's requirement that their toddler group leader share the group's religion will not significantly reduce the job prospects of non-religious child care workers. The main detriment is the offence caused to others by allowing such practices to continue. However, in the absence of other harms, offence caused by the bare knowledge that religious practices occur should not be sufficient to determine proportionality.[157]

To the extent that the group wishes to interact with the rest of society, however, they can be expected to conform to the norms of the rest of society in terms of respect for the dignity and autonomy of others.[158] Thus if a religious group wishes to enter a contract with the state to deliver services to the public, such as medical or social services, the group should conform to the standards of respect for others that is required by the state. Thus the religious group would not be able to provide such services if the job requirements indirectly discriminate against women or against gay or lesbian workers. This requirement could be limited to cases where the religious group provides services that are paid for by the state. However, a stronger version of the argument would mean that wherever the religious group engages at all with wider society, the norms of society should be respected. Thus where a religious group offers commercial services to the public, they should be required to do so equally for all members of society. For example, a hairdressing salon staffed by religious staff would not be able to discriminate against others in its employment practices if the salon were open to the public. In contrast, a hairdresser who employs an assistant to cut the hair of others from the same religious group may be allowed to discriminate indirectly in recruitment practices, as services are only offered to members of the religious group. Thus, those who seek the advantages of access to the public market would need to respect the dignity and equality of all members of the public.[159]

Using the model of work-based religious accommodation outlined above will enable a reasonable balance to be achieved between the right to freedom of religion and other competing rights. The model is predicated on maximum respect for dignity, autonomy and equality within the public sphere, broadly defined, but retaining the right for groups, religious or not, to retreat to 'islands of exclusivity' which remain essentially private. Interpreting the relatively new UK law according to this model should result in most workplaces engaging in respect-

---

[157] See discussion above at pp 62–66.

[158] See S Wessels, 'The Collision of Religious Exercise and Governmental Nondiscrimination Policies' (1989) 41 *Stanford LR* 1201, who draws a distinction between the inward-looking and outward-looking activities of religious organisations, and suggests that inward-looking activities should be free from government restrictions, but that outward-looking activities, where the group has chosen to step outside its internal life, should be subject to non-discrimination rules.

[159] See the discussion of the position in the USA and Canada in ch 6, where religious requirements can only be imposed for work in the not-for-profit activities of religious organisations.

ful pluralism,[160] where religious practice can be accommodated alongside other equality and dignity rights. Where religious groups wish to dissociate from the rest of society, they should remain free to do so, out of respect for their religious freedom. However, any intolerant religious practices will be significantly burdened as they will not be able to gain any benefits from engagement with the wider society.[161]

It has been noted that religious discrimination and freedom of religion are closely linked. Later chapters consider the current law on religious discrimination at work in the UK and beyond, and assess the extent to which protection matches the model developed above. First, the human rights protection for freedom of religion under the European Convention on Human Rights will be considered, together with an assessment of the extent to which its jurisprudence can apply in the UK and in the work context.

---

[160]  D A Hicks, *Religion and the Workplace: Pluralism Spirituality, Leadership* (Cambridge and New York, CUP, 2003).

[161]  It should be noted that although some of the observations may be of use in the wider debate over how to reconcile competing rights, any conclusions suggested here are offered in the limited context of reconciling conflicting rights at work.

# 4

## Freedom of Religion at Work and the European Convention on Human Rights

The right to freedom of religion is granted extensive protection within international law, demonstrated by its inclusion in the Universal Declaration of Human Rights, the European Convention on Human Rights and the International Covenant on Civil and Political Rights.[1] The focus of this chapter is on the protection provided by the European Convention on Human Rights (ECHR) for religious freedom,[2] and the extent to which it may apply to the work relationship. This necessitates an examination of the way in which the ECHR case law can be used directly in the domestic context, via the Human Rights Act 1998.

## I  Freedom of Religion and the Human Rights Act 1998

Under the Human Rights Act 1998 (HRA) the ECHR is partially incorporated into domestic law.[3] This means that where a Convention right is infringed at work, rather than having to make an application directly to the court in Strasbourg, an applicant will be able to use the ECHR in domestic courts. The HRA provides individual rights of action against public authorities[4] for breach of Convention rights, as well as requiring statutes to be interpreted to comply with the Convention,[5] and the common law to be developed in harmony with Convention jurisprudence. In addition, where a question to be determined by a court or tribunal might affect the exercise by a religious organisation of the Convention right to freedom of thought, conscience and religion, the court should have particular regard to the importance of that right.[6]

---

[1]  Art 18 UDHR, Art 9 ECHR, Art 18 ICCPR.

[2]  See ch 2 for a discussion of the meaning of religion in the case law of the ECHR.

[3]  The discussion here is brief. For more detail on how the HRA works to incorporate the ECHR into domestic law, see J Wadham, H Mountfield and A Edmundson, *Blackstone's Guide to the Human Rights Act 1998* (3rd edn) (Oxford, OUP, 2003). See also L Vickers, *Freedom of Expression and Employment* (Oxford, OUP, 2002).

[4]  Section 6.

[5]  Section 3 HRA 1998.

[6]  Section 13. Given that under the HRA a court should have regard to the rights under Art 9, it is not particularly clear what this section adds to the general protection, although it does suggest that where religious employers seek to rely on religious rights, the importance of the right to religious freedom should be considered.

Employees of public bodies who believe their right to freedom of religion under Article 9 is interfered with by their employer have an independent cause of action under the HRA. Accordingly, those who work for government departments, local government, health authorities, education authorities and the police can claim directly against their employer for any breach of their Convention rights.

The range of employees potentially covered by this provision is wider than just the traditional public sector. The term 'public authority' includes any body whose functions are 'of a public nature',[7] thus covering many private organisations. For example, organisations such as the former public utilities and private sector prisons come within this category. They are hybrid in nature, due to their private ownership coupled with provision of publicly funded services.

Despite the broad definition of 'public authorities' within the HRA, the ambit of protection for employees is narrowed by the distinction it draws between acts of a public nature and those of a private nature. The distinction does not apply in the context of overtly public authorities, such as local government, but an otherwise private body, which is a public authority because it carries out some public functions, is only bound to comply with the Convention in relation to those public functions. Acts of a private nature carried out by hybrid bodies are therefore not susceptible to a direct claim under the HRA; and it is fairly well established that employment matters are viewed as private in nature.[8] Thus employees in private organisations will be unable to make direct claims against their employers for breaches of their Article 9 rights in the workplace, whether or not their employers fulfil public functions. This avoids the creation of an anomaly whereby only some of the staff in a private sector organisation would be covered by the HRA, with others left unprotected, depending on whether the part of the business they work in is public in nature in terms of the services provided. However, an alternative anomaly is created, whereby staff doing the same job, such as working as a prison officer, may or may not be protected by the HRA depending on whether their employer is part of the public or private sector.[9]

Although the existence of such anomalies in the protection provided to human rights within the work context is far from satisfactory, there is more potential for using the HRA in relation to private sector employment than might be apparent on first sight. This is due to the fact that courts and tribunals are viewed as public authorities,[10] meaning that they are themselves bound to uphold Convention

---

[7] Section 6 (3). The exact division between public and private sector remains elusive. See H Woolf, 'Public Law—Private Law: Why the Divide?' [1986] *PL* 220; G Morris and S Fredman, 'The Costs of Exclusivity' [1994] *PL* 69 and 'Public or Private? State Employees and Judicial Review' (1991) 107 *LQR* 298; D Oliver, 'Common Values in Public and Private Law and the Public/Private Divide' [1997] *PL* 630; A Grear 'Theorising the Rainbow? The Puzzle of the Public-Private Divide' (2003) 9 *Res Publica* 169. For a general discussion of the impact of public law on employment law, see P Davies and M Freedland, 'The Impact of Public Law on Labour Law 1972–1997' [1997] *ILJ* 311.

[8] *McClaren v Home Office* [1990] ICR 824 establishes that employment disputes are viewed as private matters in relation to judicial review.

[9] See further, L Vickers, *Freedom of Expression and Employment* (Oxford, OUP, 2002) 74–76.

[10] Section 6.

rights in hearings, regardless of whether the parties are public or private in nature. Consequently, the Convention must be taken into account in interpreting the common law and statute, even where the subject matter of the dispute is of a private nature. This provides significant potential for Convention rights to be taken into account within the work context, regardless of the nature of the employer.

The most obvious example of the effect of the HRA in the employment relationship can be found in the statutory remedy of unfair dismissal, and the fairness of a dismissal under section 98(4) Employment Rights Act 1996. In assessing the fairness of a dismissal, Employment Tribunals will need to consider the question of whether the dismissal infringes one of the Convention rights, in order to comply with their obligation as public bodies to comply with the Convention. Where a dismissal touches on a Convention right, the question of whether it was 'reasonable or unreasonable' to dismiss in the circumstances thus needs to be answered with reference to the Convention standard. For example, the fairness of dismissal should be assessed not only by reference to current employer standards, but with due regard for the employee's human rights, and making reference to the legitimacy of the aim of the employer in dismissing the employee and the proportionality of the employer's response.[11]

It is also arguable that the duty on courts and tribunals to interpret and develop the common law in accordance with the jurisprudence of the ECHR could have an effect on the development of the understanding of the contract of employment in general, and the duty of trust and confidence in particular. Hepple has suggested[12] that the duty of trust and confidence[13] might be developed to include an understanding that Convention rights are to be protected within the employment relationship, on the basis that it is unlikely that either party would envisage a relationship at odds with the fundamental rights protected in international law. Indeed, in *Johnson v Unisys*[14] Lord Hoffman referred to the fact that the employment relationship must involve the observance of fundamental human rights as well as recognising general economic interests.[15] The scope of the duty of trust and confidence within the employment relationship is still developing, and it may be that, in time, such an understanding will evolve. However, it should also be noted that other developments within employment law suggest a hesitance on the part of the judiciary to extend the scope of the duty of trust and confidence too far.[16]

The HRA thus creates potential for the right to freedom of religion under the ECHR to operate within the employment relationship, and to be protected in domestic law. Employees in the public sector have the potential to make direct

---

[11] See *Pay v Lancashire Probation Service* [2004] ICR 187 EAT, and *X v Y* [2004] EWCA Civ 662, although see also discussion of *Copsey* below at p 118.

[12] B Hepple, 'Human Rights and Employment Law' (8 June 1998) *Amicus Curiae* 19.

[13] A 'general obligation not to engage in conduct likely to undermine the trust and confidence required if the employment relationship is to continue in the manner the employment contract implicitly envisages': *Malik v BCCI* [1997] 3 All ER 1, per Lord Nicholls at 5.

[14] [2001] UKHL 13.

[15] Lord Hoffman, at para 37.

[16] For example, the overall decision in *Johnson v Unisys* [2001] UKHL 13.

claims under the Act if their Convention rights are infringed at work; and all employees, public or private sector, can expect the jurisprudence of the ECHR to be taken into account when employment disputes involve Article 9 rights.[17] In fact, domestic courts are not bound to follow the European decisions, only to take them into account. They remain free to develop their own applications of the Convention. If domestic interpretation is more restrictive than that available at the ECtHR in Strasbourg, the individual's right to appeal to the ECtHR remains, notwithstanding the existence of the HRA.

However, the fact that the rights available to individuals under Article 9 ECHR can apply within a work context will be of little consequence if the protection under Article 9 itself is inadequate. What will be seen below is that the protection under the Convention is not particularly strong. However, the fact that domestic courts are not bound by the European jurisprudence could be of significance, as it allows courts to interpret the Convention rights to give the best protection to religious freedom in the domestic setting. Instead of being bound to follow the some-times restrictive decisions from Strasbourg, they could follow a more progressive reading of the human rights case law. This will be discussed further below. First, the protection under the ECHR will be considered.

# II  Protection of Freedom of Religion Under the ECHR

The ECHR provides two bases for the protection of religious interests: Article 9, the right to freedom to freedom of thought, conscience and religion; and Article 14, the right not to be discriminated against in the enjoyment of Convention rights on grounds including religious grounds. The right to freedom of religion under Article 9 is divided between what is known as the *forum internum*, an absolute right, referring to the right to have inner thoughts and beliefs, and the *forum externum*, referring to the right to manifest religion. The right to manifest is not an absolute right, and can be restricted where necessary and proportionate to protect others' rights.[18]

Before looking at the scope of the protection under Articles 9 and 14, the preliminary question of whether the Convention provides protection in the work-place will be considered.

## The Application of the ECHR to the Workplace

Although the right to freedom of religion and belief is protected under Article 9 of the Convention, the question of whether the Convention rights apply at all within

---

[17]  HRA s 2.
[18]  See in more detail below.

the workplace is contested within the case law, and the ECtHR has not taken a consistent view on this issue.[19]

The traditional view has been that the rights do not apply in the context of work, as the Convention does not cover access to employment. In effect, the freedom to leave one's job acts as sufficient protection of one's fundamental human rights. Thus in *Kosiek v Germany*,[20] and *Glasenapp v Germany*,[21] where staff were refused permanent employment because of their active membership of extreme political parties, the ECtHR held that the dismissals did not interfere with freedom of expression because the issue was one of access to the civil service, and so not covered by the Convention.[22] The reasoning suggests that dismissal from employment involves no prima facie interference with Convention rights: the Convention rights do not apply at work, because of the freedom of the individual to resign. If there is no interference with a Convention right, then no further questions have to be asked: the case falls at the first hurdle.

This reasoning has been followed in several cases involving the Article 9 right to freedom of religion. In *Ahmad*[23] a teacher claimed that Article 9 was breached when he was refused permission to change his working hours to enable him to attend the local mosque for prayer on a Friday lunchtime. His claim was ruled inadmissible: his right to freedom of religion was not infringed as he was free to resign.[24] Again, in *Stedman*,[25] involving a dismissal for refusing to work on Sundays, the Commission took the view that there was no breach of Article 9, as the employee was free to resign. In *Bozhilov v Bulgaria*[26] the applicant's claim arising from his politically motivated dismissal was ruled inadmissible, on the basis that the Convention does not cover recruitment to the civil service, and so the dismissal could not give rise to a claim.[27]

---

[19] Until 1998 cases under the ECHR were first heard by the European Commission on Human Rights (ECommHR), to determine whether cases were admissible or inadmissible as being 'manifestly unfounded'. Admissible cases were then subject to attempts to reach friendly settlement. Those not settled were heard by the European Court of Human Rights (ECtHR). From 1 November 1998 this process was replaced by a new system under Protocol 11. Cases are now heard by smaller subdivisions of the full Court. Committees of three judges make the first level decision on admissibility. Admissible cases are then heard by Chambers of seven judges, who hear the merits of cases. Where cases involve serious issues regarding the interpretation of the Convention, the case can be referred to a Grand Chamber consisting of seventeen judges. Reports of decisions of the ECtHR and the ECommHR, Chambers and the Grand Chamber are referred to below as part of the 'jurisprudence' of the Convention, with ECtHR and Grand Chamber decisions being given greater weight.

[20] Series A No 105 (1986) 9 EHRR 328.

[21] Series A No 104 (1987) 9 EHRR 25.

[22] See also *Leander v Sweden*, Series A No 116, (1987) 9 EHRR 433 where the applicant claimed that the refusal to offer him a job as a museum technician, because certain secret information allegedly made him a security risk, was in breach of Article 10. The application was dismissed on the basis that the right to recruitment to the public service was not recognised by the Convention.

[23] *Ahmad v UK* (1981) 4 EHRR 126.

[24] See discussion above at pp 45–52 on the extent to which the 'right to resign' can provide protection for religious freedom.

[25] *Stedman v UK* (1997) 23 EHRR CD168.

[26] App No 41978/98 decision 22 November 2001.

[27] See also in *Kosteski v The Former Yugoslav Republic of Macedonia* App No 55170/00 [2006] ECHR 403, which confirmed the decisions of *Ahmad* and *Stedman*.

The Court expressed similar sentiments in *Thlimmenos v Greece*.[28] Thlimmenos was refused registration as a chartered accountant because of his criminal conviction, which was the result of his religiously motivated conscientious objection to military service. Although successful in his claim, because the treatment offended against Article 14 read in conjunction with Article 9, the Court pointed out that the Convention does not protect the right to choose a particular profession.[29] The implication is that if the case had been brought under Article 9 alone, it would have been unsuccessful. In effect, the Court and Commission have taken the view that the freedom to resign, or to choose a different profession, provides adequate protection for employees' human rights.

The case law, then, seems fairly clear that work-related difficulties will not constitute an interference with the right to religious freedom, and it may well be the case that this is correct as regards the *forum internum* aspect of religious freedom.[30] However, such an approach is unduly restrictive as regards the *forum externum* or freedom to manifest religion, which in any event is not an absolute right but can be restricted in order to protect the rights of others. In such cases, it would be more appropriate to accept that religious interests are engaged at work. Indeed, it is possible to find support within other areas of the Strasbourg case law for the notion that dismissal or other work-related detriments can amount to an interference with Convention rights. The cases do not all relate to freedom of religion, but they could be used to argue at the domestic level that religious freedom should enjoy a measure of protection at work.

In *Van der Heijden v The Netherlands*[31] the Commission recognised that dismissal for exercising the right to free speech restricts and penalises speech, and can have as strong a deterrent effect as total prohibition. This was also recognised in the admissibility proceedings in *Glasenapp* where the Commission stated that:

> the scope of Article 10(1) may be wider than merely to forbid the complete interruption or prevention of freedom of expression, and may extend further to protect the individual against certain other restrictions or penalties which result directly from the expression or holding of an opinion.[32]

The fact that a dismissal can act as an interference with Convention rights was recognised in *Vogt v Germany*,[33] another freedom of speech case involving a teacher's participation in the activities of an extremist political party. Here the teacher was dismissed for her political activity, and the ECtHR decided that the dismissal amounted to an interference with her freedom of expression. Again, in *Smith and Grady v UK*,[34] the finding that the applicants' privacy rights were infringed by the ban on gay personnel in the armed forces suggests that the Court

---

[28] ECHR 2000-IV, (2001) 31 EHRR 15.
[29] *Ibid*, para 41.
[30] See discussion of *Re Parsons' Application* below at pp 95–96.
[31] (1985) DR 101.
[32] *X v Germany* App No 9228/80 (1983) 5 EHRR 471.
[33] Series A No 323 (1996) 21 EHRR 205.
[34] App Nos 33985/96 and 33986/96, ECHR 1999-VI, (2000) 29 EHRR 493.

accepted that privacy rights are protected, despite the fact that the applicants did not have to join the army, and could have resigned.

Other examples can be found in the case law which suggest that the Court recognises that Convention rights can be exercised in relation to work. These cases do not suggest that the Convention guarantees a right to a job, but merely that, where there is an interference with work, Convention rights can be preliminarily engaged. For example, in the admissibility proceedings in *Saniewski v Poland*[35] the Court implied that there is an interference with the right to freedom of religion if an employment-related penalty is suffered for its exercise. Here a schoolboy claimed that Article 9 was breached by the fact that it could be inferred from his school report that he was an atheist, because he had not followed the usual course of religious instruction at school. The consequent 'blank' mark for the course would enable future employers to infer that he was not of the dominant Catholic religion, and his employment prospects might therefore be harmed. The Court found the case inadmissible, on the basis that there was no proof that his employment prospects would in fact be impaired. However, had there been such proof, the case might have been admissible. The suggestion is, therefore, that interference with employment prospects can be an interference with Convention rights. Similarly, in *Pitkevich v Russia*[36] the Court found that the dismissal of a judge for the expression of her religious views involved an interference with her rights under Article 9. Although on the facts the dismissal was found to be proportionate and in pursuit of a legitimate aim (the judge was found, *inter alia*, to have prayed publicly during hearings, and to have promised favourable outcomes to parties who agreed to join her church), the fact that there was a prima facie breach of Article 9 is significant. The merits of the case were heard, rather than it failing on the basis that the right to freedom of religion was not engaged.

Support for the proposition that the protection of the Convention can be applied at work can also be found in the Strasbourg jurisprudence relating to other rights. For example, in *Niemietz v Germany*[37] the ECtHR considered the scope of the right to privacy, and whether it extended to cover the workplace. The case involved the question of whether the right to privacy was infringed by a search of the applicant's office. The Court held that the concept of privacy and the private sphere could be extended to cover the workplace, and should not be limited to an ' "inner circle" in which the individual may live his own personal life as he chooses'.[38] Indeed, the Court went on:

> There appears . . . to be no reason of principle why . . . the notion of 'private life' should be taken to exclude activities of a professional or business nature since it is, after all, in the course of their working lives that the majority of people have a significant, if not the greatest, opportunity of developing relationships with the outside world.[39]

[35] App No 40319/98, decision 26 June 2001.
[36] App No 47936/99, decision 8 February 2001.
[37] Series A No 251-B, (1992) 16 EHRR 7.
[38] *Ibid* para 29.
[39] *Ibid.*

At this stage the reasoning of the Court is based on the idea that the workplace is an important forum in which individuals express their identity, and as such should be a place where human rights are protected. They went on to point out that, for some individuals and in some jobs, it is not always possible to draw clear boundaries between the work persona and the private persona:

> it is not always possible to distinguish clearly which of an individual's activities form part of his professional or business life and which do not. Thus, especially in the case of a person exercising a liberal profession, his work in that context may form part and parcel of his life to such a degree that it becomes impossible to know in what capacity he is acting at a given moment of time.[40]

Clearly the finding that the workplace is, in some respects, a space in which one might expect a degree of privacy, is not equivalent to a recognition that every human right is exercisable at work. Yet the sentiment expressed by the Court in *Niemietz* does suggest an acceptance that people's work lives are sufficiently bound up with their personal lives for it to be appropriate to provide some degree of human rights protection at work.

Similar findings that dismissal or refusal of employment can amount to an interference with a Convention right can be seen in *Sidabras v Lithuania*.[41] The applicant was an employee of the Lithuanian branch of the KGB, who after Lithuania's independence was employed as a tax inspector. In 1999 he was dismissed in accordance with legislation which imposed restrictions on the employment of former KGB officers. The applicant claimed that this dismissal breached Article 8 (right to a private life), Article 10 (right to freedom of speech) and Article 14 (non-discrimination) of the ECHR. The case was put that the Convention did not guarantee a right to retain employment or to choose a profession. Yet the Court rejected this argument, and instead took the view that a far-reaching ban on taking up private-sector employment affects 'private life', because it can affect the ability to develop relationships with the outside world, and can create serious difficulties as regards the possibility of earning a living. Such effects have obvious negative repercussions on the enjoyment of a private life.[42]

The Court took the view that interference with rights within the context of work can therefore come within the protection of the Convention. The case recognises that dismissal or non-employment can amount to an interference with Convention rights, and, with *Niemietz*, demonstrates the understanding on the part of the Court of the importance of the workplace as a forum in which Convention rights should be exercisable.

Although not directly concerned with the protection of religion, the support these cases give for protecting rights within the workplace can be used to argue for the provision of a degree of protection for religious rights. The cases suggest two strands of reasoning, both of which lead to the conclusion that Convention rights

---

[40] Series A No 251-B, (1992) 16 EHRR 7, para 29.
[41] Application Nos 55480/00 and 59330/00, ECHR 2004-VIII.
[42] *Ibid* paras 47 and 48

should be protected in the work context. The first strand, reflected in the decisions in *Van der Heijden v The Netherlands*,[43] *Vogt v Germany*[44] and *Saniewski v Poland*[45] is the view that work-based restrictions on rights are significant interferences, because, in practice, they will reduce the willingness of rights-bearers to exercise their rights. Restricting people's access to a livelihood can involve as great a deterrent to the exercise of Convention rights as other legal sanctions; thus the effect of a threat of dismissal is not dissimilar, in practice, to a ban on the activity.[46]

The second strand, seen in the cases of *Niemietz*[47] and *Sidabras*,[48] reflects the view that rights should be protected because of the role work plays in the lives of rights-bearers.[49] The argument here is that the workplace does not form a separate part of an individual's life, and so the full enjoyment of human rights must include their enjoyment at work. For those whose religion infuses each part of their life, it is therefore legitimate to argue that full protection of the right to freedom of religion must entail some level of protection at work.

Both approaches provide strong support for the view that human rights should have currency in the workplace.[50] Instead of taking the view that the rights are not protected at all in the context of work, or are protected merely by the freedom to resign, the better argument is that the rights can be engaged, even though they may not ultimately prevail when set against other competing rights. There are a number of reasons why the view that human rights should be valid within the workplace is to be preferred. Several are recognised in the cases considered above: full enjoyment of rights requires their enjoyment in the workplace because work plays an important role in individual lives; and interference with job prospects or satisfaction is experienced as a significant detriment by the individual, sufficient to deter the exercise of Convention rights.

Moreover, the idea that people's freedom to leave employment can act as a valid way to safeguard Convention rights can be contested. It is certainly true in a literal sense: courts will not force employees to work and do not grant specific performance to employment contracts. Yet, most employees are financially dependent on having a job, and the option of resigning is not experienced practically as a form of freedom.[51] A further reason for protecting the right to freedom of religion in employment is that to do otherwise exposes some to greater religious disadvantage

---

[43] Above n 31.

[44] Above n 33.

[45] Above n 35.

[46] In the context of free speech, see J S Mill, *On Liberty and Other Writings*, S Collini (ed), (Cambridge, CUP, 1989) 31 and 34.

[47] Above n 37.

[48] Above n 41.

[49] See discussion above at pp 47–49 and 60–62 of the importance of work to the individual.

[50] See further L Cariolou, 'The Right Not to be Offended by Members of the British National Party: An Analysis of *Serco Ltd v Redfearn* in the Light of the European Convention of Human Rights' (2006) 36 *ILJ* 415.

[51] This is particularly so in cases such as *Thlimmenos*, above n 28, whose access to a whole profession was barred for reasons related to his religion.

than others. Failure to protect religious practice at work will tend to interfere far less with the practice of Christianity than other religions. Simple examples are that most public holidays coincide with Christian holidays, and mainstream Christianity involves no dress code to conflict with standards required by most employers. Thus failure to protect religion is likely to cause few problems for Christians. The same is not true of other religious employees such as Muslims or Hindus, for whom religious observance may require special provision.[52] The risk of discrimination between religions provides further reason to allow for the exercise of Convention rights at work.

It is therefore suggested that the restrictive approach of the ECHR is correct as regards interferences with the *forum internum*, but that domestic courts should recognise a prima facie right to manifest religion at work. This right is not an absolute right, and it can be restricted on various grounds, discussed below. In assessing the merits of each claim, the fact that it arises in the context of work will be relevant, but cases should not fail at the preliminary stage. In some cases the conclusion may be that the rights are not protected; other rights may prevail. However, using the arguments above should enable employees to move to a consideration of the merits of their cases.

Although it may be possible to overcome this preliminary difficulty in using the Convention in the work context, there remain two further obstacles. First, the Convention is a treaty which binds states, but may not apply to private sector employers. Second, employees may 'contract out' of their Convention rights upon entering employment.

## Treaty Basis of the ECHR

The fact that the Convention only binds states need not cause insuperable difficulties for private sector staff, as there is a general acceptance within Convention case law that states can be held responsible for any failure to enact legislation to protect employees from breaches of the Convention. In *Young, James and Webster v UK*[53] the state was held responsible for the failure to provide a remedy for those dismissed for non-membership of a union, in potential breach of Article 11. Thus, failure by the domestic courts to protect freedom of religion at work could similarly give rise to an Article 9 case, even where the employer is in the private sector.

---

[52] P Cumper, 'The public manifestation of religion or belief: challenges for a multi-faith society in the twenty-first century' in R O'Dair and A Lewis (eds), *Current Legal Issues* Vol 4 (Oxford, OUP, 2000).

[53] Series A No 44 (1982) 4 EHRR 38. The case did not consider whether British Rail, the employer, was a public sector employer, but worked on the basis that the government was responsible via its responsibility to enact legislation to protect its citizens' human rights.

## Contracting Out of Protection

The second difficulty in using the Convention to protect freedom of religion at work is closely related to the 'right to resign' argument, but its legal basis is different. This is the argument that when individuals enter the contract of employment they contract out of their Convention rights. For example, an employee who agrees to abide by a company dress code may be said to have contracted out of her rights to freedom of religion, at least so far as they may relate to modes of dress. The difficulty here is that if an employee can contract out of her Convention rights, there is then no need to address the question of whether the restrictions on the exercise of rights are necessary and proportionate to achieve a specified legitimate aim. The case falls at the first hurdle, as the rights are not engaged.

Although undoubtedly the case that employees may agree not to exercise their rights at work, the ECtHR has not allowed this argument to apply in an absolute manner. It seems that if national courts were to enforce or uphold rights for employers to impose, by contract, absolute restrictions on Convention rights, this would breach the state's responsibility to safeguard the rights of employees, in the same way as the absence of legislative protection for employees against the closed shop practices breached the state's obligations under the Convention in *Young, James and Webster*.[54] Instead, employees can contract out of their Convention rights, as long as the contractual restriction is capable of flexible interpretation, allowing courts to assess the proportionality and necessity of the restriction in the particular case.[55]

In *Sorensen and Rasmussen v Denmark*,[56] a case involving compulsion to join a trade union, the ECtHR accepted that a contractual agreement to opt out of Convention rights will not remove from the state the duty to protect those rights. The ECtHR commented that the fact that the applicants accepted membership of the union as one of the terms of employment did not alter the element of compulsion, as they would not have been recruited without that agreement. The court accepted that

> individuals applying for employment often find themselves in a vulnerable situation and are only too eager to comply with the terms of employment offered.[57]

It should thus be difficult to argue that employees contract out of the right to freedom of religion when entering employment, and so cannot complain at all about workplace restrictions on their freedom. Instead, the better view is that the right does survive entry to the workplace, and that any contractual duties restricting

---

[54] *Ibid.*

[55] See G Morris, 'Fundamental Rights: Exclusion by Agreement?' [2001] *ILJ* 49. On the ability to contract out of the right to free speech see *Vereniging Rechtswinkels Utrecht v The Netherlands*(1986) 46 DR 200. See also *Rommelfanger v FDR* (1989) 62 DR 151.

[56] App Nos 52562/99 and 52320/99, judgment 11 January 2006.

[57] *Ibid* para 59.

freedom of religion should only be upheld where they are necessary and proportionate in accordance with Article 9(2).

Any conclusion on the extent to which employees can rely on the protection of the ECHR within the workplace must remain tentative given the current state of legal authorities on the question. However, there are strong arguments of principle suggesting that Convention rights should be exercisable at work,[58] and support for the view can be found in ECtHR case law,[59] albeit not consistently. Given that domestic courts are not bound by Strasbourg case law, it would be open to them to consider the human rights protection for religious freedom in interpreting the extent of work-based obligations, drawing on the more generous reading of the case law set out above. The next section of this chapter works on the assumption that the argument can be made for protecting religious freedom at work under the Convention, and considers the extent of protection to be found within Articles 9 and 14 ECHR.

## III  Freedom of Religion Under Article 9

Article 9 provides:

1. Everyone has the right to freedom of thought, conscience and religion; this right includes freedom to change his religion or belief and freedom, either alone or in community with others and in public or private, to manifest his religion or belief, in worship, teaching, practice and observance.

2. Freedom to manifest one's religion or beliefs shall be subject only to such limitations as are prescribed by law and are necessary in a democratic society in the interests of public safety, for the protection of public order, health or morals, or for the protection of the rights and freedoms of others.

Freedom of religion is protected under Article 9 of the ECHR, along with freedom of thought and conscience, as one of the foundations of a 'democratic society', and as one of the 'most vital elements that go to make up the identity of believers and their conception of life', and in recognition of the importance of the pluralism that is indissociable from a democratic society.[60]

At a general level, then, Article 9 is viewed as fundamentally important because it is a reflection of individual autonomy, as well as being necessary to the pluralism of the modern world. Article 9 recognises that freedom of religion has both an individual and a collective dimension.[61] The right is to manifest religion 'either

---

[58] See discussion in ch 2 above.

[59] See discussion at pp 88–92 above.

[60] *Kokkinakis v Greece* Series A No 260-A [1993] 17 EHRR 397 at para 31.

[61] *Hasan v Bulgaria* App No 30985/96, (2002) 34 EHRR 55; *Serif v Greece* App No 38178/97 (2001) 31 EHRR 20.

alone or in community with others'. This means that the right extends to religious groups as well as to religious individuals.

The right to freedom of thought, conscience and religion, in its pure form (the *forum internum*), is an absolute right under the Convention, and refers to the right to have inner thoughts and beliefs. It is arguable that in this form the right must inevitably be absolute, particularly as beliefs and thoughts themselves are intangible in nature. The protection of the rights of the *forum internum* is aimed at preventing state interference with a person's thought and conscience, by way of state coercion to believe and brainwashing. It also prevents forcible attempts to change a person's religion or beliefs, and prohibits indoctrination by the state.[62]

Protection for the *forum internum*, although absolute, does not usually apply in the work context. In effect, the protection is provided while the employee's thoughts and beliefs remain private and unexpressed: once religious beliefs are expressed or acted upon, they are no longer part of the *forum internum*, and the protection is no longer absolute. However, it has been argued that both a requirement to reveal one's religion, and discrimination on the basis of religion, involve interference with the *forum internum*.[63] Thus far, the ECtHR has not taken this approach, taking instead the view (discussed above) that disadvantageous treatment at work does not amount to an interference with human rights.

Although this approach was criticised above in relation to the *forum externum*, in relation to the *forum internum* it is probably correct. The protection is absolute and so direct discrimination on grounds of religious belief would become absolutely prohibited; there is no mechanism for allowing for genuine occupational requirements, or any other justification in the Article 9(1) framework for the *forum internum*. One effect of this would be that any measures for positive action on grounds of religion would have to be disallowed, however beneficial in terms of furthering other interests. This question was considered in the Northern Irish case *Re Parsons' Application*,[64] involving the appointment of police under the Police (Northern Ireland) Act 2000. The Chief Constable of the Police Service of Northern Ireland must appoint half the police from those treated as Roman Catholic, and half from those not so treated.[65] Parsons was in the pool of those who were not Roman Catholic and was not appointed.[66] He challenged the case as breaching Article 9, on the basis that he had been treated less favourably because of his religion. In rejecting the case, the Court of Appeal in Northern Ireland held that Article 9 was not engaged. Discrimination on religious grounds did not constrain Parsons from holding a particular belief, nor did it induce him to change faith, and so the protection of the absolute right to believe was not infringed. Had

---

[62] P van Dijk and F van Hoof, *Theory and Practice of the European Convention on Human Rights* (2nd edn) (The Hague, Kluwer, 1990) 541 *ff*.

[63] B G Tahzib, *Freedom of Religion and Belief: Ensuring Effective International Protection* (The Hague, Kluwer Law International, 1996).

[64] [2003] NICA 20.

[65] See discussion at p 143 below.

[66] The pool of qualified Roman Catholic applicants was smaller, so he was able to show that had he been Roman Catholic he might have been appointed (para 7).

they held that discrimination can interfere with the absolute right, the democrat-ically agreed method to address religious inequality and division in Northern Ireland would have had to be prohibited. It is suggested that the decision on the question of whether there is an infringement of the *forum internum* as a result of employment discrimination was correct. Employment discrimination should not amount to an interference with the absolute right to believe. However, this is not to say that it cannot amount to an interference with the qualified right to manifest religion, as discussed below.

Indeed, most of the cases raising freedom of religion under the ECHR have involved the qualified right to manifest religion in worship, teaching, practice and observance alone or with others, subject to the restrictions set out in Article 9(2). It is the freedom to manifest religion which has the most potential to affect reli-gious people in the workforce but, even so, the Convention by no means provides a guarantee that the right can be of great use in the context of work.

Before establishing a right to manifest religion at work, employees will need to overcome a number of hurdles, or filters. The preliminary hurdle of showing that the right to exercise freedom of religion applies at all at work has been discussed above. Although it was argued that the right should exist in this context, it was not established beyond doubt that this is the case. Assuming that this hurdle can be overcome, a second hurdle is establishing that the contested conduct or activity is a manifestation of religion. If this is the case, the employee will, thirdly, need to show that any restriction does not come within the restrictions set out in Article 9(2). These hurdles are significant, and success in using the ECHR to protect the right to exercise freedom of religion at work is far from certain. Each step will be considered in turn, with reference to the current state of the case law of the ECHR. As with the question of whether the protection applies to work, the case law is somewhat restrictive. Having set out the current approach, an alternative, more progressive reading of the case law will be suggested.

## Manifestation of Religion

The right to manifest religion or belief has several aspects to it. It covers worship, teaching, practice and observance, whether in public or in private. It is the mani-festation of belief which is most likely to give rise to conflict in the workplace, and to be the cause of interference by the employer. For example, a work uniform may interfere with a religious employee's right to manifest her religion. Similarly, the employee who requires time off for religious observance, who requires special dietary provision, or who tries to convert her colleagues, may all claim to be man-ifesting their religion. The religious employer who requires religious observance by employees also infringes the right to manifest another religion or no religion.

If it is accepted, as suggested above, that the right to freedom of religion can be exercised at work, then the extent to which an employer may be required, under the Convention, to accommodate the religious needs of staff will be determined in part by whether such requests are indeed manifestations of religion. The difficulty for employees is that the interpretation of the term 'manifestation' under the ECHR is fairly restrictive. If the activity is found instead to be merely 'religiously motivated' then it will not be a manifestation of religion, and the employer will be under no obligation to accommodate it. Any failure to accommodate will not breach the ECHR as there will be no interference with the *forum internum*, nor with the right to manifest religion.

Much will therefore turn on the scope of the term 'manifestation' in worship, teaching, practice and observance. Clearly, the core manifestations of religion are unlikely to arise at work. Article 9 is a general right to freedom of religion, not focused on work, so it aims to protect the freedom of religious people to worship, practice and teach their religion in religious services and rituals. The right restricts the power of the state to prohibit religious activity, the running of churches, mosques, temples and other religious organisations and the teaching of religious doctrine. It is unlikely that any of these manifestations will be carried out in the workplace, unless the worker is a cleric or otherwise employed to carry out religious observance.

However, some manifestations could occur in the secular workplace, for example where a religious employee attempts to convert others or at least explain her faith to colleagues; where an individual wears particular types of clothes; follows dietary laws; or requests days or shorter periods off work for religious activity. In more contentious cases, a manifestation could involve requesting to work with others of the same religion, or requiring separation from non-believers. The question of whether an employer can ignore such requests, or can only do so when necessary and proportionate for a legitimate aim, will be determined by whether such behaviour 'manifests' religion or not.

The ECHR has taken a very restrictive view of this question in its case law, and as a result a number of difficulties are caused for employees seeking to gain protection under Article 9. The first difficulty is demonstrated in *Arrowsmith v UK*[67] in which the ECHR distinguished between conduct which is motivated by religion, and that which is a manifestation of the religion. That which is merely motivated by religion is not protected by Article 9, and so restrictions imposed by the employer on religiously motivated activity do not offend the ECHR. Thus even if the argument that the right to freedom of religion has currency at work is accepted, it is only the manifestation of religion that is protected, not religiously motivated conduct.

In *Arrowsmith*, the applicant was stopped from distributing pacifist leaflets to soldiers, advocating a withdrawal of soldiers from Northern Ireland. Arrowsmith was a committed pacifist, and claimed that distribution of the leaflets manifested her pacifist beliefs. It was not disputed that the pacifist beliefs were capable of protection under Article 9, but it was the Court's view that distributing leaflets was not a manifestation of those beliefs. The activity was motivated by pacifism, but it was

---

[67] *Arrowsmith v United Kingdom* (App No 7050/75) [1978] 3 EHRR 218.

not an expression of the views themselves. Thus Arrowsmith could not claim that her right to manifest religion or belief was infringed.

Following *Arrowsmith* it would seem that if behaviour is not required by a religion as part of religious observance, it can be restricted without breaching Article 9. Arrowsmith could continue to hold pacifist beliefs even if she did not distribute her leaflets. This approach raises severe problems for those who seek protection for religious rights at work, because in many cases it is the accommodation of religiously inspired behaviour that is requested, not pure religious observance. For example, a request by a Christian to wear a cross at work is usually religiously inspired, rather than a requirement of the Christian faith.[68]

The approach in *Arrowsmith* is unfortunate for many reasons. First, it unduly restricts the exercise of religious freedom by imposing an additional filter before the proportionality of any restriction can be considered. The manifestation of religion is not an absolute right, but is always subject to a restriction where prescribed by law and proportionate in the interests of public safety, for the protection of public order, health or morals, or for the protection of the rights and freedoms of others. Too restrictive an interpretation of 'manifestation' means that cases are lost before the proportionality of restrictions can be considered. As with the question of whether religion can be protected at all at work, it would be preferable to allow a wider definition of manifestation of religion, to include religiously motivated behaviour, and then impose such restrictions on the behaviour as are proportionate and necessary.

It is also arguable that to create a binary divide between religious manifestation and religiously motivated behaviour involves an inappropriately restrictive view of religion and its role in life. The distinction may accord with some understandings of religion, in which the focus is on observing rules, but does not fit well at all with a broader understanding of religion. To illustrate the problem, examples can be drawn from Christianity, but similar examples could be used from other religious traditions. Christianity can be viewed as involving a set of rules which one must obey, including, for example, to love one's neighbour, to attend church, to pray, to give alms, to forgive, and to abstain from sexual immorality. Some of these rules are, arguably, manifestations of the religion, such as church attendance and prayer. Impeding an individual's ability to attend prayers would therefore be an infringement of their religious practice and would need to be justified. Other rules either do not require positive behaviour (for example, they may consist in abstaining from certain behaviour) or they take place purely in the *forum internum* (for example, forgiveness) and so are harder to interfere with, but also less likely to cause difficulties at work. The difficulty arises with more all-encompassing religious mandates, such as to 'love one's neighbour'. This is a clear Christian obligation, but there is no fixed way to measure compliance. Activities by an employee, such as offering to pray for someone, which can be inspired by the instruction to

---

[68] An individual could argue that wearing a cross is mandated according to his or her personal beliefs, but the wearing of a cross is not understood to be a requirement of mainstream Christianity.

love one's neighbour, are likely to be said to be religiously inspired or motivated rather than manifestations of the religion. This is because the general rule to love one's neighbour is a clear religious obligation, but there is no clear set of instructions for compliance with that obligation.[69] Determining what is motivated and what is mandated in such circumstances is far from easy.

A further difficulty caused by the interpretation in *Arrowsmith* is that the question of what is necessary for a religion, and what is only motivated by it, can be difficult to determine. In some cases even adherents of the same religion may not agree. For example, the question of whether church attendance is obligatory is not one on which Christians agree. The danger apparent in the ECHR case law is that the court determines what is religiously mandated and, in contrast, what is religiously motivated, rather than leaving this to be determined by the conscience of the religious adherent. For example, in *Valsamis v Greece*[70] the ECtHR decided that the refusal by Jehovah's Witness children to take part in a military parade was merely religiously motivated, rather than required by their religion. The penalty imposed on them for their refusal to participate did not infringe Article 9 as, according to the Court, there was no interference with religious observance or practice.

The approach in that case is very controversial.[71] First, it may cause difficulties for minority and less well-known religions, where there is no clear line of authority on the faith's requirements. Second, the approach suggests that a court has the expertise to decide what is required by a religion, and suggests that the Court can determine what significance a certain practice has for the individual. The Court, in effect, endowed the military parade in *Valsamis* with a particular meaning for the individuals concerned, and deemed their objections to be motivated by religion rather than forming part of their religious practice. This is surely unsatisfactory: it is not the for the court to determine the meaning of particular activities for the individuals concerned. Even for religions where lines of authority are well established, the question of what is required by a religious faith cannot be answered easily. After all, a person may individually believe that certain conduct is required by their faith, even though others of the same faith disagree. The wearing of a head covering by Muslim women is a clear example of conduct which some feel, as a matter of faith, is required conduct, and others do not.

In *Valsamis* the Court itself determined that the parade did not offend the religious views of the children.[72] But it must surely be wrong for a court to be the arbiter of what an applicant believes, and arbiter of the significance of any particular activity with regard to those beliefs. Such an approach is also surprising given the absolute protection under the Convention for belief itself as part of the *forum internum*.

---

[69]  See discussion of *Devine v Home Office* at p 123 below.

[70]  (1997) 24 EHRR 294.

[71]  See S Stavros, 'Freedom of Religion and Claims for Exemption from Generally Applicable Neutral Laws: Lessons from Across the Pond' (1997) 6 EHRLR 607.

[72]  '. . . it can discern nothing, either in the purpose of the parade or in the arrangements for it, which could offend the applicants' pacifist convictions . . .' (1997) 24 EHRR 294 at para 31.

Of course, it can be hard to determine exactly what the requirements of a religion are. In the case of well-known religions, a practical answer may be to determine the question by reference to the formal authorities of the religion. However, this can cause difficulties for newer minority religions, where there may be no accepted religious code of behaviour.[73] Moreover, allowing formal authorities to determine the content of religious belief may also cause difficulties to those of more traditional faiths. Again if one takes an example from Christianity, the issue can be illustrated by the case of *Williamson v Secretary of State for Education and Employment*,[74] which involved the use of corporal punishment in private Christian schools. Clearly, not all Christians share the view that Christianity requires such disciplinary methods; indeed the judge at the first hearing of the case took this approach. However, as accepted in the Court of Appeal, the particular Christians involved in the case did believe that corporal punishment should be used in the discipline of children. It is preferable, if religious freedom is to be respected, to accept the views of the individual as to the content of their beliefs, even if those views are eccentric or controversial. The need to restrict the manifestation of those beliefs can then be dealt with in the second stage of enquiry, namely whether it is proportionate to allow the behaviour, in the light of any conflicting rights. To allow a court to determine the content of religious belief means that the question of proportionality is never reached, and the proper parameters for the protection of religion are not fully explored.

The case law on the manifestation of religion is clear: a division is made between activity which amounts to a manifestation of religion, which is protected; and that which is merely 'motivated' by religion, which is not. However, the approach is controversial for a number of reasons, not least the fact that it requires courts to make inappropriate decisions about which side of the line any particularly belief falls. An alternative and preferable approach would be to enable a wider range of religious behaviour to be considered as 'manifesting' belief. The parameters of protection for those beliefs would then be determined by a consideration of the proportionality of any restriction in comparison with the rights with which it competes, as detailed in Article 9(2). However, given the fact that such an interpretation of Article 9(2) would not accord with *Arrowsmith*, such an interpretation may be unlikely (although technically open to domestic courts, if they choose not to be bound by the more restrictive case law). This means that the potential for using Article 9 to protect religion at work remains limited, unless the employee practice in question is clearly a manifestation of religion.

## Article 9(2)

Despite the difficulties discussed above, in some cases it will be the case that an employer's actions will have interfered with the manifestation of religion at work.

---

[73] See P Cumper, above n 52, at 325.
[74] [2002] EWCA Civ 1926.

For example, refusal to accommodate prayer times, dress codes, and time off for religious observance may all be classed as interferences with the manifestation of religion. In such cases, the further question arises of whether the interference can be justified in accordance with Article 9(2), and the ECHR approach to the question will now be considered.

An interference with religious freedom will not breach the Convention if the limitations imposed are prescribed by law and are necessary in a democratic society in the interests of public safety, for the protection of public order, health or morals, or for the protection of the rights and freedoms of others. In effect, limitations are allowed as long as they are for a legitimate aim, and are necessary and proportionate to the achievement of that aim. All three conditions have to be met before a restriction or interference with freedom of religion can be acceptable under the Convention.

## Prescribed by Law

*The Sunday Times v UK*[75] contains the classic definition of what is needed for a restriction to be 'prescribed by law':

> First the law must be adequately accessible: the citizen must be able to have an indication that is adequate in the circumstances of the legal rules applicable to a given case. Secondly, a norm cannot be regarded as a 'law' unless it is formulated with sufficient precision to enable the citizen to regulate his conduct: he must be able to foresee, to a degree that is reasonable in the circumstances, the consequences which a given action may entail. Those consequences need not be foreseeable with absolute certainty: experience shows this to be unattainable.[76]

The interference with religious freedom that employees may experience is very likely to meet this description. Employees could face disciplinary action or dismissal for breaching dress codes; or they could face dismissal for refusal to work at particular times. Some expressions of religious affiliation could offend codes of behaviour at work,[77] for example if it amounts to harassment of other staff. The laws relating to unfair dismissal, discrimination or harassment that may be engaged in such cases are not without uncertainty, as outcomes at times are difficult to predict, but they are probably within the bounds of acceptable uncertainty envisaged by the ECHR. The law governing the workplace is sufficiently foreseeable: sufficient guidance can be drawn from case law, which provides for the parameters within which judicial discretion is exercised, for the outcome to be predicted with an acceptable degree of certainty.[78]

---

[75] *Sunday Times v UK* Series A No 30 (1979) 2 EHRR 245.

[76] *Ibid* at para 49. See also *Hodgson and others v UK* (1987) 51 DR 136 where the Commission said that 'The mere fact that a legislative provision may give rise to problems of interpretation does not mean that it is so vague and imprecise as to lack the quality of "law" in this sense'.

[77] In *Barthold v Germany* Series A No 90 (1985) 7 EHRR 383 the 'law' was not limited to national laws but extended to professional rules and codes of conduct. Discipline or dismissal of an employee may therefore be 'prescribed by law' where this is provided for by a professional code of conduct.

[78] See also *Goodwin v UK* ECHR 1996-II, 483 (1996) 22 EHRR 123, para 31 *ff.*

### Legitimate Aims in Article 9(2)

The purpose most likely to be applicable in the context of freedom of religion within the work context is the protection of the rights of others. Precisely which 'rights of others' need such protection is not specified, and there seems to be no requirement that the rights of others have to be legally enforceable rights. The restrictions on religion have to be prescribed by sufficiently clear laws, but the aims of those rules do not have to be specified with the same degree of clarity.[79] Religious rights may, of course, conflict with others' equality rights, such as rights to gender and sexual orientation equality.[80] The right of the employer to enjoy a degree of managerial prerogative in the running of the business will be a 'right of others' that should be balanced against the right to freedom of religion, as may be the rights of other staff to work in an environment in which their equality and dignity are respected.[81] A similar, somewhat vague, 'right' that has been recognised in the context of the workplace is a right that was infringed by a male employee who wished to wear what are conventionally considered 'female' clothes. This was said to protect the right of the employer 'to protect its own proper functioning and carrying out of its duties on behalf of the public', again a right which is not an enforceable free-standing right.[82] Other rights of others which may be protected by restrictions on the full enjoyment of religious freedom are rights not to be put under pressure by another's observance. For example, in *Sahin v Turkey*[83] the Court noted that the wearing of a headscarf may put other students under pressure to adopt more fundamentalist approaches to their faith.[84]

It would seem, then, that many of the restrictions on religion at work will be prescribed by law and will, potentially, serve a legitimate aim. It is therefore in relation to the necessity and proportionality of the interference that the supervision of the ECHR will take place.

### Necessity in a Democratic Society

The standard of review by the ECHR under this heading is fairly high. 'Necessary' means more than just 'useful', 'reasonable', or 'desirable': for any restriction to be necessary, it must be proportionate to the legitimate aim pursued.[85]

---

[79] In the context of freedom of speech see *Ahmed v UK* ECHR 1998-VI 2195 (2000) 29 EHRR 1, where the right of members of the public to effective political democracy was accepted as 'rights of others', a right which was not set out with any clarity. The danger of allowing the rights of others to be interpreted too vaguely means that the concept risks 'being stretched so far as to lose almost all distinct meaning': see the joint dissenting opinion of Judges Spielmann, Pekkanen and Van Dijk at para 1.

[80] *Dahlab v Switzerland* App No 42393/98 ECHR 2001 V, decision 15 February 2001.

[81] See discussion at pp 55–66 above of potential rights which can compete with rights to religious freedom in the workplace.

[82] See *Kara v UK* App No 36528/97, decision 22 October 1998.

[83] App No 44774/98, judgment 10 November 2005.

[84] This issue was also in play in *R (On the application of Begum) v Headteacher and Governors of Denbigh High School* [2006] UKHL 15.

[85] *Handyside v UK* Series A 24 (1981) 1 EHRR 737 at para 48.

Despite the high level of review suggested by the ECHR the Court has also recognised that states need a certain flexibility in their observance of the Convention. Thus a 'margin of appreciation' is allowed to states in setting the parameters of their domestic law. The concept of the 'margin of appreciation' allows flexibility to states in the interpretation of the Convention, although if used too extensively it has the potential to undermine the protection afforded by the Convention.[86] The theory is that this flexibility is limited, being at all times subject to European supervision, but in religion cases the ECtHR has allowed a fairly wide margin to operate,[87] perhaps reflecting the lack of consensus across Europe about how religion should be treated.

Despite the fact that the ECtHR case law has been very restrictive in its interpretation of the protection afforded by Article 9, some guidance on the interpretation of proportionality can be garnered from the cases reported, even though some of the cases were found inadmissible. Guidance can also be found from case law relating to other Convention rights which are exercised in the context of the workplace. The case law suggests that the following issues may be relevant: the nature of the restriction on religion; the nature of the applicant's job; the relationship between the religious expression and the applicant's job; and the nature of the religious belief.

*The Nature of the Restriction on Religion*    Interference with religious freedom at work can vary, and could range from a complete ban on those of certain beliefs from working at the establishment, to more minor refusals to accommodate forms of religious practice at work. The case law of the ECHR in relation to other human rights, for example, freedom of expression, indicates that where the exercise of the right is prohibited altogether, the sanction is more likely to be found to be unnecessary. For example, in *Lingens*[88] criminal proceedings brought in respect of the writing of articles criticising a senior politician effectively meant that freedom of speech was barred altogether, and so the proceedings were found to breach Article 10. In contrast, where speech has not been totally banned, the protection of the Convention has been more limited.[89]

It is clear that work-based restrictions on religious freedom will never amount to an absolute ban on belief. As recognised in *Ahmad*[90] and *Stedman*[91] the freedom of the applicants to resign effectively guarantees their Convention rights, as

---

[86]  See H C Yourow, *The Margin of Appreciation Doctrine in the Dynamics of European Human Rights Jurisprudence* (Dordrecht, Martinus Nijhoff Publishers, 1996); T A O'Donnell, 'The Margin of Appreciation Doctrine: Standard in the Jurisprudence of the European Court of Human Rights' [1982] *Human Rights Quarterly* 474; and T H Jones, 'The Devaluation of Human Rights Under the European Convention' [1995] *PL* 430. See also P W Edge, 'The European Court of Human Rights and Religious Rights' (1998) 47 *ICLQ* 680.

[87]  C Evans, *Freedom of Religion under the ECHR* (Oxford, OUP, 2001) 143–44.

[88]  Series A 103 (1986) 8 EHRR 407.

[89]  *Vereniging Rechtswinkels Utrecht v Netherlands*, above n 55. Note, however, that it was not an employment case.

[90]  Above n 23.

[91]  Above n 25.

they remain free to exercise the right after their employment has ended. Such an argument is very unhelpful to applicants if applied at too early a stage in the determination of a case, as it prevents fuller consideration of the merits of the case, as argued above. However, it is clear that the right to freedom of religion is not a right to an unburdened freedom, and it is acceptable for the exercise of the right to include some cost to the religious adherent. Thus, the fact that the employee is not forced to work can act as some level of protection for the individual. The argument that the employee will not be forced to enter a workplace must be addressed at some point in any consideration of the scope of the right to freedom of religion at work. But the better place for the issue to be considered is in terms of the proportionality of the restriction on the right, rather than acting as an initial filter to all claims, as would be suggested by the approach in *Ahmed* and *Stedman*.

*The Nature of the Applicant's Job*   Strasbourg case law has recognised that some jobs will involve a greater restriction on religious freedom than others. For example, in *Pitkevich v Russia*[92] the dismissal of a judge for the expression of her religious views was proportionate. In the context of her work as a judge, where it was necessary for her to uphold the impartiality and authority of the judiciary, it was proportionate to dismiss her. For example, she had prayed publicly during hearings and promised favourable outcomes to parties who agreed to join her church. She had intimidated parties in court and had criticised the morality of parties to proceedings concerning family matters. The outcome of the case is not surprising, and shows that the ECtHR will take into account the nature of the job in determining proportionality.

Other jobs which have been identified within the case law in which greater restrictions on religious freedom may be proportionate are teaching, and the armed services.[93] In *Kalaç v Turkey*[94] a military judge was compulsorily retired for breaches of discipline and scandalous conduct. Kalaç's conduct and attitude had 'revealed that he had adopted unlawful fundamentalist opinions'.[95] The Court found that Kalaç's forced retirement did not breach his freedom of religion, in part because he had accepted some limitation on his fundamental freedoms by accepting, of his own accord, to pursue a military career.[96]

In relation to teaching, in *Dahlab v Switzerland*[97] the applicant was a teacher of young children. The particular position of a teacher, with influence on the intellectual and emotional development of children, was relevant to the decision of the Court that a restriction on wearing the headscarf as an expression of the Muslim faith was proportionate. Similarly, although not an employment case, in *Sahin*[98]

---

[92] Above n 36.
[93] See *Larissis v Greece* ECHR 1998-I 65 discussed below at p 105.
[94] Case No 61/1996/680/870, 1 July 1997.
[95] *Ibid* at para 8.
[96] See also *Yanasik v Turkey* (1993) 74 DR 14.
[97] Above n 80.
[98] *Sahin v Turkey* above n 83.

the observation was made that students may feel under pressure to adopt stricter approaches to the religion if others wear the headscarf.[99] Thus the fact that religious behaviour may influence others seems to have been important in the reasoning in the cases. The argument may not be the same for those who wear the headscarf in forms of employment where they have less influence on others; after all, the influence of a teacher on young children may be different from the influence exercised by individuals in most other jobs. The position may also be different for those working for state employers whose dress may carry more of a connotation that the state endorses the behaviour.[100]

*The Relationship Between the Religious Expression and the Applicant's Job*    A further related factor that influences the outcome of cases on freedom of religion within the work context is the relationship between the religious expression and the applicant's job. Where the religious expression takes place outside work, it is easier to argue that any infringement related to work is disproportionate. However, the converse is also true: where the religious activity affects the individual's work, then restrictions are more likely to be proportionate. An example of the ECtHR taking into account the nature of the job in assessing whether Article 9 has been breached can be seen in *Larissis v Greece*,[101] where the conviction of a group of military officers for proselytism of the men in their command was said not to infringe the officers' right to freedom of religion. Here the ECtHR took the view that the proselytism amounted to an abuse of power by the officers.

Similarly, in *Pitkevich*[102] the dismissal was clearly a result of the judge's conduct in post. The Court explicitly pointed out that the facts that warranted her dismissal related exclusively to her official activities and did not concern any expression of her religious views in private. Again, it is the fact that her religious expression interfered with her conduct at work that was relevant to the finding that the dismissal was proportionate.

*The Nature of the Employer*    Where the employer is the state, the need for impartiality and neutrality in terms of religion is, arguably, greater. Although it can also be argued that state employers should reflect the make-up of the society which it governs,[103] this argument has not been accepted by the ECHR. In *Dahlab v Switzerland*[104] one factor in deciding that the prohibition on the teacher wearing a headscarf was that she was a 'representative of the state'. In *Sahin* it was also accepted that the public university should reflect the secular nature of the state, and this argument was given significant weight in determining whether the

---

[99] This issue was also in play in *R (On the application of Begum) v Headteacher and Governors of Denbigh High School* [2006] UKHL 15.
[100] This issue is discussed further in ch 3 at pp 67–69.
[101] Above n 93.
[102] Above n 36.
[103] See discussion of public sector employers in ch 3 at pp 67–69.
[104] Above n 80.

restriction on religious expression reflected in the headscarf ban was proportionate. The desire of the state to be religiously neutral is a matter over which the Court gives states a significant margin of appreciation, as it is a matter on which practice across the member states varies.

The nature of the employer may also be relevant, where the employer is religious in nature. The ECHR case law gives clear protection to religious communities in choosing their own leaders. Where a religious body acts as an employer, it may be that greater religious restrictions on employees will be accepted, in order to reflect the community's religious interests.[105]

*The Nature of the Religious Belief*   It has been argued above that the court should not be the arbiter of what an individual believes. Instead, for the protection to be meaningful, each individual's beliefs need protection. However, this is clearly not the same as providing equal protection to all beliefs. Those beliefs which interfere with the rights and freedoms of others will be given less protection than those which are compatible with others' freedoms.[106] This is reflected in the statement by the Court in *Serif v Greece*[107] that the 'role of authorities [where communities are divided] is not to remove the cause of tension by eliminating pluralism, but to ensure that the competing groups tolerate each other'.[108] This suggests that where religious views are intolerant of others, the Court will be more willing to find that a restriction is proportionate.

A similar sentiment is reflected in *Kalaç v Turkey*[109] where the Court referred to the fact that the decision to retire Kalaç, a military judge with connections to a fundamentalist sect, was not based on his religious beliefs 'but on his conduct *and attitude*'.[110] Cross-reference is then made to the statement by the Government that:

> the protection of Article 9 could not extend, in the case of a serviceman, to membership of a fundamentalist movement, in so far as its members' activities were likely to upset the army's hierarchical equilibrium.[111]

The Court itself does not say that fundamentalist views are given less protection, but the reference to the applicant's attitude, with the cross-reference to the Government's argument on the point, suggests a degree of support for the view that interference with intolerant religious views is more likely to be found to be proportionate when balanced against other interests in accordance with Article 9(2).

The nature of the belief, in the sense that a religious practice exercised at work can be a 'manifestation' of religion or can be merely 'motivated' by religion, may

---

[105]   *Hasan* above n 61 at para 62; see also *Serif* above n 61.
[106]   See Article 17 ECHR, and the discussion in Cariolou, above n 50.
[107]   Above n 61.
[108]   *Serif*, above n 61, at para 53.
[109]   Case No 61/1996/680/870, 1 July 1997
[110]   *Ibid*, at para 30 (emphasis added).
[111]   *Ibid*, at paras 25 and 30.

also be relevant to the question of proportionality. In effect, the importance of the practice to the individual may be relevant in assessing whether it is proportionate to restrict particular behaviour. Although the distinction between motivated behaviour and manifestation was criticised above, the idea that some religious practices are more fundamental to believers than others is inescapable. However, it is submitted that it is better treated as relevant to the question of proportionality, than entering the equation at the definitional stage, as was the case in *Valsamis*, where the fact that behaviour was not a manifestation of religion meant that any question of protection was precluded. More appropriate protection for religious interests would be provided by allowing religious practices to be protected as long as it is proportionate to do so in the light of other competing interests. The question of how fundamental the religious practice is to religious belief will then be relevant in assessing proportionality.[112]

## Application of Article 9(2) in the Workplace

Having established how the ECHR should apply the concept of proportionality in general to the exercise of freedom of religion at work, it is finally necessary to apply that reasoning to a number of practical issues that could arise regarding the exercise of freedom of religion at work. These are: determining a person's religion; the extent to which employers can be required to accommodate religious practice, such as days off for religious observance, compliance with religious dress requirements or refusal to participate in certain work tasks; and determining the scope of the rights of religious organisations to determine their own employment requirements.

### Determining a Person's Religion

One question which is likely to arise is whether a particular set of beliefs can be classed as a 'religion or belief'. The Court and Commission on Human Rights have taken a fairly broad approach here, recognising as a 'religion or belief' atheism,[113] Druidism,[114] Divine Light Zentrum,[115] Scientology,[116] Krishna Consciousness,[117] pacifism,[118] and veganism.[119]

Apart from deciding whether a particular set of convictions is protected under Article 9, difficulties can arise where there is disagreement over what constitutes a genuine religious observance. The ECtHR has not always been consistent in its approach on this issue. In *Metropolitan Church of Bessarabia v Moldova*[120] the

---

[112] See discussion on whether a practice is mandated by the religion in ch 3 at pp 73–74.
[113] *Angelini v Sweden* (1988) 10 EHRR 123 (Eur Comm HR).
[114] *Chappell v UK* (1988) 10 EHRR 510 (Eur Comm HR); *Pendragon v UK* (1998) EHRR CD 179.
[115] *Swami Omkaramamda and the Divine Light Zentrum v Switzerland* (1981) 25 DR 105.
[116] *X and the Church of Scientology v Sweden* (1976) 16 DR 68.
[117] *ISKCON v UK* (1994) 76A DR 90.
[118] *Arrowsmith v UK* above n 67.
[119] *H v UK* (1993) 16 EHRR CD 44.
[120] (2002) 35 EHRR 306, 335.

ECtHR noted that it is not for the state to determine whether religious views are legitimate. However, as discussed above, in other cases the Court, while not questioning the validity of the religious views, has become involved in questioning the meaning of the religious person's beliefs, in terms of whether conduct is a manifestation of religion or merely motivated by religion.

The difficulties for the Court in determining what an applicant believes are illustrated by the facts of *Kosteski v Former Yugoslav Republic of Macedonia*.[121] Here the applicant was disciplined for taking time off for the observance of a Muslim festival. The case was ruled inadmissible for various reasons,[122] but of relevance here was the dispute over whether the applicant really was Muslim. The respondent state claimed that the applicant was not a Muslim, because he had taken Christian holidays in the past, and showed no signs of belonging to the Muslim faith; he had a Christian name, had no knowledge of the Muslim faith, and did not follow Muslim dietary rules. The applicant claimed that he took Christian holidays as businesses were closed on those days so he could not work; pointed out that he had not chosen his name, which was given at birth, after which time beliefs could change; and that to require a good level of knowledge of the rules of a religion before one's religious rights were protected could cause difficulties for uneducated people. Moreover, he claimed that having to prove his faith in this way was an interference with his religious freedom. The Court held that in the context of requesting a benefit awarded on the basis of religion, it was not inappropriate for the employer to require the employee to substantiate his claim to hold a religious belief. However, the case illustrates a common problem for courts in becoming involved in deciding what someone believes, and the meaning to be attributed to their actions or inactions.

Another example of the ECHR approach here can be seen in the case of *Sahin v Turkey*[123] where the Grand Chamber took the view that wearing a headscarf, as part of Muslim religious observance, is contrary to notions of sexual equality.[124] However, as the dissenting judge pointed out,[125] it is not the role of the Court to determine the meaning in general of wearing a headscarf, and it should be wary of doing so.[126]

## Accommodation of Religious Practice

The jurisprudence of the Convention suggests that it is acceptable to put a 'cost' on religious observance, although this will need to be proportionate. Given the

---

[121] Above n 27.

[122] Including the fact that the religion did not require Muslims to abstain from working during the festival. On the question of whether it is for the Court to determine such issues, see discussion at p 99 above.

[123] Above n 83.

[124] *Ibid*, paras 115 and 116.

[125] Dissenting opinion of Judge Tulkens, para 12.

[126] See discussion at pp 158–164 for the approach to this question under the Employment Equality (Religion and Belief) Regulations 2003.

broad support within the Convention jurisprudence for religious rights, as important in a plural democracy, it would seem that the ECHR could be used to support an argument that employers should take reasonable and proportionate steps to accommodate religious practice within the workplace. However, although employers may be required to accommodate some levels of religious observance, it is also acceptable if such observance remains difficult for the employee, as long as it is not impossible.

*Dress Codes*   The ECommHR has accepted that dress codes can involve the right to free expression,[127] but have given little weight to the importance of dress codes as an aspect of freedom of expression, when weighed against other rights. In *Kara v UK*[128] it was accepted that dress codes could involve an aspect of personal expression, but the Commission did not find it to be disproportionate to interfere with the right in order to protect the rights of the employer to present a particular image. In *Stevens* expulsion from school did not breach the ECHR, in part because the student was not expressing an opinion or idea through his refusal to wear a school tie. The cases suggest a sympathy towards dress codes as expressing identity, but that the rights involved are not strong, and can be trumped by other rights.

In relation to religion, it would seem that the interests are stronger; the wearing of a headscarf expresses a religious view, and it is more likely that the interference would be disproportionate. However, the cases that have been brought before the ECHR on this point have not resulted in findings in favour of applicants seeking to uphold a right to wear the headscarf at work. However, in each case, the rights of others have been strengthened by the particular context of the case. For example, in *Dahlab v Switzerland*[129] the applicant was a teacher of young children. The particular position of a teacher, with influence on the intellectual and emotional development of children, was relevant to the decision of the Court that a restriction on wearing the headscarf was proportionate. Similarly, in the context of higher education in the cases of *Sahin* and *Karaduman v Turkey*,[130] the court took the view that where some are allowed to wear the headscarf, this can put others under pressure to adopt more fundamentalist approaches to their faith.[131] Thus it was the influence on others, together with the political implications of the wearing of the headscarf in the Turkish context, that seems to have been decisive. It should be noted, however, that in *Sahin* the Grand Chamber was of the opinion that the matter was one which was to be dealt with using the margin of appreciation. In effect, it recognised the strength of argument both in favour of and against the ban on headscarves, and the range of treatment given to the issue across Europe, where the issue is controversial and highly contested. The Grand Chamber took the view

[127]  *Stevens v UK* (1986) 46 DR 245.
[128]  Above n 82.
[129]  Above n 80.
[130]  App No 16278/90, (1993) 74 DR 93
[131]  This issue was also in play in *R (On the application of Begum) v Headteacher and Governors of Denbigh High School* [2006] UKHL 15

that where opinion in a democratic society can reasonably differ widely, especially on issues relating to the relationship between church and state, the issue is best left for local determination.

The debate may not take the same form for those who wear the headscarf in the context of other forms of employment, or in countries where the headscarf has only religious rather than political significance. Where those who see the head-scarf-wearing employee are other colleagues, or adult members of the public, the interests of others to be set against the interest of the employee in enjoying freedom to manifest religion are far less strong.[132]

*Hours of Work*   In relation to time off work for religious observance, the ECHR seems to recognise this as a manifestation of religion, but accepts that it may be accommodated by the employee taking unpaid time off. In *Konttinen v Finland*[133] the applicant sought to change his working hours to enable him to observe the Seventh Day Adventist Sabbath, which prohibits working from sunset on Friday. The Commission found that it was unreasonable to expect the employer to accommodate the rules of different denominations at work, and that it may impose an unfair burden on the employer and other employees. They found that the freedom of religion of Konttinen was adequately protected by his freedom to resign.

*Refusal of Work Tasks*   Refusal of staff to participate in certain tasks, such as a refusal by a doctor to take part in medical processes linked to abortion, have not given rise to case law in the ECHR. It may be that where it is easy to accommodate requests not to be involved in certain types of activity, such accommodation would be required on the part of the employer as a proportionate response to the religious needs of the employee. However, it is likely that there will also be an onus on the employee not to undertake work which he or she is unable fully to perform on religious grounds. An employee who worked in a clinic which carries out abortion is unlikely to have had her religious freedom unlawfully infringed if she refuses to participate in any abortion-related work. Her freedom of religion is safeguarded by her freedom to resign, not because the right to enjoy religious freedom has no currency in employment, but because restricting her religious freedom is proportionate to protect the rights of others. This approach was taken in *Knudsen v Norway*,[134] where a clergyman refused to carry out public functions such as marriages in protest at new abortion laws. The ECommHR found that there was no breach of Article 9 as Knudsen's religious freedom was protected by his freedom to leave his job.

---

[132] This issue is discussed in more detail in ch 3.
[133] (1996) 87 DR 68.
[134] (1985) 42 DR 247.

## The Right of Religious Organisations to Determine their own Employment Requirements

Statements from the ECHR make clear the commitment under the Convention to the idea that the right to freedom of religion includes the right to manifest religion collectively with others:

> the autonomous existence of religious communities is indispensable for pluralism in a democratic society and is thus an issue at the very heart of the protection which article 9 affords.[135]

Accordingly, it would seem clear that, under the Convention, groups of religious people should be entitled to form religious organisations, and as a natural corollary should be able to act as employers. This is particularly the case where the employment is of religious personnel.

The ECHR has been clear that it is not for the court to interfere with a religious group's freedom to appoint its own leaders.[136] A corollary of this freedom is that where a religious organisation is created, the court will uphold its rights to appoint leaders in accordance with its own rules. The refusal of an individual to comply with the teaching of a particular group can result in the individual's exclusion from the group, without infringing the individual's freedom of religion. An individual's right to freedom of religion does not extend to the freedom to be a member of a religious organisation with whose tenets he does not agree. In the context of employment, this means that if an employee of a religious organisation does not comply with the teaching of the organisation, his rights to remain in the organisation will not be protected. For example, the dismissal of a minister of the established Church in Norway for revoking his oath of loyalty did not breach Article 9.[137]

Apart from the employment by religious bodies of priests or other ministers, the ECHR also provides support for religious ethos organisations, such as religious hospitals, to run their organisations along religious lines. The support given under the ECHR for the freedom of religious employers to determine their employment requirements is illustrated by the case of *Rommelfanger v FDR*,[138] where a doctor who worked for a Roman Catholic hospital was dismissed for publicly disapproving of the Church's attitude to abortion. He was unsuccessful in his complaint that the dismissal breached his freedom of expression, and the Commission was very clear that the employer was able to set requirements on staff that they comply with the employer's religious ethos:

---

[135] *Hasan* above n 61 para 62; see also *Serif* above n 61.

[136] '[I]n the Court's view, punishing a person for merely acting as the religious leader of a group that willingly followed him can hardly be considered compatible with the demands of religious pluralism in a democratic society': *Serif* above n 61, para 51. See also *Hasan* above n 61.

[137] *Knudsen v Norway*, above n 134.

[138] (1989) 62 DR 151.

> If, as in the present case, the employer is an organisation based on certain convictions and value judgments which it considers as essential for the performance of its function in society, it is in fact in line with the requirements of the convention to give appropriate scope also to the freedom of expression of the employer.[139]

Although *Rommelfanger* involved arguments based on freedom of speech, if the case is read in conjunction with those which recognise the collective dimension to freedom of religion, it would seem to suggest that religious organisations are granted extensive freedom to determine their activities within the Convention jurisprudence.

## Harassment under the ECHR

One final way in which religious interests may be infringed in the workplace is by religious harassment. The question arises whether the experience of harassment, albeit unpleasant, can be understood to involve an infringement of a person's freedom of religion. If so, the employer would need to take action to prevent it. If there is no interference with freedom of religion the employer may still be under a duty to take action, in order to meet employment equality obligations, but that duty will not be reinforced by the need to respect freedom of religion. The difficulty with viewing harassment as involving a breach of freedom of religion is that harassment does not prevent the religious person from believing, nor does it directly prevent the practice or manifestation of religion. The only situation where rules relating to harassment will directly infringe freedom of religion is where religious staff are prevented from proselytising at work in order to save others from religious offence. Here, preventing the 'harasser' from expressing her religious views may infringe her freedom to manifest her religion.

Any link between harassment and freedom of religion is therefore not direct. Yet, it would seem that an implicit link does exist. This is because it is unlikely that full religious freedom can be enjoyed by a person whose life is made miserable by constant harassment. The proposition that harassment may involve a degree of interference with freedom of religion was recognised, to a limited degree, in *Otto Preminger Institute v Austria*.[140] Here the Court accepted that the state was entitled to seize a blasphemous film, and did not thereby infringe the film-maker's freedom of expression, because it was likely to cause offence to the religious feelings of a section of the public. In its decision, the Court makes clear that full enjoyment of the right to freedom of religion includes a right not to be unnecessarily offended:

> the manner in which religious beliefs and doctrines are opposed or denied is a matter which may engage the responsibility of the State . . . Indeed, in extreme cases the effect of particular methods of opposing or denying religious beliefs can be such as to inhibit those who hold such beliefs from exercising their freedom to hold and express them.[141]

---

[139] See *Rommelfanger, ibid.*
[140] Series A No 295A (1995) 19 EHRR 34.
[141] *Ibid* para 47.

The Court suggests that the right to freedom of religion may include a right not to have one's religious views needlessly offended. However, it is also clear that the right is not absolute in nature. The court prefaced its comments with the view that:

> those who choose to exercise the freedom to manifest their religion . . . must tolerate and accept the denial by others of their religious beliefs and even the propagation by others of doctrines hostile to their faith.[142]

It would seem then that the ECtHR accepts that the right to freedom of religion may be engaged in cases of serious religious harassment at work, if the harassment reaches a level which could be said to inhibit the freedom of religious staff to manifest their religion. Of course, the right is only protected where it is proportionate to do so, and it will need to be weighed against the competing right to freedom of speech and the rights of other workers. It may be that the ability of an employee to claim that Article 9 is breached will depend on whether she can also show a breach of Article 14, considered below.

# IV  Protection Against Religious Discrimination Under Article 14

Article 14 states:

> The enjoyment of the rights and freedoms set forth in this Convention shall be secured without discrimination on any ground such as sex, race, colour, language, religion, political or other opinion, national or social origin, association with a national minority, property, birth or other status.

Article 14 ECHR provides a right not to be discriminated against in the enjoyment of Convention rights on a number of grounds including religion. It does not provide a free-standing right to non-discrimination, but is dependent on a breach of one of the Convention rights. In this respect it can be regarded as a 'parasitic' right. To some extent the jurisprudence relating to Article 14 has been limited as a result because in many cases, although discrimination issues may arise, Article 14 is not considered by the ECtHR once it has found a breach of the substantive right. It is seen to be unnecessary to determine the Article 14 discrimination issue once the applicant has been found to have succeeded on one head of the claim.

Yet, despite this, Article 14 does retain some potential to protect the religious employee within the workplace. First, it seems that in some cases Article 14 can be used to expand the scope of the protection provided by the substantive article. In cases where there may be no breach of the individual substantive Convention right, a breach is found once the two articles are read together.[143] Article 14

---

[142] *Ibid* para 47.
[143] *Belgian Linguistics v Belgium* Series A No 6 (1979) 1 EHRR 252

effectively places on states an obligation to provide full enjoyment of the Convention rights to all, regardless of status. For example, basic protection for freedom of religion may be provided to all and so, read on its own, a state may not be in breach of the Convention. However, if some religious groups are provided with superior protection then Article 14 is breached; those with lesser protection are discriminated against in their enjoyment of the right, even though they are not denied the right altogether.

The effect of this is that the range of behaviour that can be protected under the substantive article may be expanded, because it is not just refusal to protect the right that is prohibited: anything less than 'full embodiment' of the right may give rise to a claim if the reduction from full embodiment is on one of the prohibited grounds.[144]

## Article 14 in the Employment Context

The broader understanding of what may amount to an infringement of the substantive Convention rights, when read with Article 14, may lead to a wider level of protection for religion within the employment context. First, it may help to show that the Convention should be enjoyed in the workplace. Although the Convention case law is divided on the question of whether adequate protection for religion is provided by a right to resign, if a claim is based on Article 14 the claim may well be strengthened. The Convention may not guarantee a job, but if, for example, those of the dominant religion enjoy unencumbered access to the job market, those of other religions should enjoy similar access. To do otherwise is to treat them less favourably in the enjoyment of their Article 9 rights.

The broader understanding of what may amount to an interference with Convention rights which is added by reference to Article 14 may also have an effect on the question of whether harassment involves an interference with freedom of religion, discussed above. Article 9 read with Article 14 allows for a finding that freedom has been infringed where there may be no direct interference, but where the Convention right is given something less than full embodiment or enjoyment. As discussed above, being subjected to harassment for one's religious beliefs may not prevent one from holding those beliefs, but interferes to a lesser extent. Yet being subjected to harassment for one's religious beliefs is not consistent with the full embodiment of religious freedom.

In the employment context, Articles 8, 9 and 10 are the Convention articles which are most likely to be infringed, discriminatorily, on grounds of religion. In *Sidabras v Lithuania*,[145] discussed above, the Court considered the Article 8 right to a private life where the applicant was dismissed due to his former employment

---

[144] 'The word "enjoyment", within the meaning of Article 14, must cover all situations that may arise between, at the one extreme, plain refusal of a right protected by the Convention and, at the other, full embodiment of that right in the domestic system': *Airey v Ireland* Series A No 32, 2 EHRR 305.

[145] Above n 41.

as a KGB officer. It took a very broad view of the substantive right, interpreting the ban on employment as an infringement of the applicant's 'private life' on the basis that it affected Siderbras's ability to develop relationships with the outside world, and could create serious difficulties in earning a living.[146] It may be that this broad understanding of the scope of the right to a private life was reached because the case was heard in the context of a claim that the interference was discriminatory.

An example of the use of Article 14 in conjunction with Article 9 can be found in *Thlimmenos v Greece*,[147] where Thlimmenos was refused registration as a chartered accountant because of his criminal conviction. The conviction was the result of his religiously motivated refusal to participate in military service, a criminal offence in Greece. The ECtHR found that refusal to register Thlimmenos as an accountant amounted to discriminatory treatment on grounds of religion. The Court implied that taken under Article 9 alone the case may not have succeeded, on the grounds that there is no right to a job under the Convention; but read in conjunction with Article 14, it was clear that the treatment was discriminatory. Thlimmenos's exercise of his freedom of religion led to a criminal conviction which affected his ability to work in his chosen profession. The exercise of freedom of religion by other citizens did not result in criminal convictions, and so did not affect their ability to work as they wished. To this extent, then, Thlimmenos suffered discrimination.

The Court in *Thlimmenos*[148] developed a broad understanding of the concept of discrimination and equality, recognising for the first time in ECHR jurisprudence that equal treatment extends beyond treating likes alike, to include treating those who are different differently. Thlimmenos was different from other job applicants with a criminal conviction as his was the result of religious observance. Non-discrimination required that he be treated differently, by ignoring his conviction for the purposes of registration as an accountant. This expanded idea of what is required for equal treatment in the enjoyment of religious freedom may have an effect on the understanding of the scope of an employer's duty to accommodate religion within the workplace.

Although *Thlimmenos* provides a more comprehensive understanding of discrimination, the case law of Article 14 is clear that discrimination does not arise in every case of different treatment or inappropriate similar treatment. It will arise where there is a difference in treatment, which does not pursue a legitimate aim. Further,

> Article 14 is ... violated when it is established that there is no reasonable relationship of proportionality between the means employed and the aim sought to be realised.[149]

In relation to the other factors which determine whether there has been discrimination, such as the presence of a legitimate aim for the treatment in question, and

---

[146] *Ibid*, paras 47 and 48
[147] Above n 28.
[148] Above n 28.
[149] Above n 143, at 284.

its proportionality, the factors that have already been discussed will also be considered in deciding whether discrimination can be justified, factors such as the nature of the religious conduct and the nature of the employer. As with Article 9, the ECtHR allows states a margin of appreciation in assessing the proportionality of any justification. Article 14 may not therefore add very much to the substantive protection in this regard. What Article 14 does add, however, is a broadening of the scope of protection by allowing a claim to arise even where there is no breach of a substantive Convention right. It also adds to the protection of religion at work by creating an avenue whereby an applicant can make a claim based on the fact that he does not fully enjoy the right to freedom of religion, even though there is not a total interference with the right.

# V  Conclusion

The ECHR case law on freedom of religion recognises in general terms its fundamental importance as a reflection of individual autonomy and as necessary for the pluralism of the modern world. It also provides strong recognition of the right to freedom of religion as a right that can be enjoyed communally.

Yet in many respects the jurisprudence does not suggest that religious freedom should enjoy strong protection at work. Significant hurdles must be overcome before an employee will be able to rely on Article 9 to protect the exercise of freedom of religion at work: not only must one show that the right applies at work in the first place, but one must also show that the practice in issue is a manifestation of religion, rather than merely a practice which is motivated by religion. Once over these considerable hurdles, the right to freedom of religion must be balanced against the rights of others, and the proportionately of any restriction must be assessed. The hurdles are significant, and success is by no means certain. In particular, the employee will persistently come up against the argument that freedom of religion is protected by the freedom to resign. The Convention does not guarantee the right to a job, and ultimately the freedom to resign undoubtedly does act as a guarantee of freedom of religion and belief.

Use of Article 14 in conjunction with Article 9 may help to overcome some of these difficulties, for example by broadening the range of behaviour that may be viewed as infringing the Convention protection, to include behaviour that denies the employee the full embodiment of their rights. However, this benefit is only partial, because whether a case is brought under Article 9 alone or with Article 14, behaviour by an employer can be justified where it amounts to a proportionate means of achieving a legitimate aim.

To an extent, the limited protection for religious interests at work provided by the ECHR reflects a lack of consensus in Europe on the proper scope of the protection of Article 9. This lack of consensus is often apparent in the use of the 'margin of appreciation'. The lack of consensus, and the consequent use of the 'margin of appreciation', means that the ECtHR is weak in setting standards for the protection of religious rights, particularly in contexts where the restrictions on religion are not absolute in nature. The fact that absolute freedom is protected by the right to resign leaves the ECtHR free to find lesser breaches of the right to be within the margin of appreciation. For example, in the cases relating to the wearing of headscarves at work, the ECtHR has found the restrictions to be within the margin of appreciation. Such a finding does not deem the restriction to be a correct response by an employer: it merely finds that the restriction does not breach the Convention. In effect, the ECtHR does not set standards for protection,[150] but seems to reflect ambivalence, or at least a lack of unanimity among states as to what the correct response to the issue should be.

In the domestic context, using the HRA, courts are not, however, bound to follow the restrictive interpretations of the ECHR.[151] There is thus more potential to develop more progressive protection for religious interests. There are two reasons why this may be appropriate. First, a more progressive reading of the case law would enable domestic courts to draw on the broader statements of principle in the ECHR case law which support the protection of religious rights in the workplace. Second, the reliance by the ECtHR on the margin of appreciation is inappropriate in the domestic setting.

In terms of the more progressive reading of the case law, examples have been given in the earlier discussion of the case law. For example, a better level of protection can be given in the context of work by relying on the case law which accepts that rights need protection at work.[152] Or the fact that the employee may be free to resign should not prevent the merits of the case from being heard but should instead be relevant to proportionality. Similarly, removing the artificial divide between religious manifestation and religiously motivated behaviour would allow for a fuller understanding of religion and religious practice and their role in life. The importance of the practice to the religion in question is relevant to proportionality, but the divide between manifestation and motive should not be determinative.

In relation to the 'margin of appreciation' it is clear that the ECtHR has been unwilling to rule on contentious matters such as whether banning the wearing of headscarves infringes human rights.[153] Given the range of opinion across Europe, this may well be the correct stance: the language of fundamental human rights is very strong, and the Court may well wish to avoid ruling in such strong terms on

---

[150] A Lester, 'Universality versus Subsidiarity: A Reply' [1998] *EHRLR* 73, 78, and P van Dijk and F van Hoof, *Theory and Practice of the European Convention on Human Rights* (2nd edn) (The Netherlands, Kluwer, 1990) and N Lavender, 'The Problem of the Margin of Appreciation' [1997] *EHRLR* 380.

[151] Section 2 HRA 1998. Domestic courts can provide greater protection than that available under the ECHR, but cannot provide less.

[152] See the cases discussed above at pp 88–92.

[153] The variety of practice with regard to the acceptance of the wearing of headscarves across Europe is huge. See L Vickers, *Religion and Belief in Employment—The EU Law* (European Commission, 2007).

matters which are so divisive and contested in the realms of both social theory and political reality.[154] However, in the domestic context, these matters can be viewed differently. A domestic court is not bound to impose a margin of appreciation in reaching its decisions, although where cases are not clear cut courts have a discretionary area of judgment in deciding whether Convention rights have been infringed.[155] In exercising their oversight, courts should ensure that concerns about religious freedom have been given due consideration, but need not be bound by standards applied in other states.[156] This means that domestic courts can look to the ECHR case law for guidance on the principles to be considered when assessing whether a particular practice infringes religious freedom, without needing to take into account the range of practice across Europe.

Whether or not domestic courts take the opportunity to move beyond the ECHR case law in the longer term remains to be seen, but to date they have not done so. In *Copsey v WWB Devon Clays Ltd*[157] the Court of Appeal referred to the ECHR case law in deciding a case involving an employee who had been dismissed for refusing to work on Sundays. The Court would not consider the argument that the employee's religious interests had been infringed by the dismissal, on the basis that the ECHR case law does not apply to the work relationship. Mummery LJ reached this conclusion reluctantly and stated that were it not for the 'clear' Commission decisions in *Ahmad* and *Stedman* relating to requests for changes in working hours, he would have found that Article 9 was engaged in the case, so that the employer would have needed to justify any interference with religious freedom in accordance with Article 9(2). Rix LJ was reluctant to follow the 'ambivalent collection of authorities'.[158] Instead, he would have preferred an analysis based on reference to Article 9 principles in interpreting the standard of fairness of any dismissal. However, despite these reservations, the court felt bound by the ECHR case law.

In sum, any conclusion on the extent to which employees can rely directly on the protection for the right to freedom of religion within the workplace must remain tentative given the current state of legal authorities on the question.[159] While it is suggested that the arguments for allowing reference to the ECHR in cases involving employment are strong, those arguments have not been consistently accepted in domestic courts. However, although the scope of the right to

---

[154] For the range of debate on the issue of human rights and the headscarf, see M Mahlmann, 'Religious Tolerance, Pluralist Society and the Neutrality of the State: The Federal Constitutional Court's Decision in the Headscarf Case' 4(11) *German Law Journal*; D McGoldrick, *Human Rights and Religion: The Islamic Headscarf Debate in Europe* (Oxford, Hart Publishing, 2006).

[155] See *R v DPP ex parte Kebilene* [2000] 2 AC 326, discussed in L Vickers, *Freedom of Expression and Employment* (Oxford, OUP, 2002), ch 3.

[156] For an example of the approach see *R (On the application of Begum) v Headteacher and Governors of Denbigh High School* [2006] UKHL 15. See the discussion of the role of the margin of appreciation in the domestic context in Vickers, *ibid*, 105–106.

[157] [2005] EWCA Civ 932.

[158] Citing his own judgment in *R (Williamson) v Secretary of State for Education and Employment* [2002] EWCA Civ 1926 at para 202.

[159] Contrast *Copsey v WWB Devon Clays Ltd* (above n 157) and *X v Y* (n 11).

freedom of religion may be of limited direct use in the employment context, it may be of considerable use indirectly. In particular, an appreciation of the right to freedom of religion may be of significance in determining the proper parameters of the protection against religious discrimination. Thus the HRA may be used in the domestic context to interpret the Employment Equality (Religion and Belief) Regulations 2003. With regard to the Regulations, religious interests are being protected in the employment context. It is clear that, notwithstanding the periodic reluctance of the ECtHR to apply the Convention to the workplace, the Regulations should be interpreted to comply with Article 9. This is required both under the HRA and because the Directive which the Regulations implement should in turn be interpreted to comply with the principles established under the ECHR.[160] The provisions of the Regulations are discussed in detail in the following chapter.

---

[160] Article 6(2) EU Treaty, and Recital 1 Employment Equality Directive 2000/78.

# 5

## Protection Against Religious Discrimination in the UK

The Employment Equality Directive[1] requires all Member States to protect against discrimination on grounds of religion and belief in employment, occupation and vocational training. In response, the Employment Equality (Religion or Belief) Regulations 2003, ('the Regulations') were introduced in Great Britain and came into force in December 2003. Provisions protecting against discrimination on grounds of religion and political opinion were already in force in Northern Ireland,[2] and amending legislation was introduced there to ensure compliance with the Directive.[3] The aim of this chapter is to assess the extent to which the approach in the UK, based on the Employment Equality Directive, provides the level of protection for religious interests that was advocated in chapter three, and whether the difficult task of reconciling different interests has been appropriately achieved. The focus is on the Employment Equality (Religion and Belief) Regulations 2003, which do not apply in Northern Ireland.[4] However the protection in Northern Ireland is very similar and where differences occur these will be indicated.

Clearly, the Regulations were introduced to transpose the provisions of the Directive, so at times it will be necessary to consider the wording of this parent

---

[1] 2000/78/EC establishing a general framework for equal treatment in employment and occupation [2000] OJ L303/16 ('the Directive').

[2] Legislation to protect against discrimination on grounds of religion or belief was introduced in Northern Ireland in 1976 and is currently governed by the Fair Employment and Treatment (Northern Ireland) Order 1998 (FETO). The FETO requires registration of all employers with 10 or more employees, and requires all registered employers to monitor the composition of their workforce by persons belonging to either the Roman Catholic or Protestant communities and by sex. The Equality Commission for Northern Ireland has powers of enquiry and investigation, and powers to recommend or require employers to take affirmative action in a specified period. There are also extensive duties on public authorities to promote religious equality. See A McColgan, *Discrimination Law* (Oxford, Hart Publishing, 2005) 668–687.

[3] The Fair Employment and Treatment (Amendment) Regulations (NI) 2003 (SI 2003 No 520), which amended the definition of harassment and indirect discrimination to bring it into line with the Directive.

[4] Northern Ireland has long had protection against discrimination on grounds of religion, dating from the Government of Ireland Act 1920, through the Fair Employment Acts of 1976 and 1989 to the FETO 1998. Although this gives rise to extensive experience of dealing with religious discrimination, the historical and political context of the protection is peculiar to Northern Ireland, and so this experience is not always of direct relevance to the rest of the UK.

document to see why the Regulations have been framed as they have. In addition, although the focus is on the British Regulations, it will be interesting briefly to compare the approach of other EU jurisdictions which have, at times, transposed the Directive differently, but this will be considered in more detail in chapter six.

Prior to the implementation of the Regulations, and in the absence in Great Britain of any provisions relating directly to religious discrimination, the only protection available against discrimination on religious grounds was race discrimination. For some religious groups, who share a common ethnicity, protection could be granted on grounds of ethnic origin rather than religion. Thus Sikhs and Jews have been defined as both ethnic or racial groups and as religious groups.[5] These religious groups can therefore find protection under the Race Relations Act 1976. In contrast, Muslims are not an ethnic group,[6] although, because in the UK the Muslim population is predominantly Asian, there have been findings in domestic law that discrimination against Muslims may amount to indirect race discrimination.[7] The clear lack of consistency between different religious groups is overcome with the introduction of protection against discrimination on grounds of religion in the Regulations.

The Regulations apply to all employers, religious or secular, and to the public as well as the private sector. They protect employees, and all those who contract personally to do work. They also apply to partnerships, office-holders, agency workers and other categories of worker not always protected by employment-related legislation.[8] There is an exception where there is a 'genuine occupational requirement' for an employee to be of a particular religion or belief. However, this exception is only allowed where it is proportionate to impose the requirement.

# I  Protection Under the Employment Equality (Religion and Belief) Regulations 2003

## Definition of Religion and Belief

As discussed in chapter two above, the Regulations do not define 'religion and belief', although the expectation is that they will be interpreted to comply with the definitions used by the ECtHR.[9] The lack of a formal definition provides flexibility to those interpreting the Regulations, and means that the courts will not be bound by definitions that could be under-inclusive, or could become outdated.

---

[5] See *Mandla v Lee* [1983] 2 AC 548 and *Seide v Gillette* [1980] IRLR 427. In determining the meaning of 'ethnic group' in the UK one of the factors considered was whether the group shared a religion.

[6] *Tariq v Young* Case 247738/88.

[7] *J H Walker v Hussain* [1996] IRLR 11.

[8] See Regs 6 to 20 for coverage of the Regulations.

[9] For the approach under the ECHR see C Evans, *Freedom of Religion under the European Convention on Human Rights* (Oxford, OUP, 2001) ch 4.

The lack of definition reflects the absence of definition in the Directive, which provides the potential for inconsistent treatment of religious groups across Europe. A belief system such as Scientology is a clear example of a belief which has already been subject to inconsistent treatment within Europe.[10] The lack of a domestic definition leaves the Regulations vulnerable to inconsistent interpretations within the domestic jurisdiction.

In an early case brought under the Regulations, an applicant for work as an executive officer at the Home Office was rejected because of a potential conflict of interest with his previous work advising on potential asylum seekers. He claimed his sympathy for disadvantaged asylum seekers was a demonstration of the Christian virtue of charity, and that his rejection was therefore on grounds of religion. The tribunal took the view that the beliefs were too vague and ill-defined to give rise to a claim of religious discrimination.[11]

Some of the difficulties caused by the lack of a clear definition of religion will be overcome because the protection also covers *belief*. However, it would be unlikely that beliefs as vague as those in *Devine* would be covered by the term 'belief'. As discussed above, moving to the term 'belief' does not avoid problems of definition, but merely shifts the location of the debate to the divide between beliefs with sufficient 'cogency, seriousness, cohesion and importance'[12] to warrant protection and those without.

The Regulations do not cover discrimination on grounds of political opinions or beliefs.[13] However, it can be difficult at times to draw distinctions between religious or other beliefs, and political opinions. For example, drawing distinctions between religion and politics can be difficult when considering liberation theology; and on matters such as abortion, beliefs may span the religious and the political. Distinguishing between beliefs and political beliefs can be equally troublesome: for example, communism may comprise cogent, serious and cohesive beliefs but is also a belief about the government of the state.

In the Northern Irish context, religion and politics are closely related, and here the legal protection extends to cover political opinion. Even here, however, the boundaries may not be clear. In *Gill v Northern Ireland Council for Ethnic Minorities*[14] the Northern Irish Court of Appeal rejected a claim that discrimination had occurred on grounds of political opinion where an individual had not

[10] For example, Scientology is recognised as a religion using the definitions in Italy (see the Country Report for Italy, published by the European Network of Legal Experts in the non-discrimination field (Human European Consultancy, Migration Policy Group, 2006)) and in Australia (*The Church of the New Faith v The Commission of Pay-roll Tax (Victoria)* [1982–3] 154 CLR 120), but is not recognised in the German Labour Courts ( Federal Labour Court, *Bundesarbeitsgericht* March 22 1995, *Neue Juristische Wochenschrift* 1996, 143, Country Report Germany European Network of Legal Experts in the non-discrimination field (Human European Consultancy, Migration Policy Group, 2005)), nor by the UK with respect to the laws on charitable status (see the decision of the Charity Commissioners of 17 November 1999).

[11] *Devine v Home Office* ET Case No 2302061/2004 (9 August 2004).

[12] *X, Y and Z v UK* (1982) 31 DR 50, and *Campbell and Cosans v UK* (1982) 4 EHRR 293.

[13] See *Baggs v Fudge* Employment Tribunal (Bristol) Case No 1400114/05.

[14] [2002] IRLR 74.

been offered a job because of differences in approach to race relations. The applicant advocated an anti-racist stance, whereas the local council (and the successful applicant) favoured a more 'culturally sensitive' approach. The Court defined political opinions as those concerning the government of the state or matters of public policy, rather than differing approaches to race relations.

Although the outer limits of the definition of belief are not clear, the Regulations clearly cover atheism and other non-religious viewpoints. Amendments to the Regulations in the Equality Act 2006[15] state that references to religion or belief include reference to a lack of a religion or belief. This does more than provide that the Regulations cover atheists. It would seem additionally to cover absence of a belief in a specific religion, so, for example, an employer who will only employ Christians discriminates against any applicant who is not a Christian.

## Direct Discrimination

Direct discrimination involves less favourable treatment on grounds of religion or belief. Examples of the behaviour covered would be refusal to employ, train, or promote staff on the basis of religion. Employment decisions based on stereotypical views of how those of a particular religion will behave would also be directly discriminatory. As the Regulations cover both religious employers and secular employers, the definition of direct discrimination will cover the religious employer who refuses to employ a person of a different religion,[16] and the secular employer who refuses to employ religious people. Inconsistencies in the employment of religious staff will also be covered. For example, the employment of members of staff of one religion, coupled with a refusal to employ those of another, will amount to direct discrimination.

Direct discrimination is defined as less favourable treatment 'on grounds of . . . religion or belief'.[17] It thus covers not only less favourable treatment on the grounds of a person's actual religion or belief, but also treatment based on the discriminator's perception of a person's religion, a perception which may of course be mistaken. It also covers discrimination based on another person's religion. Thus discrimination based on an association with people of a particular religion (for example, discrimination against someone married to a member of a religious group) is covered, as is discrimination based on refusal to comply with a discriminatory instruction.[18] The Regulations also provide that an employer can discriminate against a worker even if they share the same religion.

As originally drafted, and according to the wording of the Directive, discrimination 'on grounds of religion' could be taken to include discrimination based on

---

[15] S 77 Equality Act 2006.
[16] Although this may be covered by the 'genuine occupational requirement' exception discussed below.
[17] Reg 3 (1)(a) as amended by s 77 Equality Act 2006.
[18] cf under the RRA: *Showboat Entertainment Centre v Owens* [1984] 1 WLR 384.

the employer's religious views. This could, for example, cover a Catholic employer dismissing a (non-religious) employee for living in an extra-marital relationship, on the basis of the employer's religious view that remarriage was wrong. Such action would have been discriminatory and only lawful if there was a proportionate and genuine occupational requirement for the treatment. However, this was changed in the final version of the Regulations and the change confirmed in an amendment to the Regulations introduced in the Equality Act 2006.[19] Direct discrimination now no longer occurs where it is based on the employer's religion: discrimination only occurs where 'on the grounds of the religion or belief of B or of any other person except A . . . A treats B less favourably than he treats or would treat other persons'.

This makes clear that discrimination on the grounds of the employer's religion remains outside the remit of the Religion and Belief Regulations. It would seem therefore to remain legal. It is not clear why this is the case, and why discriminatory employment decisions based on the religious views of the employer should be treated differently from discriminatory employment practices based on the employer's views about the employee's religion or lack of religion.

However, the limitation on the remit of the Regulations may not be very significant, because discrimination on the basis of the employer's religion may well be recast as discrimination on the basis of the employee's religion, or lack of it. For example, the refusal by a Christian employer to employ an applicant who lives in an extra-marital relationship, because the employer believes that this lifestyle is sinful, could be said to amount to discrimination against the applicant because of the applicant's beliefs, as well as on grounds of the potential employer's beliefs. Given that 'religion or belief' is defined to include a lack of belief, then the absence of a religious belief on the part of the applicant that living in an extra-marital relationship is immoral could be the ground on which the applicant is refused the job. In effect, the fact that 'religion and belief' covers 'lack of belief' means that where the applicant does not share the employer's belief this becomes a form of 'belief' on the applicant's part. If the applicant shared the same religious views as the employer he could be employed. Because he does not, he is discriminated against.[20]

Even if such an argument is not accepted, any discrimination based on an employer's religious views will still be subject to review under other non-discrimination legislation to ensure that such treatment does not lead to discrimination on other grounds. For example, a religious employer who refuses to employ gay employees, because of his own religious views, will usually be discriminating unlawfully under the Sexual Orientation Regulations.

---

[19]  Reg 3(2), introduced in the final version of the Regulations, stated that in relation to direct discrimination, 'the reference . . . to religion or belief does not include [the discriminator's] religion or belief'. This is removed by s 77 Equality Act 2006 as otiose following the introduction of a new Reg 3(1).

[20]  Of course, an employee may share the belief that the lifestyle is sinful, but continue with the practice in any event. In such a case, the discrimination is on the basis of the employer's belief, and not on the basis of the employee's lack of shared belief, and remains lawful.

The definition of direct discrimination does not provide any general exceptions or justifications. However, specific exceptions exist where, having regard to the nature of the employment or the context in which it is carried out, being of a particular religion or belief is a genuine and determining occupational requirement and it is proportionate to apply that requirement in the particular case.[21] Thus requiring that a priest be Catholic, or that a teacher of Islam be Muslim, would not involve unlawful direct discrimination. Moreover, a slightly wider exception exists where the employer is a church or an organisation the ethos of which is based on religion or belief. The scope of these exceptions is discussed in more detail below.

## Indirect Discrimination

Indirect discrimination is defined to cover the application of a provision, criterion or practice which is applied equally to those not of the same religion, but which puts persons of the religion in question at a particular disadvantage compared to others, and which cannot be shown to be a proportionate means of achieving a legitimate aim.[22] The wording accords with other new definitions of indirect discrimination[23] and will mean that indirectly discriminatory preferences will be covered by the Regulations as well as absolute bars to employment.[24]

Indirect discrimination addresses the fact that discrimination is not always directly caused. Inherent in its meaning is the idea of disparate impact,[25] the idea that certain requirements will be harder for some to comply with than others. It reflects the fact that treating everyone the same may not achieve full equality, but may instead create inequality, or at least allow inequality to remain, because of a failure to recognise the difficulties some groups may have in meeting what may appear to be neutral requirements.[26]

The disadvantages suffered by religious staff may not be that employers refuse to employ or promote them directly because of their religion; instead, difficulty can arise because it is harder for religious staff to comply with some requirements imposed at work, even though those requirements are religiously neutral and applied to all staff. For example, an employer may not refuse to employ Christians, but a requirement to work on Sundays may make it harder for some Christians to take up the employment. Similarly, a uniform for female staff which consists of a

---

[21] Reg 7(2).

[22] Reg 3(1)(b). The wording of the Directive is: 'where an apparently neutral provision, criterion or practice would put persons of a particular religion or belief . . . at a particular disadvantage compared with other persons' unless it can be justified: Art 2(2).

[23] eg the new s 1 RRA provided by the Race Relations Act 1976 (Amendment) Regulations 2003 which applies to discrimination on grounds of race or ethnic or national origins.

[24] Contrast the position under the original RRA 1976 in *Perera v Civil Service Commission* [1983] IRLR 166 and still applicable to discrimination on grounds of colour and nationality.

[25] The concept of disparate impact discrimination was developed in the USA in *Griggs v Duke Power Company* 401 US 424 (1971).

[26] For an overview of the development of the concept of indirect discrimination see S Fredman, *Discrimination Law* (Oxford, OUP, 2002).

skirt and short-sleeved top would not amount to a bar on the employment of Muslim women, but could act as a barrier to their entry into the particular employment. Protection from indirect discrimination is designed to address the neutral employment requirements which create particular difficulty for some staff. It reflects the fact that neutral rules which are generally applied can have a particularly detrimental impact on some religious groups. Clearly, such requirements are sometimes necessary, and so the concept of indirect discrimination includes an element of justification. A hospital will need to employ some staff to work on Sundays, for example, and so a requirement to work on Sundays will be capable of justification.

In order to establish indirect discrimination an applicant must show that the neutral work requirement operates to the disadvantage of the particular religious group. The fact that an employee can, in fact, comply with a requirement will not prevent a claim being made[27]; the focus is on whether it is harder for the employee to comply in practice, and so puts the applicant at a disadvantage in comparison with others. Thus, Christian workers are clearly physically able to work on Sundays, but to do so may interfere with their religious observance. It is the practical difficulty in complying with a requirement to work on Sundays which would be the cause of discrimination, and any claim would not be blocked by the fact that compliance is physically possible.

Although cases cannot be ruled out by the physical possibility of compliance with a work requirement, applicants will need to show that they are put at a 'particular disadvantage' before indirect discrimination is made out. This wording is designed to overcome the difficulties caused by earlier definitions of indirect sex discrimination which required proof that the proportion of women who could comply with a work-based requirement was 'considerably smaller' than the proportion of men who could comply. Had such a definition been used for indirect religious discrimination, an applicant claiming that a requirement to work on Sundays was discriminatory would need to have shown that a considerably smaller proportion of Christians could work on Sundays than others. With respect to sex discrimination, this caused a number of difficulties. First, the question of what was meant by 'considerably' smaller, and the evidence needed to prove this, were both highly contested, as was the question of who should comprise the comparator group with which the applicant would be compared.[28] The wording in the Regulations is designed to make it easier for applicants to prove indirect discrimination, requiring only that the applicant show that the requirement puts the religious person at a

---

[27] Note that under earlier definitions of indirect discrimination contained in the Sex Discrimination Act 1975 and the Race Relations Act 1976 the applicant had to show that there was a requirement with which he or she could not comply. However, early case law decided that this covered requirements with which the applicant had difficulty complying as well as requirements with which he or she could not comply at all: *Price v Civil Service Commission* [1978] ICR 27.

[28] These issues generated much case law with respect to sex discrimination; for example, see: *Jones v University of Manchester* [1993] IRLR 218; *R v Secretary of State for Employment ex parte Seymour Smith* [2000] IRLR 263 HL; *London Underground v Edwards* (No 2) [1998] IRLR 364 HL; and *Barry v Midland Bank* [1999] IRLR 581 HL.

particular disadvantage compared to others. Exact statistical proof of the extent to which it is harder to comply is not needed, nor is there a need to find a comparator group which can be proven statistically to find it easier to comply with the requirement.

Despite the attempts to make the indirect discrimination provisions more user-friendly in the Religion and Belief Regulations (as well as in amendments to the Race Relations Act[29] and the Sex Discrimination Act[30]) hurdles still remain for applicants attempting to bring claims of indirect discrimination. It is clear that the levels of statistical analysis needed to prove the disparate impact of neutral requirements under older definitions should not be required. Nonetheless, applicants will need to have some evidence of 'particular disadvantage'.[31] They will still need to be able to show that the requirement causes them difficulty in comparison to others, and will need to be able to point to a group of 'others' in comparison with whom they are at a disadvantage.

The question of who the comparator(s) should be is not clear. The Regulations provide that the comparison of the religious person's case with another 'must be such that the relevant circumstances in the one case are the same, or not materially different, in the other'.[32] However, there can be difficulty in determining when the circumstances are 'materially different', and it may be that the factor which demonstrates the disparate impact is the factor which a court determines makes the comparator's case different.

In some cases the disadvantage caused to a religious person may be clear when compared to a non-religious person: for example, an employer who refuses to allow a form of dress (such as a head covering) puts at a clear disadvantage those whose religion requires such a form of dress (such as some Sikhs and Muslims), when compared with those, religious or not, who do not have a religion-based dress code. However, in other cases, the disadvantage may only become apparent if one chooses a more specific comparator. Complications may arise where comparisons are made in the UK between the dominant Christian religion and other religions. Many Christian festivals and customs have been so widely adopted that they are almost universally celebrated as largely secular or cultural occasions. Thus, the normal working week involves a day off on Sunday, and Christmas and Easter are almost universally celebrated, with most businesses closed, even if most celebrations are not religious in nature. This means that comparisons with treatment of other religions becomes complex: is treatment of one religion different from another, if one religion's practice is effectively treated as cultural rather than only religious? For example, a refusal to allow any workers to take Saturdays off may not amount to less favourable treatment even though Jewish workers and

---

[29] Race Relations Act (Amendment) Regulations 2003 (SI 1626).

[30] Employment Equality (Sex Discrimination) Regulations 2005 (SI 2467).

[31] Under the Equality Act 2006 the definition of indirect discrimination for the purposes of non-discrimination in the provision of goods and services refers only to 'disadvantage' rather than 'particular disadvantage'. It is unclear what effect the removal of the word 'particular' will have.

[32] Reg 3(3).

Seventh Day Adventists are all prevented from taking their religious day of rest off work: all staff wanting Saturday off are treated the same. However, if compared with Christians, the treatment may be disadvantageous because they can take their religious day of rest off work. However, it might be suggested that the two religious groups are not in comparable situations: it is arguable that having Sunday off is not a religious accommodation granted to Christians, but merely the acceptance of a cultural norm.[33] Thus one might say that a Christian's circumstances are materially different from those of a Jewish or Seventh Day Adventist member of staff: his religious observance can be carried out during time that is traditionally non-working time, and so the comparison for the purposes of indirect discrimination is not valid. How courts will determine the question of whether cases are comparable or not has the potential to be complex, and it is not yet clear how courts will deal with the question.

It would seem that if the Regulations are to adequately protect against discrimination on religious grounds, then once less favourable treatment can be shown in comparison with another group, this should be sufficient, whether that comparison is with those of a majority religion, a minority religion, an established religion or no religion. Such an approach would also accord with the aim of reducing the extent to which cases can be taken over by the technicalities of proving that working practices impact disproportionately on particular groups. The change in definition of indirect discrimination, to avoid complex statistical proof of proportions of the population who can and cannot comply with work requirements, aims to make it easier to claim indirect discrimination. This aim will be undermined if an overly complex system develops for determining whether differences between groups of comparators are 'material'. Thus, the best outcome in the example above is to accept that the Jewish or Seventh Day Adventist worker is at a particular disadvantage in comparison with Christians, as a requirement to work on Saturdays is particularly disadvantageous for them. However, in justifying any requirement, an employer can point to the cultural norm[34] of working on Saturday and resting on Sunday. Hence it would be preferable to view the issue as one of justification rather than a problem of finding the correct comparator.[35] This way the interests of equality and religious freedom can be assessed in determining whether a requirement is justified, rather than having cases fall at the first hurdle of establishing that there was different treatment.

An additional problem with regard to showing particular disadvantage can arise with respect to the use of indirect discrimination by those who have an individualised religious belief, which is not shared by others. The wording of the Regulations suggests that, before indirect discrimination can be made out, the applicant must show that a neutral requirement is imposed which puts or would put *persons* of the same religion at a particular disadvantage. This suggests that

---

[33] See the observations of the ECommHR in *Ahmad v UK* (1982) 4 EHRR 126 para 28.

[34] Albeit one based on a religious tradition.

[35] An additional benefit of such an approach to any applicant is that the burden of justifying any discrimination will be on the respondent.

there must be some sort of group disadvantage suffered by the applicant. This certainly accords with the traditional view of indirect discrimination as addressing group disadvantage. The wording is the same in relation to sex and race discrimination, where it will rarely create difficulties, as there will be others in the same group as the applicant. However, in the context of religious discrimination, this restriction could be of some significance. If an individual has a personal religious or philosophical belief which makes it difficult for her to comply with a particular work requirement, it may be hard to use the indirect discrimination rules unless she can point to others who are also disadvantaged.

Yet nothing in the definition of religion and belief suggests that there is a minimum number of adherents before a belief system can be classified as a religion or belief under the Regulations. If freedom of religion is to be given maximum protection individual religious adherents should be protected against discriminatory treatment, whether or not others share their beliefs. It may be that the more personalised wording used in relation to disability discrimination (that of reasonable adjustments or reasonable accommodation) is more appropriate for the protection of religious interests at work. The wording allows the law on disability discrimination to reflect the individual experience of disability, and may be appropriate for use in the context of religious discrimination if a personalised understanding of religion and belief is to be protected, as would be required if the law is to give proper protection to freedom of religion and thought. The question of whether a duty of reasonable accommodation should be introduced, or whether such a duty can be read into the Regulations, is discussed further in the final chapter.

In fact, a religious or other belief held by one person could be covered by the Regulations as currently drafted. Indirect discrimination requires that a provision 'puts or would put' persons of the religion in question at a disadvantage. Although this suggests that a group must be disadvantaged, the inclusion of the conditional ('would put' persons at a disadvantage) can be used to include provisions which disadvantage an individual applicant, and would also put persons of the same view, were there to be any, at a disadvantage. This way, the protection against indirect discrimination need not be limited to those who can find a group who hold the same religious or other beliefs. The benefit of such an interpretation, albeit a somewhat awkward one,[36] is that it allows those who hold religious or other beliefs, which may not be shared by others, to be protected against indirect discrimination. Such a reading does not run counter to the aims of the definition, which is phrased as it is because it was developed with respect to sex and race where there are always those of the 'other' group. Where finding a group of people with exactly the same characteristics is difficult, such as in the context of disability, the more personalised 'accommodation' test is used. Interpreting indirect

---

[36] The duty to interpret legislation to accord with the European Convention on Human Rights, imposed by s 3 Human Rights Act allows for even strained interpretations to be upheld. Here, to do so may be necessary in order to interpret the Regulations to accord with the rights and freedoms protected by Art 9. See further ch 4 on the ECHR.

discrimination as suggested above enables the protection to extend to individual religious or other beliefs.

Of course, any assessment of the proportionality of imposing a provision which disadvantages the holder of a particular religious or other belief is likely to take into account the number of individuals affected. If an employer refuses to adapt a uniform rule to reflect the dress codes of a large proportion of the local workforce, such a refusal may be viewed as disproportionate; failure to accommodate one employee's religious views may be more easily regarded as proportionate.

## Justification

Even if a work requirement does put a person at a disadvantage, there will only be unlawful indirect discrimination where the requirement cannot be justified. Once the employee has shown that a practice puts her at a disadvantage, then it is for the employer to show that the requirement is a proportionate means of achieving a legitimate aim. This means that appropriate and necessary requirements can be imposed, even though they may give rise to disadvantage to some groups. In effect, the test of justification enables any work requirements that will adversely affect the right to freedom of religion and belief to be subject to review in the light of the factual and contextual factors discussed in chapter three above.

The ACAS guidelines on the Regulations suggest that a requirement in a small company for staff to work late on Fridays in order to analyse end-of-week data from the USA, would be justified even though it may put certain religious staff at a disadvantage because of their need to be involved in religious observance on Friday evenings. Assuming that the data needs immediate analysis, the practice would be justified as an appropriate way to serve a legitimate business need. In such a case, the size of the undertaking means that common accommodations for religious practice such as flexible working and shift swaps are not possible.

The need for justification should ensure that job requirements are appropriate to the job in question, and should prevent the imposition of unnecessary requirements that have a disproportionate impact on those of any particular religion or belief. The wording of the justification standard in the Regulations differs from that used in the Directive, where any indirectly discriminatory practice must be 'objectively justified by a legitimate aim and the means of achieving that aim [must be] appropriate and necessary'.[37] The wording of the Regulations suggests less emphasis on the necessity of any practice before the proportionality is assessed. However, it will be for a tribunal to assess in any particular case whether a requirement is proportionate, and in making that assessment it will be necessary to interpret the Regulations to comply with the Directive. Hence, the difference in wording need not be particularly significant in practice.[38]

The Regulations have the potential to be interpreted to give appropriate protection against religious discrimination, and to provide proper protection for

---

[37] Art 2(2)(b).
[38] Given this, however, it is not clear why different wording was adopted.

freedom of religion. The extent to which they do so will depend on the extent to which courts and tribunals are able to take into account the factors discussed in chapter three above when assessing whether any religious requirements imposed at work are proportionate. In particular, there is scope for the standard of justification to be developed to reflect interests other than pure economic interests of the employer. For example, it is arguable that at times indirect discrimination may be justifiable because of the need to protect the interests of other staff. In particular, the negative aspect of freedom of religion may be important, allowing practices which aim to provide a 'religion-free' environment to be justified. For example, if a workplace operates in an area where there is religious tension between different groups, it may be justifiable to require a secular workplace, even though this causes disadvantage to religious interests. Or an employer may wish to project a secular image to the public. Although there may be some economic reasons for this, it may also be motivated by the employer's own views, or the views of the majority of staff. If the rights of all parties are to be respected, it may be that the indirectly discriminatory effect of such a policy can be justified, as serving the legitimate aim of upholding the 'rights of others', even in the absence of a business or economic case. Conversely, the adverse effect of a requirement to work in an overtly religious atmosphere which may be experienced as a disadvantage by an atheist working for a religious employer may be justified as necessary to uphold the religious freedom of the employer.

The standard of justification with its test of proportionality should allow the contextual issues identified in chapter three to be taken into account in assessing proportionality. Issues that may be relevant include whether the employer is a monopoly employer, whether the employer operates in the public or private sector, and the socio-economic context in which the discrimination has occurred.

However, the freedom of tribunals and courts to interpret the Regulations to balance appropriately the interests of religious freedom as well as equality may be tempered by the need for consistency as between different grounds of discrimination. With regard to sex discrimination the standard of justification is very high: any requirement must have a legitimate aim, the means chosen for achieving that objective must correspond to a real need on the part of the undertaking, must be appropriate with a view to achieving the objective in question, and must be necessary to that end.[39] Economic cost or customer preference will not usually justify indirect sex discrimination. If such a level of justification is required for religious indirect discrimination cases, it may be very difficult for courts to achieve the more complex balancing of interests that is necessary adequately to take into account the varied and competing interests that arise with regard to religious discrimination.[40]

Yet, if different standards of justification are developed for different grounds of discrimination, this will lead to inconsistencies in treatment as between different

[39] *Bilka-Kaufhaus v Weber von Hartz* [1986] ECR 1607–1631, [1986] ECR 1607.

[40] For example, accommodating religion at work can put at a disadvantage those whose non-belief means they want a neutral workplace. This means that justification of any indirect discrimination will always be complex.

grounds of discrimination within the domestic and European jurisdictions.[41] The wording of the Employment Equality Directive suggests that one standard is expected for all grounds, with the specific exception of age and disability for which special provision is made. The lack of specific provisions for justification of religion suggests that a uniform approach to justification is expected. However, if the competing interests discussed in chapter three are to be properly reconciled, the development of varied standards of justification will be necessary, albeit at the cost of simplicity.[42]

## Proving Justification

One particular matter that is likely to arise in the context of religious discrimination is the question of whether employers can justify potentially discriminatory work requirements on the basis of a general benefit, or whether they will be required to prove that the justification covers the individual worker in question. For example, a requirement that telephone switchboard staff work Monday to Friday from 9 am until 5 pm may be potentially justified on the basis that the service is needed during normal working hours, even though it may disadvantage a member of staff who needs to leave at 4 pm in the winter for religious reasons. Once a person can show that because of her religion she has suffered disadvantage, the burden of proof shifts to the employer to show that the practice can be justified. In this example the employer may be able to show that the requirement is necessary as it enables the switchboard to be fully operational during normal working hours. The question which then arises is whether the employee can require the employer to justify the imposition of the general rule to her particular case. For example, she may be able to show that there are fewer calls to the switchboard after 4 pm on a Friday, and so they can be handled by colleagues, so that the general justification should not be applied to her case.

Requiring the employer to justify the imposition of the rule to the particular case will put a greater burden on the employer to justify practices which operate to the detriment of religious staff, and would create a greater degree of protection for religious interests at work. Given the often individualised nature of religious discrimination, a burden on the employer to justify requirements that disadvantage religious staff on an individualised basis might be appropriate. It would make the protection for religious discrimination more akin to that available for disability discrimination where a duty to accommodate disability imposes a duty on the employer to make individual adaptations, where reasonable, to adjust the workplace or work practices to the individual needs of the disabled person.

---

[41] For example, the ECJ has suggested that there should be uniform application of the various equality provisions across the EU: see *Chacón Navas v Eurest Colectividades SA* [2006] C-13/05, para 40, a case involving the definition of disability.

[42] In the consultation paper produced as part of the Discrimination Law Review (*Discrimination Law Review, A Framework for Fairness: Proposals for a Single Equality Bill for Great Britain*, London, Department for Communities and Local Government, 2007), the suggestion is made that a Single Equality Act should, as far as possible, have one set of definitions to apply to all grounds.

The question of whether there is a burden on employers to prove that a general justification applies to the case of an individual applicant was considered by the ECJ in *Cadman v Health and Safety Executive*[43] in the context of equal pay. Here, a pay scheme which awarded enhanced pay for long service was found to be indirectly discriminatory against women, who tend to change jobs more often, or who may start careers late, and so have less opportunity to become eligible for the higher rates of pay. The practice was justified on the basis that longer length of service and experience enables better performance of duties. It was accepted that this was capable of justifying the long service pay system. However, Mrs Cadman argued that the employer needed to prove not only that longer service could be equated to better performance, but that in her particular case this was so: could she, for example, argue that she in fact acquired skills faster than normal, or had gained skills through alternative experience, so the general rule should not apply in her individual case? The Advocate General's opinion was that to require justification as between every employee was too burdensome on employers: if a rule was justified, in general, that would be sufficient. Such an interpretation of the burden of proving that a practice is justified would mean that it would be difficult to use the indirect discrimination rules to protect against discrimination in cases where an individual's profile does not match the norm. However, the approach was not followed in the judgment of the full chamber of the European Court of Justice, which held that an indirectly discriminatory requirement can be required to be justified vis-à-vis the individual, once it is shown to have disparate impact, if the individual can provide evidence capable of raising serious doubts that the general justification applies in the individual case.

The possibility of an individualised justification rule with regard to indirect discrimination[44] gives greater potential for the Regulations to be effective to protect members of small or minority religious groups. However, such an approach could cause difficulties if applied in religion and belief cases, especially where justification is based not on economic reasons but on the need to protect the rights of others. If one takes the example of a ban on the wearing of religious symbols at work, the justification could be based on the religious freedom of the employer and the desire to protect the negative freedom from religion of other staff. For example, an employer may wish to promote a secular image, and to protect staff from pressure to dress in a religious manner at work. It may be difficult for an employer to be able to show that a ban on religious dress imposed on one individual member of staff is necessary to achieve the overall aim, even though at a general level such an approach may be justified. Even though it would be for the applicant to show that the general justification of the rule should not be applied in the particular case, the potential need to justify every rule with respect to every individual applicant may not set the correct balance between competing interests at stake in the workplace, particularly in the light of the fact that a workplace restriction on religious

---

[43] *Cadman v Health & Safety Executive* [2006] IRLR 969.
[44] *Ibid,* at paras 37–40.

freedom is not absolute. Again, it may be that the use of standards of justification developed in the context of race and sex discrimination are not appropriate for direct transplantation into the context of religion and belief.

## Exceptions to the Non-Discrimination Duties

The Regulations contain a two-tier system of exceptions to the duty not to discriminate on grounds of religion or belief, where being of a particular religion or belief is a genuine occupational requirement for the job in question. The first exception applies to all employers and is narrow in its remit. A second, broader, exception is provided for organisations with a religious ethos.

Regulation 7(2) provides the more general exception; the non-discrimination duty does not apply where:

> having regard to the nature of the employment or the context in which it is carried out—
>
> (a) being of a particular religion is a genuine and determining occupational requirement of the job; and
>
> (b) it is proportionate to apply that requirement in the particular case.

Under this provision, an organisation undertaking Muslim youth work could refuse to employ non-Muslim youth workers. Similar provisions apply to the other heads of discrimination, such as sexual orientation, so for example it could be argued that an organisation providing a counselling and support service for gay and lesbian clients could refuse to employ a heterosexual counsellor.[45]

The exception to the principle of non-discrimination contained in Regulation 7(2) is narrow. It only applies where there is a very clear connection between the work to be done and the characteristics required: the occupational requirement must be genuine *and determining*. This means that the need to be of a specific religion or belief must be a defining characteristic of the job.

Any occupational requirement to be of a particular religion must also be *proportionate*, a concept that is likely to be interpreted in the same way as the proportionality of any justification of indirect discrimination. This will mean that the imposition of an occupational requirement must not only be genuine, but will need to serve a legitimate aim. There will need to be a real need on the part of the undertaking to impose the religious occupational requirement, and it will need to be appropriate and necessary to impose the requirement in order to achieve that aim.[46]

The high standards of justification imposed by the requirement of proportionality mean that it will be necessary to consider the requirements of the job very closely before being able to use the exception. Certainly, while a mosque may require its religious teachers to be Muslim, a requirement that the cleaner be Muslim would not be allowed under this exception. Moreover, Regulation 7(2)

---

[45] Reg 7 Employment Equality (Sexual Orientation) Regulations 2003.
[46] *Bilka-Kaufhaus v Weber von Hartz* above n 39.

will not allow discrimination in favour of those who share a religion just because people wish to work with like-minded colleagues. So a Muslim factory owner, or a Christian coffee shop owner, would not be allowed to discriminate on grounds of religion in recruiting workers under Regulation 7(2).

Although religious people may argue that they bring a specifically religious approach to their work, it cannot realistically be claimed that being of a particular religion is a determining occupational requirement for many jobs. Under Regulation 7(2) religious discrimination is only really likely to be lawful in cases of those employed in religious service, whose job involves teaching or promoting the religion, or being involved in religious observance. The fact that the religious requirement must be 'determining' means that the religious nature of the job must be a defining aspect of the job.

The presence of an exception in the form of Regulation 7(2) is uncontroversial; similar 'genuine occupational requirement' exceptions are contained in the Employment Equality (Sexual Orientation) Regulations 2003, as well as in the RRA and SDA.

More controversial is the additional exception for organisations with a religious ethos contained in Regulation 7(3), where the requirement of proportionality is retained, but regard has to be had to the religious ethos of the organisation and the context of the employment in deciding whether 'being of a particular religion or belief is a genuine occupational requirement for the job', and the occupational requirement does *not* have to be determining. This suggests a less rigorous approach in deciding whether the particular job requires a particular characteristic than that required by Regulation 7(2), where the emphasis is clearly on the nature of the job itself.

In relation to religious employers it may be possible to argue that a workplace is, for example, Muslim or Hindu, because its staff are all from the same religion, and it operates according to a religious code. Such a religious employer would be able to require that all staff share the religion, even categories of staff such as secretarial or catering staff for whom religion is not a determining requirement. This type of employer does currently exist, for example, religious bookshops, and religious medical practices which run their workplaces according to the religious principles of the workers. Also, many religious organisations such as churches employ ancillary staff in jobs which are not religious in nature, such as administrative staff, cleaners, etc. The imposition of a requirement to be of a particular religion would not meet the demands of Regulation 7(2) as having a shared religion is not a determining characteristic of these jobs, but it may meet the requirements of Regulation 7(3).

The provision of a broader exception for religious employers is explicitly made in the Employment Equality Directive. After setting out the wider religious ethos exception, Article 4(2) states that:

> the Directive shall thus not prejudice the right of churches and other public or private organisations, the ethos of which is based on religion or belief, acting in conformity with

national constitutions and laws, to require individuals working for them to act in good faith and with loyalty to the organisation's ethos.

The presence of religious ethos employers is widespread in the UK and across Europe, in particular religious schools, religious hospitals and hospices. Some freedom for them to continue to require loyalty from their staff towards the religion was felt to be necessary.[47]

Regulation 7(3) allows greater latitude to employers to create discrimination on much wider grounds: employers can create religiously homogenous workplaces without a need to show that the religion requires workers to work in a religious environment, or clients to receive religious goods or services. A Christian solicitor's firm might thus be able to employ only Christians, without having to make the case that being a Christian is a defining characteristic of the job.

Regulation 7(3) is not without limitations, however. Although not necessarily 'determining', any requirement must be genuine and occupational, and therefore must be linked to the job in question. It will be difficult to argue that all staff must share the religion. For example, in a religious medical practice it may be that one could require that the partners be Muslim, but it would be more difficult to argue this in relation to support staff. An understanding of the faith, and sympathy for its practice, could be required, but it would be difficult to show that a shared faith is necessary.

Religious requirements imposed on ancillary staff are thus only likely to be proportionate if it can be shown that all such staff participate in the religious purposes of the organisation. For example, if all staff offer religious support to each other, or participate in common prayers or other religious observance, then it may be proportionate to require a common religion across the workplace. However, a mere preference for working with those of the same religion will be unlikely to be sufficient.

The exception only applies to organisations with a religious ethos, and any discrimination will need to be proportionate. Again, the imposition of a religious requirement must be genuinely necessary for the purposes of preserving the religious ethos of the organisation. Clearly, religious requirements which are used as a cover for other forms of discrimination will not be exempted.[48] Nor should employers impose additional religious duties on staff in order to enable them to employ co-religionists.

---

[47] Indeed, some states in Europe already excepted religious organisations from constitutional requirements of equality on the grounds that the freedom of religion of such organisations should not be fettered. For example, in Germany, legal provisions do not apply to religious communities without qualification. See further discussion at pp 213–216 below.

[48] For example, although Christianity is not a white-only religion, a requirement that employees be Christian in areas with high Asian Muslim or Hindu populations would be likely to generate a largely white workforce, and so could be used as a cover for race discrimination. Clearly, where this is the case, the exception in Reg 7(3) would not apply.

## Religious Requirements which Discriminate on Other Grounds

At times, religious requirements, which may satisfy the exception for genuine occupational requirements, will come into conflict with other rights created under the Employment Equality Directive or other anti-discrimination provisions. In the Directive, Article 4(2), concerning the additional exception for religious ethos organisations, contains a specific statement that the use of the genuine occupational requirement by a religious organisation 'should not justify discrimination on another ground'. There is no equivalent injunction in the Religion and Belief Regulations. However, this does not mean that discrimination on other grounds in the name of religion is allowed: the fact that a religious requirement may be allowed as a genuine occupational requirement under the Religion and Belief Regulations does not act as a defence to any claim on other grounds of discrimination.

For example, an employer who sets religious observance as a preference in making an appointment in order to maintain the religious ethos of the organisation (under Regulation 7(3)), may indirectly discriminate on grounds of sexual orientation where the religion in question is hostile to homosexuality. Religious prohibitions on divorce or cohabitation outside marriage could lead to indirect discrimination on grounds of marital status.[49] A preference for workers to share an employer's faith, which includes a belief that women should not work, will involve indirect sex discrimination as women of that faith are unlikely to apply. Any attempt to justify such treatment will need to meet the high standards required to justify sex or sexual orientation discrimination. It is rarely going to be proportionate to allow such indirect discrimination. The net effect is that where indirect discrimination results, the creation of religiously homogenous workplaces is not allowed. For example, partners in a Christian legal practice who believe that homosexuality is incompatible with biblical teaching will not be protected if they refuse to engage a gay partner.

It may be possible, in specialised circumstances, for indirect discrimination caused by the creation of religious ethos organisations to be capable of justification, bearing in mind the contextual and other factors that courts or tribunals may take into account in determining proportionality. It was suggested in chapter three that discriminatory religious groups should at times be allowed to retreat from mainstream society to create 'islands of exclusivity',[50] remaining free to enter into employment relationships with others of the same faith, and without being required to provide employment for those of other religions or lifestyles. Although others' interests may be infringed by their practice, where this is not to a significant

---

[49] Discrimination on grounds of marital status per se is not unlawful in the UK. Discrimination against those who are married is unlawful under the SDA. This means that discrimination on the grounds of being single, for example, remains lawful.

[50] A Esau, ' "Islands of Exclusivity": Religious Organizations and Employment Discrimination' (1993) 33 *Univ British Columbia LR* 719.

extent it may be proportionate to tolerate these infringements in order to maintain religious freedom for the group.

For example, if a male employer, from a religious group which believes that men and women should not work together, wishes to employ only a co-religionist this will indirectly discriminate against women. If the wish to employ co-religionists is allowed as a genuine occupational requirement, then the sex discrimination is indirect: only male co-religionists will apply, because female co-religionists will not wish to work with the male employer. In assessing justification, the factors suggested in chapter three should be taken into account. Members of the religious group will find it very difficult to work elsewhere, as their refusal to work with women makes them virtually unemployable in the secular world, so their interests are served by allowing the practice. If the employer is not a state or large employer, there is likely to be an absence of economic harm to women, and so the harm caused is largely that of 'bare knowledge' offence, caused by the fact that what is generally viewed as an unacceptable practice can be tolerated within society.[51] In such limited circumstances, it may be that the discrimination could be viewed as proportionate.

However, in the vast majority of cases, although the Religion and Belief Regulations allow for genuine occupational requirements to be imposed by religious employers in order to maintain the religious ethos of the organisation, such requirements will not be lawful if they result in indirect discrimination on other grounds. Thus a Christian medical practice which would not employ gay doctors, or a Muslim solicitor's firm which will not employ a lesbian Muslim, will usually not be acting lawfully. The requirement to be Christian or Muslim may be lawful, but the indirect sexual orientation discrimination will be very difficult to justify. It was suggested in chapter three that discrimination on other grounds should not be proportionate where employers have access to the public market, and expect to gain economically from interaction with wider society. Only where they have retreated from the general society to an 'island of exclusivity' should it be proportionate to discriminate indirectly on other grounds. Such cases will be very limited, but their existence is necessary if sufficient religious freedom is to be enjoyed by religious groups whose beliefs may conflict with the norms of the rest of society in terms of respect for the dignity and autonomy of others.

## Special Exceptions for those Employed for the Purposes of Religion

Although where a genuine religious occupational requirement discriminates directly on other grounds it will be unlawful, a further exception is provided in the Sex Discrimination Act to cover 'employment for purposes of an organised religion'. This is limited to restrictions imposed so as to comply with the doctrines of the religion, or (because of the nature of the employment and the context in which it is carried out) so as to avoid conflicting with the strongly held religious

---

[51] See discussion at pp 62–66 above.

convictions of a significant number of the religion's followers.[52] In effect, discrimination against women is accepted where its is part of the belief system that such discrimination is necessary; for example, this would apply to the Catholic Church, where it is a doctrine of the religion that only men can act as priests.

A similar exception is included to take account of religious beliefs regarding sexual orientation. Regulation 7(3) of the Sexual Orientation Regulations provides that there is no sexual orientation discrimination where the employment is for the purposes of an organised religion, and the employer applies a requirement related to sexual orientation so as to comply with the doctrines of the religion, or (because of the nature of the employment and the context in which it is carried out), so as to avoid conflicting with the strongly held religious convictions of a significant number of the religion's followers.

These exceptions to sex and sexual orientation discrimination apply only to the appointment of religious personnel for the purposes of an organised religion. This refers to the appointment of clergy, or their equivalent for other religious groups. Thus it will cover the appointment of religious leaders both where the religion prohibits homosexual practice, and where the religion itself tolerates it, but many within the faith do not. It covers requirements 'related to' sexual orientation, and so could cover attitudes to sexual orientation as well as the sexual orientation of applicants themselves. For example, an Anglican church may wish to appoint a priest who does not support the ordination of gay clergy, and such a requirement would be covered, even though it does not relate to the sexual orientation of the priest himself.

Concerns that this provision could cover a wide range of workers employed by religious organisations, such as teachers or nurses in religious foundations, were alleviated by the decision of the English High Court in the *Amicus* case,[53] which limited the words 'for the purposes of a religion' to the appointment of religious leaders and teachers such as priests and imams. Discrimination on grounds of sexual orientation in any other context will amount to sexual orientation discrimination.

It is quite arguable that the special exception for the appointment of clergy (and their equivalents) was unnecessary, as requirements relating to the sexual orientation of religious personnel would have been covered in any event by the general genuine occupational requirement provision. It would be expected that where a church chooses to restrict employment of priests to heterosexuals, in order to comply with religious doctrine, such a requirement would be found to be proportionate: having regard to the nature of the employment (being a priest) being heterosexual would be a 'genuine and determining occupational requirement', and it would be 'proportionate to apply that requirement in the particular case', particularly if freedom of religion of the adherents, and the religious autonomy of the religious group, were to be taken into account in assessing proportionality.

---

[52] S 19 SDA 1975, as amended by Reg 20 Employment Equality (Sex Discrimination) Regulations 2005.

[53] *R (on the application of Amicus-MSF and others) v Secretary of State for Trade and Industry and others* [2004] IRLR 430.

The wording extends beyond compliance with the tenets of the religion, to encompass the need to avoid conflicting with the strongly held religious convictions of a significant number of the religion's followers. Again, this can be criticised as both imprecise and as providing too broad an exception to the non-discrimination principle. For example, it is not clear what will amount to 'a significant number of followers', and it could be argued that exceptions should not be given to cover religious convictions which do not amount to the tenets of a religion. However, the wording merely reflects the need adequately to protect the religious autonomy of religious adherents, and the fact that not all members of a religious group will have exactly the same views on issues of sexuality and gender. For example, the Anglican Church accepts the ordination of both women and gay clergy, but recognises that this is not accepted by all Anglicans. The wording of the provision means that an Anglican church can specify in appointments that it would prefer to have a male priest, even though this is not 'required' by the tenets of Anglicanism. If freedom of religion is to be protected at an individual level, this must be the correct approach, as the alternatives are less attractive. One alternative is to restrict the protection to those who agree with the mainstream teaching of a religion, thereby failing to protect the freedom of religion of minorities within faith groups. The second alternative is, for example, to allow Anglicans who reject the ordination of women to argue that this is a tenet of their religion (even if not of other Anglicans). This could give rise to difficulties for tribunals who may then be drawn into decisions regarding the true tenets of a religion, questions which are not appropriate for decision by secular courts.

The provision of a special exemption for religious bodies to the non-discrimination principles of the SDA or Sexual Orientation Regulations may appear to give special treatment to religious bodies. Concerns about special treatment were more acute when they included the possibility that the provisions could be used to cover non-religious posts such as teachers or nurses in religious foundations. However, once restricted to the appointment of religious leaders or clergy, any special treatment becomes more apparent than real: a gender or sexual orientation requirement imposed on the appointment to religious office would come within the general 'genuine occupational requirement' in any event. It should be proportionate to allow religious bodies to appoint their leaders or clergy according to the tenets of the religion.

In fact, it may be that the 'special treatment' will work to reduce the extent to which religious convictions can be used to justify the imposition of requirements related to sexual orientation or gender in the name of religion or belief. Left to develop freely, the argument that respect for religious belief can justify indirect discrimination on grounds of sexuality or gender might have led to broader exceptions for religious ethos organisations. However, by creating a special exception to recognise this religious argument, but then restricting its use to the appointment of clergy or their equivalent, the use of the argument that sexual orientation or gender discrimination is needed to protect religious interests has been strictly curbed. Of course, the need to protect religious freedom can still be used to argue for exemption, but its specific recognition and restriction in Regulation 7(3)[54] may make it much harder to do so successfully. The legislation as interpreted in *Amicus* provides a clear steer that religious convictions can be used to justify discrimination on grounds of sexual orientation or gender, but only in the strictly limited circumstances of the appointment of clergy.[55]

## Exceptions to Non-Discrimination in Northern Ireland

The FETO does not apply to ministers of religion, nor to the recruitment of teachers, and special provisions apply to appointments to the police force. The exception for clergy meets the requirements of Article 4 of the Directive, as it is clear that discrimination on religious grounds will be proportionate in such circumstances. In relation to the police and the recruitment of teachers, this is provided for under the special provisions of Article 15 of the Directive, to reflect the under-representation of one of the religious communities in the police force, and to maintain the balance of employment opportunities for teachers in Northern Ireland.

Article 70 of FETO also provides a more general exception where 'the essential nature of the job requires it to be done by a person holding, or not holding, a particular religious belief'. Unlike the exceptions provided in the Directive and the Regulations, there is no requirement of proportionality, and thus the FETO exception is more narrowly drawn than that under Article 4 of the Directive and Regulation 7 of the Religion and Belief Regulations, particularly as there is no equivalent of the broader religious ethos exception of Regulation 7(3) and Article 4(2).[56]

## Determining Whether a Person Meets a Religious Requirement

In addition to showing that the religious requirement is a genuine (and in the case of Regulation 7(2), determining) occupational requirement and that it is proportionate in the particular case, the Regulations state that it must also be the case that:

> either the person to whom that requirement is applied does not meet it, or the employer is not satisfied, and in all the circumstances it is reasonable for him not to be satisfied, that that person meets it (paragraph (c)).

This provision addresses the fact that, unlike sex and race discrimination, in relation to religious belief (and sexual orientation, where the new wording appears again), it may be difficult to determine for certain whether someone complies with

---

[54] As restrictively interpreted in the *Amicus* case.

[55] Or the equivalent of clergy for other religions.

[56] In evidence to the House of Lords Select Committee on the EU the former chairman of Northern Ireland's Fair Employment Commission said that Article 70 had not led to any cases of any significant difficulties (HL Select Committee on the EU, 1999–2000, 9th Report, para 110).

an occupational requirement. It may be clear that a female applicant does not meet a requirement to be male, but it may not be clear that a person does not meet the religious requirements of an organisation. A person could claim, in good faith, to be of a particular religion (for example, he could be baptised into the Christian church, but not attend church regularly), but the employer may disagree that the individual is of the required religion. Without this additional regulation it was not clear how an employer could determine whether the person complies with the requirement set.

The additional regulation also addresses the problem that the question of whether or not the applicant complies with the faith could be determined by fine theological judgments, on which even the parties do not agree. Again, the applicant may be of the view that he complies, but the employer may disagree. In such circumstances, Regulations 7(2)(c) and 7(3)(c) allow the matter to be determined by the employer, as long as in the circumstances the assessment is reasonable.

It could be said that the section creates too much discretion for employers to discriminate. A reliance on the 'reasonable view of the employer' runs the risk of employees being discriminated against on the basis of prejudice masked as religious scruple. However, it is not clear whether any alternative would improve matters. If tribunals were to decide whether staff meet the religious requirements of the employer, they may end up involved in determining complex issues of religious doctrine. Allowing employees to decide if they meet a requirement would not accord with the treatment of other job requirements, where the employer decides whether the applicant has the qualifications for the job. Given the lack of viable alternatives, leaving the question to the employer, limited by the requirement that any decision must be reasonable, is probably the best answer to what could otherwise be a vexed question.

In Northern Ireland the question of how to determine the religion of applicants has arisen in the context of monitoring the religious make-up of the workforce and determining eligibility for the affirmative action programme in the police. In this context, the determination is made by the employer. Under the Police (Northern Ireland) Act 2000 the Chief Constable must appoint, from a pool of qualified applicants, one half from those treated as Roman Catholic, and the other half from those not so treated. In deciding who should be treated as Roman Catholic, candidates are asked to self-designate. If they choose not to, the Chief Constable can use the 'residuary method' of deciding which community the individual belongs to, using surnames, schools attended, sporting or leisure pursuits and address.[57] The provisions of the Police (NI) Act have been challenged as incompatible with the ECHR, but the claim was unsuccessful. The provisions were a proportionate interference with religious freedom because of the long-standing problem of imbalance in the police force.[58] The use of the residual method of determining

---

[57] The types of information suggested to be used to determine an individual's community are specified in Sch 3 Fair Employment (Monitoring) Regulations (Northern Ireland) 1999.

[58] *Re Parsons' Application* [2003] NICA 20.

religious affiliation, where an individual has not self-designated, does appear open to the use of stereotype, but it was accepted in *Re Parsons' Application*.[59]

## Ascertaining an Organisation's Religious Ethos

The Regulations are clear on how a tribunal should determine whether a person has a particular religion, but are less clear on how to determine an organisation's religious ethos. In many cases the issue will be clear: a publisher which publishes Christian teaching and devotional materials and which starts each day with staff prayers could reasonably be presumed to have a Christian ethos; and a Hindu charity should easily establish a religious ethos. Refusal to employ a non-believer may be proportionate, if regard is had to the religious ethos of the organisation.

However, difficulties may arise where discrimination takes place on more subtle grounds, particularly if discrimination occurs within one religious tradition. For example, a Catholic charity wishing to employ Catholics will discriminate against Protestant Christians as well as non-Christians; and an Anglican church that does not acknowledge the priesthood of women will discriminate if it refuses to employ an Anglican who supports the ordination of women. Whether such discrimination is proportionate 'having regard to' the religious ethos of the employer is unclear. A tribunal could take the view that the Christian ethos will be adequately maintained in both cases by the appointment of a person who shares the same general religion (in this case, Christianity). Thus any refusal to employ would be discriminatory, as it would be disproportionate having regard to the organisation's religious ethos. Alternatively, it could be argued that the employer and employee do not share the same religious ethos, despite both being Anglican Christians, and that the need to respect the religious ethos of the organisation justifies the religious discrimination involved in the refusal to employ. Which approach is taken will depend on how many shades of religious opinion tribunals are prepared to recognise.

As with the determination of a person's own religious views, if full protection for religious freedom is to be given, tribunals should err on the side of recognising many different shades of religious opinion. The fact that religious groups identify as having a separate religious ethos from others within the same religion should be sufficient to determine that such a religious ethos exists. Individuals should be taken to adhere to a religion or belief, even though they dissent from a majority religious view. Allowing the individual to determine his or her religious identity in this way gives maximum protection to individual freedom of religion. Objectivity can be introduced into the equation by the need for any religious ethos requirement for the job to be genuine and proportionate, rather than by the refusal to recognise the subtleties and intricacies of religious difference.

---

[59] *Re Parsons' Application* [2003] NICA 20.

## Victimisation

The Religion and Belief Regulations not only protect against direct and indirect discrimination as they are usually understood, but also provide protection for those who suffer victimisation for making use of their provisions. Victimisation, defined as a form of discrimination in the Regulations, occurs where a person is treated less favourably for bringing proceedings or giving evidence under the Act, alleging that acts of discrimination have occurred and for doing 'anything under or by reference to [the] Regulations in relation to [the discriminator] or any other person'.[60] Protection is only lost if an allegation is neither true nor made in good faith.[61]

## Harassment

A final form of discrimination covered by the Regulations is harassment on grounds of religion. Similar provisions are contained in the legislation covering discrimination on all other grounds.

Under the definition in the Regulations, harassment is defined as follows:

(1) a person ('A') subjects another person ('B') to harassment where, on grounds of religion or belief, A engages in unwanted conduct which has the purpose or effect of—

    (a) violating B's dignity; or

    (b) creating an intimidating, hostile, degrading, humiliating or offensive environment for B.

(2) Conduct shall be regarded as having [this] effect only if, having regard to all the circumstances, including in particular the perception of B, it should reasonably be considered as having that effect.[62]

The legal understanding of harassment developed in the context of racial and sexual harassment, as a form of discrimination: to harass someone was to treat them less favourably than others. Particular difficulties had developed within this framework for dealing with harassment due to the need to find others in comparison with whom a victim of harassment had been treated less favourably. Thus, for example, sexual behaviour which both men and women may have found offensive would not be covered by a definition based on less favourable treatment.[63]

The new definition used in the Regulations, and for harassment on other grounds too, is based on the concept of 'dignity' and the creation of a hostile

---

[60] Reg 4. Equivalent protection is given in relation to other grounds of discrimination.
[61] Reg 4(2).
[62] Reg 5.
[63] *Stewart v Cleveland Guest (Engineering) Ltd* [1996] ICR 535, where the display of nude pin-ups was found not to amount to sexual harassment because it was not discriminatory: men may also have been offended.

environment.[64] This would seem a more appropriate basis for protection, with a focus on the hostile or offensive environment created at work by harassment, and the infringement of dignity which is involved. Behaviour which those of different groups will all find offensive can therefore be covered.

Although basing the protection against harassment on dignity rather than disadvantage is an improvement on previous definitions, harassment is another area, like justification of indirect discrimination, where a common definition for all grounds may not produce the best protection for religious interests.[65] A number of difficulties in creating a right not to be subjected to religious harassment can be identified. The first is that as well as the 'victim' of harassment having a right to be free from harassment, both the 'victim' and the 'harasser' enjoy the right to freedom of religion. At times these rights will conflict. For example, drawing on examples from US case law, an employee who, for religious reasons, tells colleagues that she believes their lifestyles to be sinful,[66] could be exercising the right to manifest her religion, and to free speech, but could simultaneously cause offence. Or a religious employer who prints religious verses on pay slips[67] could be exercising a right to religious freedom, whilst offending non-believing staff. Of course, where rights conflict, the exercise of freedom of religion is only protected where it is proportionate, and a court could find that restrictions in cases such as these are proportionate. Nonetheless, it is clear that the presence of a 'right to freedom of religion' may act as a complicating factor in cases of religious harassment.

Another difficulty is that religious harassment can arise from both religious speech and 'secular' speech, and from religious staff or non-religious staff. For example, in the USA, a Catholic employee, motivated by her religious beliefs, decided to wear a badge with a picture of an aborted foetus on it,[68] behaviour which her colleagues found offensive. The conduct of the employee was not overtly religious, but it nonetheless accorded with the definition of religious harassment.[69] Those harassed were not religious, but her behaviour was religiously motivated.

---

[64] On the benefits of basing protection against harassment on the concept of dignity rather than on the concept of discrimination or less favourable treatment, see R Ehrenreich, 'Dignity and Discrimination: Toward a Pluralistic Understanding of Workplace Harassment' (1999) 88 *Geo LJ* 1, and L Clarke, 'Harassment, Sexual Harassment, and the Employment Equality (Sex Discrimination) Regulations 2005' (2006) 35 *ILJ* 161.

[65] For a full discussion of religious harassment, see L Vickers, 'Is All Harassment Equal? The Case of Religious Harassment' (2006) 65(3) *CLJ* 579, upon which much of the following section is based.

[66] See, for example, the facts of the US case, *Chalmers v Tulon Co of Richmond* 101 F 3d 1012 (4th Cir 1996). Chalmers sent letters to colleagues saying that they had done immoral things and needed to repent.

[67] See, for example, the US case, *Brown Transport Corp v Commonwealth* 133 Pa Comm 545, A 2d 555 (1990). Here a Jewish employee objected to bible verses appearing on pay slips, and on religious articles appearing in a company newsletter. The employee complained, and was later sacked. He claimed he was subject to religious harassment, by being subjected to the religious speech of the employer. He was successful.

[68] *Wilson v US West Communications* 58 F 3d 1337 (1995). She was dismissed, and the dismissal was held to be lawful.

[69] The religious employee ('A') has subjected the non-religious person ('B') to harassment because, on grounds of religion (the badge-wearing is religiously motivated), she has engaged in unwanted conduct (the wearing of the badge) which has the effect of creating an offensive environment for B. See Reg 5(2) below.

Although the definition of harassment contained in the Regulations is common to all grounds of discrimination, it is possible to interpret it to take into account the range of competing interests that arise in the specific context of religious harassment. The content of the Regulation on harassment set out above is considered in detail below, together with a suggested interpretation that should enable tribunals to take full account of the varied interests that compete where religious matters are considered.

Harassment at work can cover a wide range of conduct. The archetypal case of harassment would probably involve making rude comments about religious dress, religious beliefs or religious practices. The perpetrators are usually colleagues who are either aiming to create a hostile environment or merely careless about causing offence, and who are doing so by speech or action. In more severe cases harassment can go beyond verbal attacks to physical assault.

Harassment must be 'on grounds of religion'. In this regard, the Regulations do not fully transpose the Framework Directive which uses the term 'related to' rather than 'on grounds of' religion and belief.[70] The term 'related to' is broader in scope, and does not carry the suggestion that there needs to be a causal link between religion and the harassing behaviour. Under the Directive, harassment may be unlawful because the behaviour is religious in nature and is offensive to the 'victim'. There is no need to show a causal link, such as that the harasser directed the behaviour at the victim because of his or her religion. The fact that the protection under the Directive is broader than that under the Regulations as currently drafted has been accepted in domestic courts.[71] In the absence of amending regulations, the best approach is to interpret the current Regulations so as not to require that harassment be motivated in any way by religion. For what follows the term 'related to religion' will be used, in recognition that the Regulations are likely to be amended and, in the meantime, are likely to be interpreted to comply with the Directive.

As well as harassment related to a victim's actual religion or belief, the wording will cover harassment related to the harasser's perception of a person's religion, a perception which could be mistaken. It would also cover harassment related to a person's association with people of a particular religion. For example, a worker could be harassed because his child has converted to a new religion.[72] Moreover, it is not limited to harassment of a religious person by a person of no religion or vice versa. It could also cover harassment by a person of the same religion as the victim, but whose interpretation differs. For example, an evangelical Christian could persistently attempt to persuade another Christian of the rightness of her

[70] See *EOC v Secretary of State for Trade and Industry* [2007] EWHC 483 (Admin); Clarke, above n 64. The relevant part of the Employment Equality (Sex Discrimination) Regulations 2005 is due to be amended in the light of the judicial review case, but by December 2007 the amendment was still awaited.

[71] See *EOC v Secretary of State for Trade and Industry* [2007] EWHC 483 (Admin) at para 7 where it was accepted that the argument brought in relation to sexual harassment applies equally to religious harassment.

[72] See Clarke, above n 64.

version of the faith; or a Muslim who wears a headscarf could harass a Muslim colleague who does not.

It is not clear from the definition whether harassment includes harassment related to the harasser's religion or only harassment related to the victim's religion. It would seem that religious harassment can occur where the 'perpetrator' is uninterested in the victim's religion, but is interested in promoting her own religious views. One example is the badge-wearing case discussed above; another would be a strict Catholic who creates a hostile environment for a non-religious colleague who has remarried after divorce. Here the harassment is related to religion: not the religion of the victim, but that of the harasser. In the definition of direct discrimination the Regulations state that 'the reference . . . to religion or belief does not include [the discriminator's] religion or belief'.[73] However, no such statement is made in relation to harassment. Thus it would seem that harassment can be 'related to' religion where it is based on the harasser's religious views. If a hostile environment is thereby created, even if not intentionally, then religious harassment will have occurred in accordance with the definition in the Regulations.

In order to come within the definition of harassment, unwanted conduct must have the purpose or effect of violating dignity, or creating an intimidating, hostile, degrading, humiliating or offensive environment for the victim. These terms are not themselves defined, and are somewhat opaque. Although using the concept of violated dignity to define the harm of harassment is an improvement on the concept of comparative harm, the content of the term itself is not easy to define.[74] The idea of human dignity refers to the intrinsic, incomparable and indelible worth of all individuals. Respect for this human quality should mean that the individual should not be treated as of less worth than others. Although it may lack clear content, using the concept of dignity to define the meaning of harassment can be useful; it suggests that where a person subjects another to treatment which communicates to them a lack of worth, this can be actionable. Moreover, the very lack of clear content in the term 'dignity' can also mean that it can be interpreted in a way that takes into account the various conflicting interests that may arise in harassment cases, such as the need to maintain the rights and freedoms of others, as well as the dignity of all members of staff. For example, in assessing whether dignity has been violated, a tribunal may consider the nature of the offence caused: harassing behaviour is more likely to violate dignity where it mocks the religious views of the 'victim', than if it seeks to engage in debate about religious issues.

The second form of harassment, creating an 'intimidating', 'hostile' or 'degrading' environment suggests that fairly high levels of harm to the victim will need to be caused. The alternative terms 'humiliating' and 'offensive' are suggestive of a more subjective understanding, and leave open the possibility that the victim could be humiliated or offended by behaviour which others may not understand to be harmful. The fact that the question of whether an offensive, hostile or humil-

---

[73] Reg 3(2).
[74] See discussion in ch 3 at p 37 above.

iating environment is created may be contested is addressed by Regulation 5(2): account should be taken of the victim's perception of the offensive conduct, but an objective 'reasonableness' standard is retained to protect against unreasonable claims of harassment by hypersensitive victims.[75] The reference to the perception of the victim means that the test has a subjective element, and it is likely that victims will be able to claim that conduct is unwanted or offensive when it comes from one person, even though the same conduct was inoffensive or acceptable when it came from another.[76] Moreover, it would appear that a single incident, if severe enough, will be capable of creating a hostile, degrading or offensive environment.[77]

The use of a subjective test of 'offensiveness' is particularly appropriate in the context of religious harassment, given the relative lack of shared or established understanding of the likely effects of certain behaviour on religious people. In relation to sexual and racial harassment, some common understanding of racial and sexual harassment issues has developed over time: in *Insitu Cleaning v Heads*[78] the EAT had no hesitation in saying that references to a man's bald head could not be equated with a coarse reference to the size of a woman's breasts.[79] They were able to call on common understandings of the level of offence likely to be caused. This may not be clear in the case of religious harassment. If it is not clear whether a set of views even constitutes a religion, it is unlikely to be clear in some cases whether certain behaviour would cause offence, or whether the religious adherent is being unduly sensitive. For example, calling a set of beliefs a 'cult' might be understood by some to be highly offensive, but may be no more than mildly irritating to others. Moreover, even within mainstream religions, different adherents will have very different views. For example, whether or not explicit discussion of abortion would offend would vary from Christian to Christian let alone between those of different faiths: a tribunal could not rule with any certainty whether a person who was offended was being 'unduly sensitive', and taking offence too easily.[80]

---

[75] The objective nature of the same test was challenged with respect to sexual harassment in *EOC v Secretary of State for Trade and Industry* [2007] EWHC 483 (Admin). The High Court decided that the objective nature of the test was consistent with the Directive and reflected the state of the domestic law prior to the new regulations.

[76] Such an understanding was developed in relation to sexual harassment under the previous framework for protection: *Wileman v Minilec Engineering* [1981] IRLR 145 EAT.

[77] Again, a similar understanding was developed in relation to the earlier law on sexual harassment: *Bracebridge Engineering v Darby* [1990] IRLR 3 (sexual assault); *Insitu Cleaning v Heads* [1995] IRLR 4 (offensive name calling).

[78] Above n 77.

[79] Above n 77 at 9.

[80] This may not only be a problem for lesser-known religions. Indeed, it may be that tribunals will assume that they know what will be offensive to those of the dominant Christian religion, thus failing to give due regard to the 'particular perceptions' of the victim. It is notable that some of the judges in *Williams v Secretary of State for Education and Employment* [2002] EWCA Civ 1926 (Buxton LJ in the CA, and Elias J in the first instance hearing) were prepared to determine what was and what was not required of Christianity, rather than considering the religious views of the particular claimants before them. It is unlikely that an English court or tribunal would assume expert knowledge of any other religion.

Although a subjective test allows for individual believers to be protected even though others may not find the behaviour offensive, too subjective a test would run an alternative risk. Employers and employees could be threatened by potential religious harassment claims arising from conduct which they could not have known was offensive. As a result, freedom of speech and freedom of religion at work could be significantly restricted as individuals voluntarily censor their speech for fear of causing some undefined type of offence.

This danger is reduced by the provision in Regulation 5(2) that conduct shall be regarded as offensive, hostile, etc, only if, having regard to all the circumstances, it should reasonably be considered as having that effect. The perception of the victim is only one of the circumstances to which regard is given. Other circumstances could include the need to adequately protect the freedom of speech and freedom of religion of all parties; the need to promote inclusion, diversity, tolerance and dignity at work[81]; and whether the speech was intended to hurt the victim or was part of more general speech which was overheard by the victim.

The ethos of the workplace could also be a relevant circumstance. The definition of harassment makes no mention of employer ethos, but where the employer has a religious ethos, this is likely to be relevant. For example, if a religious person who is sensitive about the drinking of alcohol and sexual behaviour in public decides to work in a night club, she will not be able to expect the same level of sensitivity to her particular religious needs as if she works for a religious bookshop. Conversely, if such an employee chooses to work for an organisation which shares her religion, she may be able to expect greater protection of her religious sensitivities.[82]

A final circumstance that may be relevant to the question of whether it is reasonable to treat the conduct as creating an offensive environment is whether the behaviour is intentional or not. Harassment does not have to be intentional to be unlawful. The conduct only needs to have the effect of violating dignity or of creating an intimidating, hostile, degrading or offensive environment. Where such an environment is caused unintentionally, a tribunal could find that, in the circumstances, it is not reasonable to find that the hostile, etc, environment was created. Or in determining whether the victim's dignity is violated, a tribunal could take into account whether the conduct was intentional. Where offence is directed at the 'victim' on purpose to offend, it will be more likely to violate dignity. Where it is unintentional there is no purpose to violate dignity, and a tribunal may find that no violation of dignity actually arose.

---

[81] See S D Jamar, 'Accommodating Religion at Work: A Principled Approach to Title VII and Religious Freedom' (1996) 40 *New York Law Sch LR* 719 on the factors to take into account in assessing harassment cases.

[82] In relation to sexual or racial harassment there are rarely going to be circumstances where the tribunal holds that the choice to work in the particular environment negates the claimant's claim. The right of the workers to be free from racism and sexism at work is more important than any 'right' of harassers to express themselves as they chose. However, in cases involving religion, the competing interest in freedom of religion means that the 'harasser' may indeed have an interest in the freedom of speech. See L Vickers, 'Is All Harassment Equal? The Case of Religious Harassment' (2006) 65(3) *CLJ* 579.

It is with respect to unintentional harassment that the difference in wording between the Directive ('related to' religion) and the Regulations ('on grounds of religion') becomes more relevant. If unwanted conduct must be 'on grounds of religion', this has a similar effect to a requirement of intentionality. The perpetrator of the harassment would have to engage in the harassing conduct because of religion, or for a religious reason. For example, an employee who seeks to convert her unwilling colleague to her religion could be harassing the colleague, because she is acting 'on grounds of religion'. The fact that she does not mean to cause any offence (indeed, she may believe that she is acting in the best interests of the 'victim' as she is trying to achieve her colleague's salvation) does not prevent this being harassment. Yet, the fact that the 'harassing' behaviour is religiously motivated means that it would be difficult to claim that it was truly 'accidental'. In contrast, a person who discusses a more 'secular' issue such as abortion or euthanasia with others, in the hearing of a religiously sensitive colleague, thereby causing offence, will not be harassing the 'victim'. This is because, although she happens to cause religious offence, she does not act 'on grounds of religion' in discussing the topic. Thus, although offence could be caused to a religious person, it will not amount to harassment because it was not done 'on grounds of religion or belief'. Similarly, a religious individual who overhears a conversation between two colleagues in which his religion is described as a cult could be highly offended. However, the conversation, if not directed at the 'victim', is difficult to describe as behaviour engaged in 'on grounds of religion'. On the other hand, in each case, the behaviour can clearly be viewed as related to religion. Thus, in each case, the behaviour could constitute harassment if the Regulations are amended or interpreted to include harassment related to religion, despite its unintentional nature.

The case of a conversation related to religion which is overheard provides a good example of the particular difficulties which arise in relation to religious harassment. With respect to sex or racial harassment, to hear racist or sexist speech might be said to be harassing, even if there was no intention for the victim to overhear. Although this may interfere with the freedom of speech of the speaker, such free speech interests do not trump the rights of victims of harassment to be free from the negative effects of such speech.[83] However, with regard to religious speech, it is more difficult to state with any certainty where the balance should lie between the right of two colleagues to discuss religion using the terminology they choose (including the word 'cult') and the right of another individual to restrict the use of such a term. It may therefore be that the term 'on grounds of religion' should be retained in the Religion and Belief Regulations, in order to preserve the correct balance between competing interests.

---

[83] Most sexual or racial harassment will not be recognised as having sufficient intrinsic value as speech to justify its protection in the face of a conflict with the rights of others. This may not be the case for religious speech. Of course, in some cases, speech may cause offence on both religious and sex related grounds, such as a debate on abortion or on whether women should be ordained as priests. See further Vickers, above n 82.

A second example of difficulties arises in relation to proselytism at work. This could involve harassment, but could also form part of the right to manifest religion held by employers and employees. It is easy to envisage that proselytism could give rise to religious harassment. While simple conversations about religion or belief are unlikely to amount to harassment, if they persist once it has been made clear that they are unwelcome it is possible that they could come within the definition of harassment: the religious employee will have engaged in unwanted conduct with the effect of creating an intimidating or offensive environment for the other person.[84] It is more likely to be viewed as intimidating if the proselytism is of a junior colleague by someone more senior. Of course, a similar problem could occur with sexual harassment if an individual persists in asking a colleague on a date, despite it being made clear that this is not welcome; but in the case of the proselytiser, the ability to spread one's faith may form part of the right to religious freedom, leading to a clash of interests that is absent in the sexual harassment example. However, although the right to manifest religion does cover 'bearing witness' and proselytism, any such right is not absolute, and is limited where it is improper.[85] Proselytism will be improper if it interferes with the rights of others to be free from harassment at work, and the fact that rights to religious freedom are engaged need not prevent a finding of harassment.

## Conclusion

While it forms an important part of the protection of religious interests at work, the prohibition of religious harassment involves many difficulties. The difficulties can be overcome by careful and purposive interpretation of the Regulations to reflect the competing interests in freedom of religion, freedom of speech and the need for dignity of all staff. The main impediment to developing such an interpretation is the competing interest in developing a common interpretation for all grounds of harassment.[86] However, if the religious interests of members of staff are to be suitably protected it may be that the interpretation of the harassment provisions will need to develop slightly independently. This way the specific contextual issues related to religion can be properly reflected.

## Scope of the Regulations

The Regulations protect against discrimination in employment and occupation. Regulation 6 provides that it is unlawful to discriminate on grounds of religion or belief in the arrangements made for determining who to employ; in the terms of

---

[84] Reg 5(1).

[85] *Kokkinakis v Greece* [1993] 17 EHRR 397.

[86] In the consultation paper produced as part of the Discrimination Law Review (*Discrimination Law Review, A Framework for Fairness: Proposals for a Single Equality Bill for Great Britain*, London, Department for Communities and Local Government, 2007), it is recognised that having a single definition for harassment may not be appropriate, and opinions on the issue are sought.

employment; and by refusing to offer employment. Once employed, it is unlawful to discriminate on grounds of religion or belief in the terms of employment afforded; in opportunities for promotion; or by dismissal or subjection to other detriment. Employment is defined in Regulation 2 more broadly than the term is defined with relation to other employment legislation.[87] As well as covering those working under a contract of service or apprenticeship, it also covers those who contract personally to do any work. This means that the Regulations will cover clergy or other ministers of religion, whose employment status has often been a source of uncertainty.

Protection extends to cover discrimination after the end of the employment relationship.[88] Thus, refusal to write a reference, or writing a poor reference, for a person on grounds of religion would be unlawful. The coverage also covers working relationships which do not fall within the definition of employment. Thus contract workers,[89] office-holders,[90] police,[91] barristers,[92] advocates[93] and partnerships[94] are all covered. Most of these groups of workers are covered by the genuine occupational requirement exception contained in Regulation 7, so that, for example, a partnership of doctors who are all Christian may be able to argue that the discrimination involved in such an arrangement is lawful as a proportionate requirement necessary to the preservation of the partnership's religious ethos.[95] Of course, the exception does not apply to the police, and interestingly, although it applies to partnerships, it does not apply to barristers. It seems that religiously homogenous solicitors' firms may be lawful, but not religiously homogenous barristers' chambers.

In addition to various forms of employment or work relationships, the Regulations cover access to further and higher education,[96] as part of the protection for vocational training which is inherent in the Directive's coverage of employment and occupation.[97] They also cover the operation of qualifications bodies, which have power to confer professional or trade qualifications, and prohibit discrimination in decisions on the conferral of such qualifications.[98] Employment agencies and careers guidance services are covered.[99]

Discrimination by trade organisations is also covered, with a prohibition on discrimination in the terms on which a person may be admitted to the organisation;

---

[87] Under the Employment Rights Act 1996, s 230 (1) 'employee' means an individual who has entered into or works under (or, where the employment has ceased, worked under) a contract of employment.

[88] Reg 21.

[89] Reg 8.

[90] Reg 10.

[91] Reg 11.

[92] Reg 13.

[93] Reg 13.

[94] Reg 14.

[95] Reg 14(4).

[96] Reg 20.

[97] Reg 17.

[98] Reg 16.

[99] Reg 18.

or by refusing to accept, or deliberately not accepting, his application for membership. This reflects that fact that admission to a trade association may give access to markets for a business or may give particular standing to a business, the denial of which could clearly cause some detriment to a religious person. However, it may be that the blanket restriction on discrimination by trade organisations will have significant consequences for religious groups.[100] A trade organisation is defined as an organisation of workers, an organisation of employers, or any other organisation whose members carry on a particular profession or trade for the purposes of which the organisation exists.[101] The exact meaning of the wording is somewhat unclear, but it may cover organisations such as the Association of Christian Lawyers, and the Muslim Doctors and Dentists Association, which include a faith requirement for membership.[102] Whether or not they are covered may depend on the extent to which such organisations provide economic benefit to members such as access to networks of clients, etc. The exception based on genuine occupational requirements does not apply to trade associations. Therefore a trade association which discriminates in terms of membership on grounds of religion or belief will not be exempted on the basis that the discrimination is necessary to preserve the religious ethos of the organisation.

## Positive Action

Regulation 25 provides that positive action in the form of providing training for those of a particular religion or belief, or encouraging those of a particular religion or belief to apply for work, remains lawful, where it prevents disadvantage, or compensates for disadvantages suffered by those of the particular religion or belief doing that work or likely to take up that work. Similar exceptions for positive action apply to trade organisations. Thus, allowing a trade organisation which is open to all to have a section to help Muslim members, for example, may be lawful if it can be shown that Muslims within the particular trade or business suffer disadvantage.

With respect to Northern Ireland, the Directive specifically includes provisions for positive action, in order to address its history of religious and political discrimination. Thus the Police (Northern Ireland) Act 2000, requiring equal numbers of recruits from the Roman Catholic community, remains lawful, and is specifically excepted from the provisions of the Directive.[103]

## Applying the Regulations to the Workplace

Areas where the Religion and Belief Regulations are likely to have an impact will be considered in turn. These are requests for time off for religious observance; the

---

[100] I am grateful to Peter Griffith for this point.
[101] Reg 15(4).
[102] It could also, arguably, cover barristers' chambers.
[103] See discussion at p 143 above, and Recital 34 and Art 15 of Directive 2000/78.

imposition of dress codes; the display of religious symbols at work; and the use of lifestyle requirements imposed by religious employers.

## Hours of Work

Refusal of requests to accommodate changes in hours of work to enable members of staff to participate in religious observance will usually amount to indirect discrimination.[104] Requests to be excused work on Friday evenings or Saturdays, and requests for time off for prayer during the working day, are likely to be common. Refusal amounts to a requirement to work to a particular timetable, which puts the religious employee at a disadvantage, and will need to be justified. In many cases there will be a legitimate aim: although many jobs can be adapted to work flexibly, many require constant presence during specific working hours. Even if there is a legitimate aim, the requirement will need to be proportionate to that aim. The question of proportionality will depend on issues such as the requirements for cover during the member of staff's absence, the ease with which shifts can be swapped between staff, the availability and cost of cover, the length of time off requested, and the frequency of requests.

Prior to the introduction of the Regulations, the leading case involving an employee requesting time off for religious observance was *Ahmad v UK*,[105] in which a school refused to allow a Muslim teacher time off on a Friday afternoon to attend a mosque for prayers. The ECommHR recognised that Article 9 can give rise, in some circumstances, to a duty to accommodate religious difference. However, in this case there was no breach of Article 9 as freedom of religion at work was guaranteed by the freedom to leave the employment.[106] The finding in the domestic hearing of the same case[107] had reached the same conclusion, although Scarman LJ in his dissenting opinion argued that requiring the employing authority to expend some effort to uphold the teacher's right to freedom of religion would be reasonable. Accommodating Mr Ahmad's request would have required some reorganisation of timetables and perhaps some teaching cover, but that would be an acceptable demand to make of the employer to safeguard Mr Ahmad's religious freedom. Under the Regulations it would seem that Scarman LJ's view, being more sensitive to religious requirements of employees, would now prevail, and it will be acceptable to require some effort by employers to accommodate their employees' religious practices.

The use of the Religion and Belief Regulations to support requests for flexible working for staff has the potential to cause difficulties for employers, particularly if justifications must be made on an individual basis. For example, as well as attempting to accommodate requests based on religion, employers will also need to try to accommodate requests for flexible working made by working parents or

[104] It could be direct discrimination if an employer allows some religious individuals time off and not others, and the reason for the different treatment is religion.
[105] (1981) 4 EHRR 126.
[106] Similar reasoning was repeated in *Stedman v UK* (1997) 23 EHRR CD168.
[107] *Ahmad v Inner London Education Authority* [1977] ICR 490.

carers.[108] An employer may be able to manage if a small number of staff work flexibly, but may not be able to allow many to do so, either because of the need to maintain a basic level of coverage of work, or because of potential fragmentation of the management process if too many staff are unavailable at different times. Thus it may not be any one particular worker whose requested flexibility cannot be accommodated, but the cumulative effect of too many requests. If justification must be individualised, this could cause difficulties: if a general justification is accepted this is less problematic for employers.[109]

Where an employer is faced with a number of requests for time off for different reasons, it is not always clear how they should be prioritised. For example, one employee could wish to have Sundays off to take part in religious observance; another to spend time in sporting activities; and another to have a day off in common with the rest of the family. It might be argued that religious interests should take priority, but this is not certain. Moreover, if the request for 'time off with the family' is recast as a request for time off for child care, the issue becomes one of gender equality, and the question of priority of interests becomes more acute.

Moreover, even in the absence of competing equality rights, the issue of time off can become very contested where there is a simultaneous secular benefit[110] to the request. Allowing Christian staff to be given priority in avoiding working on Sundays or on Christmas Day, or Seventh Day Adventists priority in not working on Saturdays, has the potential to cause resentment among other workers, who may have non-religious but very strong reasons to want the same time off. It remains to be seen whether the discontent of other workers will be a factor that allows employers to justify refusing to give priority to religious staff with regard to such requests.[111] This may be another area where different standards of justification for sex discrimination and religious discrimination should be allowed: certainly in justifying a refusal of an application to work flexibly under the working families legislation, an employer cannot rely on the discontent of other staff, although granting a request to arrive later to work, or to leave early, or to have longer holidays, could cause some discontent among those not eligible to have such requests considered.

## Sunday Working and Shop Workers

Special rules for working hours apply to shop workers with regard to requirements to work on Sundays.[112] These rules were introduced when the Sunday Trading Act 1994 relaxed the rules covering shop opening on Sundays. Similar rules protect

[108] Section 80F Employment Rights Act 1996 (as amended by the Employment Act 2002) and extended to those caring for adults by the Work and Families Act 2006.
[109] See discussion of justification at p 131–135 above.
[110] See P W Edge, *Legal Responses to Religious Difference* (Dordrecht, Kluwer Law International, 2001) 7.
[111] See discussion of the position in the USA at p 188.
[112] See H Fleming, 'Working, Praying and Sunday Rest: Has the Law Struck the Right Balance?' (2005) 9 *Edinburgh LR* 317.

those who work in betting shops.[113] The aim of the protection was to prevent shop workers and betting shop workers from being forced to work on Sundays after the rules on trading on the traditionally work-free day had been changed. The rules provide a right to those who worked in shops or betting at the time the legislation was passed to refuse to work on a Sunday, and to be protected from any adverse treatment that might result from the refusal. Thus it is automatically unfair to dismiss, select for redundancy or subject to any detriment a person who exercises the right to refuse to work on a Sunday.[114] For those employed since 1994, the right is not automatic. Staff must give three months notice[115] that they wish to opt out of Sunday working: once the notice period is served, they cannot be subjected to dismissal or any detriment for refusing to work on Sundays, nor for serving the notice. However, until the notice period is up, the employee can be required to work on Sundays, and the Sunday Trading Act rules do not protect job applicants who indicate an unwillingness to work on Sundays from being discriminated against on that basis.

Although clearly introduced to protect the religious interests of staff, the Sunday trading rules do not require staff to give any reason for wishing to avoid working on a Sunday. Thus they apply equally to those with a religious or secular motivation for refusing to work on Sundays, whilst providing no protection for those of other religions who wish to be protected for refusal to work on a holy day, or those in different sectors who do not wish to work on Sundays. The protective rules will have been of use to religious employees employed in the retail sector in 1994 when the changes to shop opening times came into force, and who wished to avoid work on Sundays for religious reasons. They will continue to be of use to those who change their beliefs during their employment in the sector, and who wish as a result to discontinue working on a Sunday. However, they will not help new staff who have an objection to Sunday working, as they will not be able to undertake service for the three month period of notice required by anyone starting work in the sector after 1994. Those who apply for work in the retail sector and who wish to avoid working on Sundays from the start of their employment, together with those who wish to take different days off, or who work in other sectors, will remain dependent on the application of the Religion and Belief Regulations for any protection, on the basis that refusal of a job because of a religious objection to the hours of work is indirectly discriminatory, as discussed above.

---

[113] The rules were introduced when the Deregulation and Contracting Out Act 1994 allowed betting on Sundays in England and Wales. The protection for shop workers was extended to Scotland in the Sunday Working (Scotland) Act 2003.

[114] Schedule 4, Sunday Trading Act 1994. The rules do not apply to those employed to work on Sundays only.

[115] The notice period is reduced to one month if the employer fails to give the employee notice of the right to opt out of Sunday working.

## Dress Codes[116]

Employers will often impose some sort of dress code on staff. This may be a uniform, or may consist of rules on hair length, grooming, or bans on the wearing of religious symbols such as crosses, headscarves, or turbans. An employee who is refused a request that a dress code be adapted to accommodate religious practice would suffer indirect discrimination. The employer's requirement that staff comply with a particular dress code would put the religious person at a particular disadvantage, and it would need to be justified. There may be a legitimate aim for a dress code, such as presenting a particular corporate image, but any refusal to adapt would also need to be proportionate. A number of interests will have to be balanced in assessing justification and proportionality. These include: the freedom of religion and freedom of expression of the employee seeking an adaptation of the dress code; the employer's freedom to create a religiously neutral workplace; the interests of staff and customers or service users to enjoy the negative aspects of freedom of religion; and the interest in promoting diversity at work. Also relevant will be the type of business (for example, public or private sector), the nature and extent of the accommodation required, whether the religious dress is necessary to the religion (rather than being common practice among the religion's adherents), and in some cases the extent to which the member of staff has contact with the public.

Much of the discussion of religious dress codes at work has involved the issue of whether or not it is lawful to dismiss female Muslim staff for wearing a headscarf.[117] More recently attention has focused on the wearing of a veil over the face.[118] The legal issues involved in restrictions on the veil are the same as those relating to the headscarf, but the factual difference in the level of covering involved will mean that the outcome, in terms of whether restrictions are proportionate, may differ. The issues which arise in cases of headscarves and veils are perhaps more complex than those which arise in relation to some other adaptations of work uniforms, or restrictions on wearing other religious insignia such as crosses, due to the fact that wearing a headscarf or veil involves an interaction with other interests such as those in gender equality. Nonetheless, the debate over the wearing of headscarves in the workplace provides a useful illustration of the array of issues which may need to be balanced in assessing the proportionality of imposing dress codes at work.

The conflicts that arise regarding the wearing of veils or headscarves at work are remarkably complex, and seemingly intractable. The reason for controversy is that a number of interests conflict in such cases, and counter-arguments can be found

---

[116] Refusal to accommodate religious dress is identified as a common form of religious discrimination experienced in employment in P Weller et al, *Religious Discrimination in England and Wales* (London, Home Office Research Study No 220, 2001).

[117] For a detailed review of the issues raised by the headscarf debate see D McGoldrick, *Human Rights and Religion: The Islamic Headscarf Debate in Europe* (Oxford, Hart Publishing, 2006).

[118] *Azmi v Kirklees Metropolitan Borough Council* [2007] ICR 1154.

to most arguments in favour of a ban. The right to religious freedom is clearly engaged when any restriction is imposed on religiously motivated choice of dress. What the headscarf debate illustrates very well, however, is the negative aspect of religious freedom and the interests of individuals who wish to be free from religion, and who prefer to work, or to have services delivered, in a non-religious environment.[119] The conflict between positive and negative aspects of freedom of religion is inescapable. For example, if schools or hospitals allow the wearing of the headscarf, this upholds the religious freedom of the wearer, but may infringe the negative aspect of religious freedom of the pupil or patient.

The legal question at stake in the context of a restriction on wearing a headscarf at work is whether such a restriction can be justified. The justification may be as to the indirectly discriminatory impact of a uniform which does not include the headscarf, or as to a genuine occupational requirement not to wear Muslim religious dress, which acts as a defence to the direct discrimination involved. In either case the question will be whether the dress code is proportionate to a legitimate aim.

Of course, the legitimate aims may involve practical issues related to the job, which may justify restrictions on the wearing of a headscarf or veil. It may be that health and safety requirements involve their removal, or it may be that communication is restricted in the case of the wearing of a veil so that its removal is necessary to the performance of the job. Assuming that performance-related requirements are not purely hypothetical, the employer will be able to show in such cases that the restriction serves a legitimate aim, and it is likely to be proportionate. In such cases the freedom of religion of the individual worker will be only to enjoy the residual protection of the freedom not to work.[120]

In the absence of practical reasons to prohibit the wearing of the veil, restrictions may still be proportionate. A number of other legitimate aims exist, some of which involve rights which may be equal in strength to the right to religious freedom claimed by those seeking to wear the headscarf or veil. Legitimate aims include the aims of providing religiously neutral workplaces, of upholding the right to freedom from religion of colleagues and service users, of ensuring equality between genders (as the headscarf or veil is a religious dress restriction imposed only on women), and of maintaining the freedom of religion of other Muslims to be free from pressure to wear more conservative religious dress. These interests may provide a legitimate aim for any restriction, but this must then be balanced against the interests of the person wearing the veil or headscarf, so that restrictions are only imposed if it is proportionate to do so.

In assessing the proportionality of any restriction, the factors identified in chapter three can be considered. One contextual factor was whether the employer is part of the public or the private sector. However, in the context of religious dress

---

[119] In *Kokkinakis v Greece* [1993] 17 EHRR 397 the ECHR recognised the need for respect for the freedom of religion of others. This requires respect for others' freedom not to be religious.

[120] See discussion at pp 45–53 above.

codes, the role of this factor is not clear. With regard to public sector or state employment, it is arguable that staff represent the state, and so the wearer of a headscarf infringes state neutrality on questions of religion, meaning that restrictions are more likely to be proportionate. However, even if staff can be taken to represent the state in this way, it is equally arguable that the state should reflect the diversity of the community it represents, and so should employ a range of religious staff to reflect its commitment to religious freedom.[121]

Moreover, it is questionable whether the wearing of a religious symbol by an individual member of staff in the public sector can really be said to imply state endorsement of those beliefs. The wearing of a visible religious symbol may suggest state support for the practice, but individual dress codes may only be a reflection of individual belief, and should perhaps be seen as a personal statement, rather than as reflecting the views of the state. If bans are proportionate in the public sector, this effectively places limits on the employment of Muslim women by the state. This may significantly interfere with their freedom to pursue their chosen profession. In some sectors, such as education and health, the state is virtually a monopoly employer: to prevent the wearing of headscarves would prevent many Muslim women from participating fully in these sectors. Moreover, if a ban on headscarves in a particular workplace means that a woman is unable to work at all, this should be taken into account in assessing the proportionality of any ban, given the importance of employment to individual economic and emotional wellbeing.[122]

One way to reduce the impact of a ban on women's employment opportunities would be to limit any dress code restrictions to staff who can be taken to represent the employer, such as senior staff. However, this would cause an alternative discrimination against Muslim women. The effect would be to concentrate their employment in areas of work with less status, such as catering or cleaning, where they are not senior enough to be taken to imply state endorsement of their religious practice.[123]

Another factor relevant to proportionality is the extent to which a restriction would affect the rights and interests of others. To be weighed in the balance here are the religious interests of Muslim women, the interest of others in freedom from religion, and the potential conflict between Muslims over the meaning to be ascribed to the wearing of the headscarf. For example, in several cases under the ECHR, reference has been made to the fact that Muslims wearing the headscarf can put under pressure those Muslims who choose not to.[124]

Another relevant factor is the question of whether allowing headscarves or veils at work is consistent with a commitment to equality. In relation to religious equality, a problem arises from the fact that a ban on the display of religious affiliation

---

[121] See discussion at pp 67–68 above.

[122] See discussion at pp 47–48 above.

[123] See D Schiek, 'Just a Piece of Cloth? German Courts and Employees with Headscarves' (2004) 33 *ILJ* 68.

[124] *Sahin v Turkey* Application No 44774/98 judgment 10 November 2005, paras 115 and 116. See also *Dahlab v Switzerland* App No 42393/98 decision 15 February 2001.

through dress will not affect all religions equally. A ban on the wearing of head-scarves, veils or other religious symbols is likely to have a greater effect on Muslims. It will not affect the majority of Christians as their beliefs do not usually require specific forms of dress. Even if they do require modesty in forms of dress, for example, this is more likely to be achieved in a manner which accords with mainstream clothing codes, and so is likely to pass unnoticed.

With reference to the need to maintain gender equality at work, the question of proportionality becomes highly contested. The issue of gender equality can be used on both sides of the argument over restricting religious dress. On the one hand, because the specific group that is affected is Muslim women,[125] it can be argued that any ban on headscarves will rarely be proportionate as it will adversely affect Muslim women while having no effect on Muslim men. If Muslim women are to achieve equality with Muslim men and non-Muslim women, they need access to work, and bans on the wearing of religious dress militate against this. After all, a ban on headscarves is unlikely to result in more Muslim women work-ing as doctors, judges, police officers or teachers. Rather than removing the veil in order to work, it is as likely that they will not enter these professions at all. Such an outcome would be counter-productive in terms of achieving women's equality. It may be that allowing Muslim women to wear the headscarf in such jobs will send a positive message about women's equality, and Muslim women's equality in par-ticular, illustrating that they are as capable as others of such work.

On the other hand, the headscarf is understood by many to be illustrative of the subjection of women to the power of men. It is therefore viewed as antithetical to the interests of women to facilitate the practice by allowing headscarves to be worn at work.[126] On this view, gender equality requires that the headscarf and veil be restricted at work, particularly with regard to the public sector, where the state's commitment to equality for women may mean that such practices should not be condoned.

In addition to equality rights, a number of other matters need to be taken into account in assessing the proportionality of any restriction on the wearing of the veil or headscarf. First are the socio-economic aspects of any case. Muslims tend to be from ethnic minorities in the UK and can suffer economic disadvantage,[127] with that economic disadvantage exacerbated by issues of gender. It may be that accommodating the religious practice of Muslim women will give them access to work and a way out of the social exclusion they may otherwise experience.[128] In particular, work within the public sector may be seen as a suitable vehicle to carry out the social policy of inclusion.

---

[125] This is a clear example of multiple discrimination: see S Fredman, 'Double Trouble: multiple discrimination and EU law' (2005) 2 *European Anti-Discrimination Law Review*.

[126] See above n 124.

[127] See *Fairness and Freedom: The Final Report of the Equalities Review, February 2007* available at: <http://www.theequalitiesreview.org.uk/publications.aspx> (accessed 22 June 2007) 78, which identi-fies Pakistani and Bangladeshi women as particularly vulnerable to inequality in the employment sphere.

[128] See the discussion of social exclusion at pp 35–36 above.

A second matter to consider is the interaction between religious freedom and freedom of expression. The wearing of a headscarf or veil is an expressive act, and it may have a number of meanings. Even as an expression of religious devotion the wearing of a veil or headscarf can have different meanings. Some believe it is required as part of their religious beliefs, for others it is not mandated by Islam but is an expression of religious commitment.[129] As well as religious meanings, wearing of religious dress may express cultural or ethnic identity; it may be used to distinguish the wearer from mainstream culture,[130] or it may have a political meaning. Some wearers may act purely from personal choice, others may act under the influence of husband, father, brothers or other women. Given the very varied meanings attached to the wearing of headscarves and veils, courts will need to be very wary of interpreting on behalf of women the meaning of their actions.[131]

Of course, the many and varied meanings of the wearing of a headscarf or veil do not only apply to the wearer. In determining whether it is proportionate to restrict the wearing of religious dress at work, the interests of others also need to be put in to the balance. For example, customers or service users may have an interest in having goods and services delivered by a politically and religiously neutral workforce. Moreover, as identified in chapter three, employers have economic and expressive rights to project a particular image to customers or clients, an image that may be secular.

Finally, the proportionality of any restriction on the wearing of religious dress at work has to be determined in light of the fact that protection of religious freedom does not extend to the provision of a job. The 'right to resign' remains the ultimate protection for religious freedom.[132] Of course, the right to resign does not provide much protection for religious freedom and there are times when the religious interests of the employee who wishes to wear a headscarf will outweigh the other interests involved. Nonetheless, the weighing of proportionality in employment cases should be undertaken in the light of the fact that the infringement of religious freedom represented by a ban on the wearing of the headscarf is an infringement of a right which itself is not an absolute right, and in a context where the rights are not exercisable in an absolute form.

Given the range of competing fundamental rights at stake, it is perhaps not surprising that where questions have arisen regarding the wearing of headscarves, the courts have rarely found bans to be in breach of freedom of religion. This can be seen across Europe. In the ECtHR case of *Sahin v Turkey*[133] a headscarf ban on students was upheld as consistent with the right to religious freedom protected by

---

[129] To adopt the terminology of the ECHR, for some it is a manifestation of religion, for others it is merely motivated by religion. See *Arrowsmith v UK* [1978] 3 EHRR 218.

[130] See *R (on the application of Begum (Shabina)) v Denbigh High School Governors* [2006] UKHL 15, for a discussion of the potential meanings of the wearing of a headscarf.

[131] See *Sahin v Turkey*, above n 124, dissenting opinion of Judge Tulkens para 12. See also M Mahlmann, 'Religious Tolerance, Pluralist Society and the Neutrality of the State: The Federal Constitutional Court's Decision in the Headscarf Case' 4(11) *German Law Journal*.

[132] See discussion at pp 45–53 above.

[133] See above n 124.

Article 9 ECHR. In Germany, Belgium and Denmark restrictions on the wearing of headscarves have been found to be lawful and proportionate even though they adversely affect Muslim women. For example, in a case involving a dismissal for wearing a headscarf, the Supreme Court in Denmark held that dismissal was not in breach of the Danish Act Prohibiting Discrimination on the Labour Market or Article 9 of the ECHR, because the dress code was enacted in order to signal that the company was politically and religiously neutral and so was objectively justified.[134]

In effect, where the issues are so contested, courts in Europe have tended to limit their role to determining whether a proper and fair procedure has been used by employers in deciding whether headscarves or other forms of religious dress should be allowed. So, for example, in Germany, the Federal Labour Court held that dismissal of a salesperson based on the wearing of a headscarf was invalid,[135] because although relying on economic loss as a justification, the employer had not shown any actual financial loss caused by the wearing of the headscarf.

Similar procedural safeguards were required by the House of Lords in the UK in upholding the legality of a refusal by a school to allow a Muslim pupil to wear a jilbab to school.[136] The case did not involve employment, but the approach is likely to be similar in such cases. Here the school had a uniform which allowed the wearing of religious dress, including a headscarf. One pupil wished to wear the more religiously conservative dress, the jilbab, a long coat-like garment. The school insisted on the correct uniform being worn, a uniform that had been agreed in consultation with the local Muslim community. The school's freedom to enforce the uniform rule was upheld by the House of Lords, because it was proportionate having regard to the individual pupil's freedom of religion, the competing interests of protecting other Muslim students from family or societal pressure to wear the more conservative style of dress, and the fact that the pupil had the option of attending a different school where the jilbab could be worn. The fact that a range of criteria had been considered by the school, including the pupil's freedom of religion, meant that the rule could be upheld.

In terms of how the wearing of headscarves should be treated under the Religion and Belief Regulations in the context of employment, the approach seems to be to require a clear objective basis for any restriction on religious dress. Any requirement regarding headscarves or veils will have to be objectively justified by a legitimate aim and the means of achieving the aim will need to be appropriate and necessary. If an employer seeks to justify on the basis of hypothetical claims (eg, customers may object) this may not be sufficient, as the employer will need to show that the requirement is necessary. This means that a real need for the ban must be established, and the means to achieve it must be narrowly tailored to

---

[134] Decision of Danish Supreme Court, 21 January 2005, 22/2004.

[135] Federal Labour Court 10 October 2002, 2 AZR 472/01.

[136] *R (on the application of Begum (Sabina)) v Denbigh High School Governors* [2006] UKHL 15. See also the decision relating to a pupil's exclusion for wearing the niqab or veil: *X (by her father and litigation friend) v The headteacher of Y school and the governors of Y school* [2006] EWHC 298 (Admin).

achieve its objective. In terms of legitimate aims, however, justification may be possible because of the wide range of additional interests that may be at stake.

This approach was taken by the EAT in one of the early cases brought under the Regulations, *Azmi v Kirklees Metropolitan Borough Council.*[137] Azmi was a teaching assistant who wanted to wear the niqab or face veil when in the presence of male colleagues. When she was dismissed for refusing the employer's request to remove the niqab when assisting in class she claimed direct and indirect discrimination but was unsuccessful.[138] Her claim that discrimination on grounds of a manifestation of belief (wearing a headscarf) is direct discrimination was unsuccessful[139]; the discrimination was indirect in nature as the refusal to allow a face covering was applied to all, but put Azmi as a Muslim woman at a particular disadvantage when compared with others. However, the Employment Tribunal and the Employment Appeal Tribunal held that the indirect discrimination was justified. The restriction on wearing the niqab was proportionate given the need to uphold the interests of the children in having the best possible education. The school had investigated to see if the quality of teaching was reduced when Azmi wore the face covering and had come to the conclusion that it was; they had also investigated whether it was possible to rearrange her timetable to enable her to assist only in classes with a female teacher and found that this was not possible.[140] In relation to the question of justification, Azmi argued that insufficient effort had been made to try to accommodate her religious requirements; for example, the school could have trialled and assessed alternative ways to improve her communication and performance when wearing the niqab. The EAT held that the school had done enough to show that the restriction on wearing face coverings was proportionate.

As discussed above, it is unclear whether the standard of justification will be uniform across different strands of discrimination. This may be of particular significance in relation to dress codes. It may be that matters such as the religious freedom, in a negative sense, of customers or other employees are taken into account in assessing whether a restriction on dress is acceptable. It is hard to see such matters as attitudes of other staff or customers being allowed to justify sex or race discrimination. On this issue again the question arises as to whether a single standard of justification for exceptions to the non-discrimination principle is possible.

---

[137] [2007] ICR 1154.

[138] She also claimed victimisation and was successful due to inadequacies on the part of the employer in dealing with her case.

[139] This must be correct. Allowing discrimination on grounds of a manifestation of religion to be direct discrimination would mean that it would not be capable of justification. Given that manifestations of religion are only protected to the extent that they are proportionate when in conflict with others' rights, it would be surprising to create an absolute right to manifest religion via the rules on direct discrimination.

[140] Other suggested ways to avoid the problems were to remove the children needing support during lessons conducted by a male teacher; for Azmi to teach with her back to the male teacher; or that she sit behind a screen. The school's view that these were not appropriate ways to deal with the difficulties posed by the wearing of the veil was supported by the EAT.

## Lifestyle Requirements

Another way in which religious issues may arise at work, apart from time off or dress codes, arises in the particular context of religious ethos employers. Where employers have an ethos based on a religion or belief, they may wish to impose on members of staff requirements relating to lifestyle. These may involve sharing the employer's faith, but may extend to other matters of private life such as sexual morality.[141] The freedom of religious employers to require the loyalty and good faith of staff is addressed by Regulation 7(3) which sets out the special genuine occupational requirement exception for religious ethos organisations. This enables religious organisations to impose on staff requirements of loyalty to the religion, requirements that would otherwise amount to direct or indirect discrimination against those of different faiths. Apart from discriminating against those of other faiths or none, lifestyle requirements will also impinge on the private lives of staff, and to this extent may be difficult to justify. For example, private matters such as divorce or remarriage could be relevant as demonstrating good standing and loyalty to the religion.

In assessing whether it is proportionate to impose such requirements a court can take into account the factors identified above as relevant to proportionality. Where an employee has chosen to work for a religious employer, it may be proportionate for the employer to make demands in terms of loyalty and lifestyle. Matters which in other contexts would clearly be private may be relevant in a workplace which has opted to share such matters between staff. For example, a Christian workplace where staff engage in prayers at the start of the day may expect staff to share fairly personal matters of faith or daily life. Where such requirements are imposed in workplaces where there is less choice for the staff member, for example the employer is virtually a monopoly employer in the particular sector, such requirements may be difficult to justify.

If a lifestyle requirement is enforced in relation to a female employee but not a male employee then this may give rise to sex discrimination. In *Percy v Church of Scotland*[142] a female minister in the Church of Scotland was asked to resign her office after an investigation into an alleged affair with a married parishioner. The questions at issue in the case related to her status as an employee and the question of whether the matter was a spiritual matter for resolution within the internal church structures, or a matter for resolution under the SDA. The basis of her sex discrimination claim was not that it was inappropriate for such private matters to give rise to disciplinary measures, but that where male ministers were known to have had extra-marital sexual relationships similar disciplinary action had not been taken. The House of Lords found that the matter was within the scope of the

---

[141] Such requirements are covered in Art 4(2) of the Directive, which states that it does not prejudice the rights of churches or other organisations with a religious ethos to require individuals working for them to act in good faith and with loyalty towards the organisation's ethos. See discussion of Reg 7(3) above at pp 136–137.

[142] *Percy v Church of Scotland Board of National Mission* [2005] UKHL 73.

Sex Discrimination Act. It is clear that the inequality of treatment of male and female priests is at the heart of the decision. The fact that disciplinary action was being taken as a result of private matters was not of such concern, given the nature of the work.

Although lifestyle requirements will often be directed at men and women, they may, in practice, have a greater impact on women, and so may involve direct or indirect sex discrimination. The presence of special protection for religious ethos organisations does not extend to the justification of discrimination on other grounds such as gender. Physiological differences and social differences can mean that lifestyle requirements can have a particular impact on women. For example, it is often only with pregnancy that a breach of a requirement to abstain from sexual activity outside marriage will become known to an employer. Discrimination against women who become pregnant when unmarried may be motivated by a desire to sanction the failure to meet a requirement in terms of lifestyle, but it will also be pregnancy-related, and may therefore amount to sex discrimination.[143] Similar problems, where gender and religion interact, could arise if a religious employer refused to employ anyone who has had an abortion.

Where a decision to dismiss a member of staff is related to pregnancy, it will amount to sex discrimination. In *O'Neill v Governors of St Thomas More RCVA Upper School*[144] a teacher in a Catholic school became pregnant and was dismissed when it became known that the father of the child was a priest. Her dismissal was found to be discriminatory on grounds of sex, because it was related to pregnancy. The employer's argument that the reason for dismissal was not the pregnancy, but the failure to comply with religious standards, was not accepted, because the pregnancy precipitated and permeated the decision to dismiss.

However, despite the finding in *O'Neill*, it is arguable that if an employer could show that dismissal would also follow a discovery that a man had failed to comply with religious standards, then such a dismissal should not automatically be found to be on grounds of pregnancy. The case of *Dekker*,[145] which established that pregnancy discrimination was direct sex discrimination, did not thereby create total immunity from dismissal for pregnant women. For example, a pregnant woman can lawfully be made redundant if the selection for redundancy is not related to the pregnancy. The protection is from dismissal or disadvantage imposed because of pregnancy, not from that which is imposed for other reasons such as redundancy. In effect, in this context, dismissal may not be for pregnancy *per se*, but may genuinely be for breach of a lifestyle requirement. In such a case, dismissal will not be directly discriminatory on grounds of sex. It may be indirectly discriminatory, if one takes the view that it is harder for women than men to conceal a breach of a lifestyle requirement where it results in pregnancy, but such indirect discrimina-

---

[143] See *Dekker v Stichting Vormingscentrum voor Jong Volwassenen (VJV-Centrum) Plus* [1990] ECR I-3941, and *O'Neill v Governors of St Thomas More RCVA Upper School* [1996] IRLR 372 discussed below.

[144] [1996] IRLR 372.

[145] Above n 143.

tion may be justifiable: to prohibit the dismissal of priests in such circumstances would involve a fairly serious erosion of autonomy of religious groups in the selection of their leaders. For example, if a female religious teacher or priest from a religious group which does not allow extra-marital relationships were to become pregnant, her dismissal would be on grounds of failure to comply with an occupational requirement of loyalty to a religious lifestyle, assuming it could be shown that a male priest would also be dismissed for engaging in such a relationship.[146]

As with any other genuine occupational requirements imposed by religious groups, the determination of whether the requirement is proportionate may depend on other factors, such as the type of job in question. Lifestyle requirements imposed by religious employers who provide public services are less likely to be proportionate than those imposed by purely private organisations. Moreover, strict lifestyle requirements are more likely to be proportionate if they are imposed on those who teach or preach the religion than if imposed on those less directly involved in religious practice. Where requirements are imposed on those more distantly linked to the mission of the religious group, they may be more difficult to justify.

## Refusal of Work Tasks

Members of staff who hold certain beliefs may ask to be removed from carrying out some types of work because they are incompatible with those beliefs. For example, staff may ask not to be involved in any work that is linked to abortion, or gambling, or other behaviour they believe is wrong. In the case of abortion or participation in embryo research, there are special provisions for conscientious objection, covering all staff involved with these procedures.

With regard to abortion, section 4(1) of the Abortion Act 1967 states: 'no person shall be under any duty . . . to participate in treatment authorised by this Act to which he has a conscientious objection'.[147] This covers doctors, nurses and other staff involved in treatment for abortion. However, the provision does not cover those not involved in 'treatment', so a secretary who refused to type a referral letter regarding an appointment for advice on abortion was not covered by the conscientious objection clause.[148] Although according to section 4 doctors and nurses cannot be required to be involved in abortion, they are expected to refer patients requesting abortion to another practitioner.[149] Thus, if a doctor or other

---

[146] The reason for Percy's success in *Percy v Church of Scotland Board of National Mission* [2005] UKHL 73 was because of evidence that where male priests had been involved in extra-marital affairs they had not been dismissed.

[147] S 38, Human Fertilisation and Embryology Act 1990 contains provisions in similar terms.

[148] *Janaway v Salford Health Authority* [1989] AC 537.

[149] See s 8 of the GMC Guide, *Good Medical Practice 2006*. 'If carrying out a particular procedure or giving advice about it conflicts with your religious or moral beliefs, and this conflict might affect the treatment or advice you provide, you must explain this to the patient and tell them they have the right to see another doctor. You must be satisfied that the patient has sufficient information to enable them to exercise that right. If it is not practical for a patient to arrange to see another doctor, you must ensure that arrangements are made for another suitably qualified colleague to take over your role.'

medical practitioner has an absolute religious objection to abortion, such that they are not willing to refer patients to other doctors who will advise on the issue, they will not be protected by the provisions in place to safeguard conscientious objection to participation in treatment. In such a case, discrimination against the individual, although linked to the employee's religion, will not necessarily amount to actionable indirect discrimination as it may be justifiable where the individual is refusing to carry out important aspects of the job.

In cases of religious objection to other tasks, refusal of staff requests to be excused from some aspects of work will be indirectly discriminatory: the employer is requiring the employee to engage in certain conduct and the employee's religious beliefs put him at a disadvantage because he cannot do so. However, any such requirement can be justified, where proportionate. Where carrying out the task in question is a significant aspect of the job, it is very likely to be justified. Where the contested duties are more tangential, it may be that the proportionate response is to allow voluntary swaps of tasks, or to redeploy the individual, especially where this can be done without disadvantage or disruption to others.[150]

# II  Religious Schools[151]

Schools with a religious ethos are very common in Britain, even within the maintained sector.[152] Over 30 per cent of maintained schools in England have a religious character.[153] These schools are largely funded by the state, although they may also receive some additional funding from the Church.[154] Thus although they have a religious input in terms of some funding and aspects of their governance, they are effectively public sector organisations.

As regards the imposition of religious requirements on staff, the position of teaching staff is covered by special regulation of the Schools Standards and Framework Act 1998 (SSFA),[155] to which the provisions of the Religion and Belief Regulations are subject. The SSFA protects teachers in non-faith schools from religious discrimination,[156] but allows faith schools to impose requirements regarding religion and belief on teaching staff, as well as allowing voluntary aided schools to require certain standards of conduct from teaching staff and non-teaching staff.[157]

---

[150]  See the discussion of this issue with respect to the position in the USA and Canada at pp 189–190 and 200 respectively.

[151]  See O Hyams, *Law of Education* (Bristol, Jordans, 2004).

[152]  Schooling in Northern Ireland is largely organised on religious lines, and the recruitment of teachers is exempt from FETO 1998.

[153]  Around 7,000 of the 22,000 maintained schools in England have a religious character: <http://findoutmore.dfes.gov.uk/2006/02/religious_educa.html> accessed 3 January 2008.

[154]  In addition, the school site and buildings will be owned by the Church.

[155]  As amended by the Education and Inspections Act 2006.

[156]  S 59 SSFA.

[157]  See s 37(2) Education and Inspections Act 2006.

The Religion and Belief Regulations thus do not add much to the position of teaching staff whose position is largely covered by the SSFA. However, they will be of relevance to non-teaching staff in non-voluntary aided schools.[158] Where the employer is a local authority, the school will be treated as any other organisation, rather than as a religious ethos organisation: even though the school is religious in nature, the employer is the local authority, and so does not have a religious ethos.[159] It will be lawful to impose genuine and determining occupational requirements of a religious nature on staff, as long as it is proportionate to do so, having regard to the demands of the particular job. The imposition of any requirement relating to religion or belief will need to be proportionate, and the type of work and level of involvement with children in the school is likely to be relevant in determining proportionality. For example, a teaching assistant or school librarian may have more involvement with children in the school than a caretaker or cleaner, even though neither is involved in direct teaching.

Teachers and some support staff are governed by the SSFA, and religious discrimination is allowed in some circumstances. The SSFA generally protects teaching staff from discrimination on grounds of religion, but it does provide some exceptions whereby schools with a religious character can discriminate in favour of staff who share the religious ethos of the school. The provisions of the SSFA are complex because of the complex taxonomy of schools, involving voluntary aided, voluntary controlled, community schools and foundation schools.[160] The rules vary depending on the type of school involved, and so a brief definition of the different types of school is necessary. All types of school are run by school governors, but there is variation in who funds the school and employs the staff. In voluntary controlled church schools, the land and buildings are owned by a church, but the local authority funds the school, employs the staff and controls admissions. In contrast, in voluntary aided church schools the land and buildings are owned by the church, and the governing body employs the staff and controls admissions, but the school is funded largely by the local authority.[161] In community schools, the local authority owns the buildings, provides funds, employs staff and controls admissions. In foundation schools, funding is provided by the local authority, but buildings are owned by the governing body, and the governing body employs the staff and controls admissions.

The distinctions between different types of schools therefore relate to questions of funding and the legal question of who employs staff. They are not based on the level of religious input.[162] Yet these distinctions have great significance in terms of

---

[158]   However, it is difficult to envisage faith requirements being imposed on those in non-faith schools.

[159]   *Glasgow City Council v McNab* UKEAT/0037/06.

[160]   Other schools which receive state funding are academies, set up under the Learning and Skills Act 2000. These are partly funded by the business sector. In addition, there are City Technology Colleges, funded directly by the Government, rather than via a local authority.

[161]   Some funding may come from the voluntary organisation, usually a church.

[162]   However, as a general rule, voluntary aided schools and voluntary controlled schools are usually faith schools. Foundation schools (many of which were formerly grant maintained schools) may or may not be faith-based, and community schools are rarely faith-based.

the extent to which schools can discriminate in favour of religious members of staff and against those who do not share the religion of the school.

The main distinction within the SSFA is between schools with a religious character and those without. With regard to community schools and other schools which do not have a religious character, the SSFA provides that teachers cannot be refused employment, dismissed or deprived of promotion or other advantage by reason of their religious beliefs, for failure to attend religious worship, or refusal to give religious education.[163] To that extent the SSFA provides similar protection to teachers in non-faith schools as would be provided under the Religion and Belief Regulations.

With regard to schools with a religious character, the main distinction is between voluntary aided schools, which have greater freedom to impose religious requirements on staff, and voluntary controlled and foundation schools, where the extent to which religion can be used as a factor in employment decisions is more limited. In religious voluntary controlled or foundation schools, religion can be taken into account in appointing the head teacher, and regard may be had to his or her 'ability and fitness to preserve and develop the religious character of the school'.[164] In addition the school can 'reserve' up to a fifth of its teaching staff who can be 'selected for their fitness and competence' to give religious education in accordance with the tenets of the faith of the school.[165] Although this may involve positive discrimination in favour of religious staff, the Act also allows that failure to comply with the tenets of the religion can be grounds for dismissal. Thus, the SSFA allows for religious discrimination in the appointment of the head teacher and reserved staff, and allows for the imposition of lifestyle requirements on them. Breach of those requirements can give grounds for dismissal. The SSFA protects other (non-reserved) teachers and support staff from discrimination on grounds of religious opinion, failure to attend religious worship, or refusal to give religious education at the school.

The freedom of voluntary aided schools to discriminate on grounds of religion is even greater, as religious requirements can be imposed on all teaching staff, not just the head and 'reserved teachers'; and special protection against discrimination in employment on grounds related to religion or religious observance has been removed.[166] Preference can be given in connection with the appointment, remuneration or promotion of all staff on the basis of religious belief and attendance at worship. Moreover, in decisions to dismiss, regard can be had to conduct which is incompatible with the precepts of the religion, or with the upholding of its tenets.[167]

---

[163] S 59 SSFA 1998 The provision applies to working as a teacher, and being employed for the purposes of the school otherwise than as a teacher.

[164] S 60 SSFA 1998, as amended by s 37 of the Education and Inspections Act 2006.

[165] S 58 SSFA 1998. After amendment by s 37 of the Education and Inspections Act 2006, if the head teacher is appointed to teach religious education, the headteacher counts as a reserved teacher. This means that the extra religious requirements can be imposed on the head teacher.

[166] See s 37(2)(b) Education and Inspections Act 2006.

[167] S 60 SSFA 1998. Note that *O'Neill*, considered above at p 166, was decided prior to the entry into force of the SSFA 1998.

Schools outside the maintained sector, independent and private schools, are governed by special provisions which give them similar powers to discriminate on grounds of religion in order to preserve the religious ethos as are given to voluntary aided religious schools.[168]

To a limited extent the rules governing the appointment and selection of teaching staff in schools parallel those which are applicable to all workers under the Religion and Belief Regulations. For community schools and others without a religious character, discrimination on grounds of religion is not allowed under the SSFA and nor would it be under the Regulations. However, for foundation and voluntary controlled schools with a religious character, the SSFA gives greater powers to schools to discriminate in favour of religious teachers than would be available if the Religion and Belief Regulations were to govern the employment status of teaching staff. The position is similar to the position under the Regulations were they to be regarded as religious ethos organisations: in appointment decisions for a head teacher reference can be made to the candidates' ability to maintain and develop the religious ethos and a requirement that a leader of a religious organisation share the religious ethos of the organisation would be likely to be proportionate, 'having regard to the nature of the employment or the context in which it is carried out'.[169] However, in *Glasgow City Council v McNab*[170] the EAT was very clear that a local authority, which is the employer in a voluntary controlled school, could not be regarded as a religious ethos employer, even though the school may have a religious ethos.[171] Under the Regulations, then, any requirement for a teacher or head teacher to be religious would need to be a genuine and determining requirement. Thus it would seem that the provisions of the SSFA impose greater restrictions on the religious freedom of teaching staff than would be the case under the Religion and Belief Regulations.

Moreover, in relation to voluntary aided schools, there are other significant areas of divergence between the SSFA and what might have been expected under the Religion and Belief Regulations. The possibility of applying faith and lifestyle requirements to all teachers[172] in such schools, whether or not they are engaged in teaching religion, seems to go beyond what might be lawful under the Religion and Belief Regulations were they to apply to such schools. Clearly, voluntary aided church schools would be covered by the exception to the non-discrimination principle in Regulation 7(3), which applies where being of a particular religion or belief is a genuine occupational requirement for the job and it is proportionate to apply the requirement to the case. But with regard to teaching subjects other than religion, it is hard to see that being of a particular religion or belief would be a

---

[168] Independent Schools (Employment of Teachers in Schools with a Religious Character) Regulations 2003 SI 2003/2037 inserts new ss 124A and 124B into the SSFA 1998.

[169] Reg 7(3) Employment Equality (Religion and Belief) Regulations 2003.

[170] UKEAT/0037/06.

[171] However, the position may not be the same where the employer is a religious organisation, but funding is received from the state (for example, a voluntary aided school).

[172] And some support staff.

genuine occupational requirement of the job. It is also difficult to see that such requirements are proportionate when compared with requirements imposed in other maintained schools.

Furthermore, it is arguable that the provisions of the SSFA go beyond what would be allowed under the Religion and Belief Regulations alone. This is because they do not contain a requirement of proportionality in their application. Moreover, if the proportionality of the religious requirements imposed on staff in maintained schools were to be assessed in the light of the factors suggested above in chapter three, it may be that they would be found to be disproportionate. This is particularly the case when one takes into account the fact that the only difference between different types of schools is in the legal constitution of the schools, rather than their commitment to a religious ethos. In practice, voluntary aided church schools may be no more 'religious' in nature than voluntary controlled ones. The question of whether they are controlled or aided often depends on the levels of financial support available from the church at the times of their adoption into the maintained sector, rather than on the religious nature of the education provided.[173] The requirements on the school to teach the national curriculum and provide for the educational needs of children are exactly the same regardless of the type of school. It is not clear why the legal status of the school should make so much difference to the equality rights of staff. It might be clearer if differences were based on the extent to which the school itself makes a particular religious belief integral to school life.

The other factor which may militate against a finding that religious requirements are proportionate is the fact that the employer in the case of maintained schools is funded by the state, and so forms part of the public sector. Exclusion from employment on grounds of religion or belief could have a major impact on teaching staff given the large proportion of schools which have a religious character. It was suggested in chapter three that where the employer is the state, it may be appropriate to reflect the diversity of the population in recruitment. Enabling state-funded employers to discriminate on religious grounds does not help achieve that end.

It is therefore arguable that were the position of school teachers to be covered only by the Religion and Belief Regulations, the level of discrimination allowed on grounds of religion would be reduced. This raises the question of whether the provisions of the SSFA are compatible with the requirements of the Employment Equality Directive. Although the provisions of Article 4(2) allow for exceptions allowing religious organisations to maintain a religious ethos and require loyalty of staff, it is arguable that the breadth of the exceptions allowed under the SSFA, for voluntary aided schools in particular, is too broad to comply with the requirement in Article 4(2) that exceptions be legitimate and justified.[174]

---

[173] For example, some voluntary aided schools are fairly 'multi-faith' in nature, with voluntary controlled schools being more exclusively Christian. The difference may depend on catchment area, decision of the governing body, the personality of the head teacher, or the history and custom of the school and its linked parish.

[174] Following the decision of the EAT in *McNab*, see n 170, that schools where the employer is the local authority cannot be viewed as religious ethos organisations, it is questionable whether the exception in Art 4(2) should apply to voluntary controlled schools.

It should be noted that the SSFA does not create any special exceptions with regard to other grounds of discrimination such as sex or sexual orientation. Thus, although the Act may allow discrimination on religious grounds, such discrimination will be unlawful if it results in indirect sex or sexual orientation discrimination. The exception for such discrimination with regard to employment for the purposes of an organised religion[175] does not extend to general employment in schools.[176]

## III  Protection of Religious Interests Which are Not Protected by the Regulations

Prior to the introduction of the Religion and Belief Regulations, religious interests were given very limited protection within the employment relationship.[177] That limited protection will still be all that protects any individual who falls outside the protection available under the Regulations, for example, an individual whose beliefs are not classified as a religion or belief, or whose treatment is found to be too tangentially related to religion to be classified as on grounds of religion or belief. The residual protection for religious interests provided by general employment law is, effectively, that available under the general law on unfair dismissal, and the way in which this protection might apply to cases with a religious dimension will now be briefly considered.[178]

The general law on unfair dismissal is not particularly helpful in protecting religious interests at work. It imposes more onerous qualifying conditions such as the requirement that applicants be employees and that they have worked for a year for the same employer before being granted protection.[179] No protection is available for less favourable treatment during the recruitment or selection process, nor is there any protection for detriment short of dismissal. Moreover, the remedies for unfair dismissal are different: reinstatement and reengagement are possible remedies but are rarely granted, and compensation is limited.

Where an employee brings a claim for unfair dismissal, he must first show that there has been a dismissal. The onus then shifts to the employer to show that there was a fair reason to dismiss. The potentially fair reasons are limited to those listed

---

[175] Reg 7(3) Employment Equality (Sexual Orientation) Regulations 2003 and s 19 Sex Discrimination Act discussed above at p 140.

[176] *R (on the application of Amicus-MSF and others) v Secretary of State for Trade and Industry and others* [2004] IRLR 430. See discussion at p 140 above.

[177] The exception would have been for those religions which could also be classified as ethnic or racial groups. Such groups will still be covered by the Race Relations Act, the provisions of which are largely parallel to those protecting against religious discrimination.

[178] For more detail on the law of unfair dismissal see S Deakin and G Morris, *Labour Law* (4th edn) (Oxford, Hart Publishing, 2005).

[179] The qualifying period was reduced from two years to one year in June 1999 by the Unfair Dismissal and Statement of Reasons (Variation of Qualifying Period) Order 1999, SI 1999 No 1476.

in section 98 ERA 1996 (as amended), namely the capability or qualification of the employee, the conduct of the employee, the retirement of the employee, the fact that the employee is redundant, that the continued employment of the employee is illegal, or some other substantial reason that justifies the dismissal of a person holding the position that the employee held.[180] This last reason acts as a catch-all provision that can be used to cover almost any reason for dismissal. Where the employer can show that the dismissal was for one of the potentially fair reasons, then the tribunal decides whether the dismissal was fair or unfair, having regard to the reasons shown by the employer and looking at whether, in the circumstances (including the size and administrative resources of the employer's undertaking) the employer acted reasonably or unreasonably in treating the reason as sufficient reason for dismissing the employee, and this is determined in accordance with the equity and substantial merits of the case.[181]

The test of fairness contained in the legislation is of key importance in assessing the extent to which a dismissal for exercising the right to freedom of religion will be fair or unfair. The test is intended to be neutral as between the parties and so it is worded to ensure that the burden of proving fairness does not rest on either party. The fairness or unfairness of the decision to treat the reason as sufficient to dismiss is a question of fact[182]; it is not the job of the tribunal to substitute its own judgment for that of the employer. It has long been accepted that there may be a range of employer responses that are reasonable and fair and that as long as the employer's decision to dismiss does not fall outside that range the decision will be fair.[183] In effect, the benchmark against which the fairness of an employer's response is being tested is that of other employers. Where it has been shown that many employers react in a certain manner to particular types of conduct the tribunal has rarely found the reaction unfair, even though the decision may have been harsh.[184]

The 'range of reasonable responses' test of fairness[185] has been criticised for merely reflecting current employer standards, rather than setting good standards.[186] Employment Tribunal members do not assess whether they think that the employer acted correctly, but decide whether the employer's actions were fair, according to the standard of the reasonable employer. By accepting that there may be a 'range' of reasonable responses, tribunals effectively accept that fairness may be of varying standards, and that practices which fall below, and even well below,

---

[180] S 98 (1) and (2) ERA.

[181] S 98(4).

[182] *UCATT v Brain* [1981] IRLR 224.

[183] *Rolls Royce Ltd v Walpole* [1980] IRLR 343; *Richmond Precision Engineering Ltd v Pearce* [1985] IRLR 179.

[184] H Collins, *Justice In Dismissal* (Oxford, OUP, 1992) ch 1. In *Haddon v Van Den Bergh Foods Ltd* [1999] IRLR 672 the Employment Tribunal found the decision to be 'harsh in the extreme', but still found it fair.

[185] Adopted in *Iceland Frozen Foods* [1982] IRLR 439.

[186] '[T]he concept of fairness . . . becomes norm-reflecting rather than norm-setting': P Elias, 'Fairness in Unfair Dismissal: Trends and Tension' (1981) 10 *ILJ* 201, 213.

the standards of best practice can still be fair.[187] It is open to employers to argue that although their actions were not ideal, when one takes into account commercial or other factors, they were within the range of responses that can be expected of reasonable employers.[188] The standard of review is therefore very different from the standard required of a tribunal assessing proportionality.

Even though the test of fairness used has been favourable to the employer, the unfair dismissal legislation nonetheless does provide a degree of protection for employees, and could be used by employees dismissed for exercising the right to freedom of religion in ways which are not protected by the Religion and Belief Regulations. The legislation requires that there be a reason for the dismissal that can, in principle, be fair, before the fairness of the actual dismissal is assessed. Where there is no good reason for dismissal, it will be unfair. For example, in *Wigan Borough Council v Davies*[189] the employer's failure to provide support to an employee to enable her to carry out her job without harassment from colleagues was found to be a breach of contract entitling the employee to claim constructive dismissal. In such circumstances, it is difficult for an employer to show that dismissal was fair.

In many cases, there will be a potentially fair reason, particularly given the 'catch-all' provision, 'some other substantial reason justifying the decision'. Thus where behaviour, even though religiously motivated, causes the employer difficulties, this may provide a substantial reason for dismissal, whether those difficulties are commercial or relate to personnel management. For example, a reason for dismissal may be found where relationships have clearly broken down between staff so that a team's ability to work together is adversely affected[190]; or employers could face pressure to dismiss from those outside the organisation, such as customers.[191] The only question then is whether the dismissal is fair, according to the test discussed above.

Although the test of fairness is favourable to employers, it will need to be interpreted in the light of the ECHR jurisprudence on religious freedom, because of the requirement imposed by the HRA on courts and tribunals to interpret domestic legislation to comply with the ECHR. Thus, when assessing whether treatment of an individual was fair or unfair, taking into account the range of reasonable responses open to an employer, the Tribunal will need to take into account the question of whether the employee's rights under Article 9 have been protected. This was confirmed in *Copsey v WWB Devon Clays Ltd.*[192] However, if protection is not available under the Regulations, it is unlikely that protection would be

---

[187]  *Post Office v Foley, HSBC Bank (formerly Midland Bank) v Madden* [2000] IRLR 827 CA.

[188]  H Collins, *Justice in Dismissal*, above n 184, 38.

[189]  [1979] IRLR 127.

[190]  *Treganowan v Robert Knee & Co. Ltd* [1975] IRLR 247.

[191]  *Scott Packing and Warehousing Co Ltd v Paterson* [1978] IRLR 166. But see *Grootcon (UK) Ltd v Keld* [1984] IRLR 302 EAT, *Wadley v Eager Electrical Ltd* [1986] IRLR 93 and *Dobie v Burns International Security Services (UK) Ltd* [1984] IRLR 329.

[192]  [2005] EWCA CIV 932. See the discussion at p 118 above.

available under the ECHR either[193]: thus using the HRA to enable interpretation of the unfair dismissal protection to comply with the ECHR is unlikely to create any greater protection for employees who fall outside the protection under the Regulations.

However, as well as assessing fairness in accordance with the standards of the ECHR, dismissals also need to be procedurally fair. If an employer fails to follow basic disciplinary procedures or is inconsistent in the treatment afforded to the employee in comparison with others, the dismissal can be unfair.

As the law is currently interpreted, employment protection is weak for employees who exercise the right to freedom of religion at work, but who do not come within the terms of the Religion and Belief Regulations. Where the legitimate interests of the employer, such as financial interests or the interest in effective management of the enterprise, are harmed by an employee's exercise of religious freedom, dismissal is likely to be found to be fair. As long as any other similar cases have been treated consistently and appropriate procedures are used, any claim of unfair dismissal will probably fail.

# IV  Conclusion

The introduction of the Religion and Belief Regulations prohibiting religious discrimination at work raises some singularly perplexing issues regarding the scope that should be granted to religious interests at work. This is largely due to the compound nature of religious discrimination and the competing interests it engages. Accommodation of religion upholds the religious freedom of the person accommodated but may simultaneously undermine the freedom of religion and belief of another. Secular employers may discriminate against religious employees. Religious groups may wish to employ those of the same religion and so may discriminate against others. Discrimination can occur between those of different religions, or those of the same faith. Moreover, cases of religious discrimination may also involve discrimination on other grounds such as sex, sexual orientation, or marital status.

The creation of religious rights via the Employment Equality Directive in the EU, and thence to the UK, means that the control of religious discrimination forms part of a general framework of equality rights. This means that not only is there inevitable interaction between equality rights, but the legal framework of protection uses virtually identical terminology for all grounds of equality, even though the religious ground involves multi-faceted interests of equality and the individual human right to freedom of religion and belief, covering both a negative

---

[193] Not least because the Regulations will be interpreted to comply with the ECHR. The facts in *Copsey* occurred before the Regulations were in force, and so had to be decided on the basis of a claim of unfair dismissal only.

and a positive right. These multiple interests mean that the proper treatment of religious interests at work is very complicated to determine, as it can depend on a range of factors such as the type of employer, and the socio-economic context of the case. The Religion and Belief Regulations need to be interpreted in the light of the range of competing interests that arise and which are identified in chapter three, including the need to uphold both a positive and a negative freedom of religion, as well as equality, autonomy, dignity and pluralism.

Under the Religion and Belief Regulations, these interests require that tolerance of difference is maximised. This means that religion and belief can be accommodated at the workplace only to the extent that they do not infringe the rights of others. In most cases, any clash between discrimination rights is resolved in favour of gender, sexual orientation and other equality rights: religious grounds cannot be used to justify discrimination on other grounds in any but the most limited circumstances.[194] However, the freedom of religious groups to act in order to uphold their religious interests through the employment relationship is provided for where it is proportionate. The need for proportionality will mean that employers will rarely be able to create religiously exclusive workplaces, and may make this very rare in the public sector (with the anomalous exception of faith schools).

The use of 'proportionality' was recommended in chapter three as an appropriate way to determine the proper scope of religious protection in the workplace. Apart from the protection against direct discrimination, the protection for religious interests at work uses sufficiently indeterminate or discretionary language for reference to the concept of proportionality to be used in the interpretation of the Regulations. 'Genuine occupational requirements' are only lawful to the extent that they are proportionate; indirect discrimination is only unlawful where it cannot be justified as proportionate, and harassment occurs, in effect, where 'in all the circumstances' it is 'reasonable' for the behaviour to have the effect of infringing a person's 'dignity'. These terms are indeterminate in nature and allow the factors relevant to proportionality to be taken into account in any assessment of whether a claim is made out. The Regulations therefore have the potential to be interpreted to accord with the model set out in chapter three. This would also accord with the best reading of the protection under the ECHR.

The only area where there is no discretionary language is direct discrimination which occurs in the absence of a genuine occupational requirement. However, the complexities of competing interests do not apply in cases of direct discrimination, as the individual will have been discriminated against purely on the basis of belief.[195] It is only once the belief is manifested that it creates any interaction with other people, giving rise to complexity. However, this results in indirect discrimination[196]

---

[194] The appointment of clergy and their equivalent: Reg 7(3) Employment Equality (Sexual Orientation) Regulations 2003 and s 19 Sex Discrimination Act 1975.

[195] The absolute nature of the protection against direct discrimination mirrors the absolute protection for the *forum internum* under Art 9 ECHR.

[196] The discrimination will be as a result of the manifestation, not the belief itself.

rather than direct discrimination, and any interference with the manifestation of religion may therefore be open to justification, if it is proportionate. In chapter three it was suggested that the reason for protecting religious interests at work was based on the importance of religious belief to individual autonomy and dignity. On this basis, being treated less favourably purely on the basis of belief is difficult to justify. Once the religious belief manifests itself in any way which interferes with the rights of others, however, complexity is introduced. That complexity can be addressed though the mechanism of the proportionality equation.

One major obstacle stands in the way of creating an approach to the protection of religious interests based on a careful and contextual balancing of the factors identified as relevant to proportionality, and that is the desire to create a uniform standard of protection for all equality rights.[197] Although the desire to be free from hierarchy in the realm of equality and diversity is laudable, attempting to interpret the scope of the religious discrimination rights to create uniformity with other areas of equality law may not be the ideal approach. Instead, interpreting Regulations to accord with the model created in chapter three would allow for a more flexible approach to the complex interplay of interests at stake when individuals seek to protect religious interests in the workplace.

In the next chapter, the protection afforded to religious interests in a number of other jurisdictions is assessed, to see what can be leant from their different legal approaches to these universally complex issues.

---

[197] See *Discrimination Law Review, A Framework for Fairness: Proposals for a Single Equality Bill for Great Britain* (London, Department for Communities and Local Government, 2007).

# 6

## Religious Interests in the Workplace: Comparative Perspectives

Previous chapters have considered the protection of religious interests in employment as protected in the UK and under the ECHR, and identified a number of difficulties which may arise in terms of interpretation and application. It will now be instructive to consider case law from other jurisdictions, to see if it provides any guidance on how to tackle the difficult questions of principle that are common across jurisdictions. Such questions include how to determine the existence of a religion; how far employers should be required to accommodate religious practice; and whether employers should be allowed to discriminate against others in order to preserve a religious ethos in the workplace.

Clearly, it can be problematic to make comparisons with other jurisdictions, especially if the historical, social and political contexts are different. In the case of the United States of America, for example, the historical and social context for the protection of religious interests differs significantly from that in Britain. Its modern state was founded in part by those arriving in North America to avoid religious persecution, and religion remains a force in politics.[1] Equally, the USA has a long constitutional commitment to the separation of church and state, in contrast to the established status of the Church of England.

Indeed, some have argued that the legal and cultural contexts in which the law operates can differ so much that comparisons between states run the risk of becoming meaningless or misleading.[2] However, when one is looking at standards relating to fundamental human rights, comparative perspectives can be useful, notwithstanding the different social contexts.[3] When considering difficulties such as how to balance conflicting rights, the experience of other jurisdictions can be helpful. International comparisons can be instructive precisely because the issues

---

[1] See S D Jamar, 'Accommodating Religion at Work: A Principled Approach to Title VII and Religious Freedom' (1996) 40 *New York Law Sch LR* 719. Moreover, the general level of employment protection in the USA is far lower than in Europe: in the USA the general rule of employment 'at will' prevails.

[2] O Kahn-Freund, 'On Uses and Misuses of Comparative Law' (1974) 37 *MLR* 1.

[3] On the extent to which judges use comparative legal perspectives in adjudicating human rights cases, see C McCrudden, 'A Common Law of Human Rights? Transnational Judicial Conversations on Constitutional Rights' (2000) 20 *OJLS* 499.

relate to universally accepted rights such as freedom of religion, and generalised concepts such as equality.

A full examination of the treatment of religious interests at work in other jurisdictions is beyond the scope of this chapter. However, in presenting an overview of the main provisions of protection, some interesting similarities and differences will be seen. Examples will be drawn from the USA, Canada, and Europe. What becomes clear from this comparative assessment is that all states share a vision of creating a plural and tolerant society. However, quite what is meant by this, and the methods used to achieve the aim, varies between states.

# I  United States of America

In the USA, anti-discrimination provisions are contained in Title VII of the Civil Rights Act 1964.[4] In addition, government workers are protected against religious discrimination under the Constitution, and many individual states have their own human rights laws which cover discrimination. In effect, there are hundreds of courts making decisions on cases involving religion, under many different local provisions, and so what can be offered here can only be a generalised view. However, Title VII of the Civil Rights Act applies in all states and to all employers, so is the focus of the discussion here.

Under Title VII, discrimination on grounds of race, colour, religion, sex or national origin is prohibited. It covers all employers with over 15 employees, those employed by the state and local government as well as private sector employers. Both direct and indirect discrimination are covered and the Act also creates a duty to make reasonable accommodation for religious practice. In addition, an exemption for 'bona fide occupational qualifications' (BFOQ) exists, enabling employers to impose requirements on staff that they adhere to a particular religion where it is necessary for the particular requirements of the job.

## Meaning of Religion

The term 'religion' includes 'all aspects of religious observance and practice, as well as belief'.[5] The protection against religious discrimination extends beyond traditional religious groups to cover other deeply held moral and ethical views, including lack of belief,[6] if the views are sincerely held with the strength of traditional religious views.[7]

---

[4]  42 USC§ 2000e-2.

[5]  S 701(j).

[6]  *Young v Southwestern Savings and Loan Association* 509 F 2d 140 (5th Cir 1975).

[7]  EEOC Guidelines, 29 CFR 16051, based on *US v Seegar* 380 US 163 (1965), and *Welsh v US* 398 US 333 (1970).

With regard to determining the belief of the employee, the US courts have held that it is not for the employer to judge the reasonableness of the employee's beliefs. Moreover, even where employees cannot point to a religious group which shares their views, this will not prevent a finding that the particular individual holds a religious view. For example, in *Van Koten v Family Health Management Inc*[8] the applicant claimed to be a member of the 'Wicca' religion. Although the employer successfully defended the claim because the employee had not told the employer of his religion, the court did accept that a person can be of a particular religion even though there is no religious group with the same views to which the employee can belong. Moreover, the fact that others of the same religion do not share exactly the same beliefs as the claimant does not prevent a claimant from bringing a discrimination claim. For example, a vow taken by a Christian to wear a badge bearing an anti-abortion message can be protected on religious grounds, even though not all Christians would take the same view of abortion.[9]

While beliefs do not need to be religious, they must be deeply held ethical views, which hold a place parallel to religion in the life of the claimant. Thus, a belief in the beneficial effects of eating cat food was not a religion or belief that needed accommodating.[10] Perhaps more useful in terms of guidance is the decision that political views such as those espoused by the Klu Klux Klan are not protected, because they are 'political and social in nature'.[11] However, a belief of a more religious nature in a white supremacist religion has been found to be capable of protection. In *Peterson v Wilmur Communications*,[12] the claimant was a 'reverend' in the World Church of the Creator, whose belief system, called 'Creativity', taught that white people are superior to others. He was employed as a manager, supervising eight people, but was dismissed after writing a column in a local paper about his religion, for which he was photographed wearing a T-shirt commemorating a man who had been involved in a racially motivated killing. Following the publication of the column, Peterson was demoted away from his supervisory role. The court held that 'Creativity' was a religion, despite the findings relating to the Klu Klux Klan, and despite the fact that it had some political aspects. His demotion, motivated because of his beliefs, was therefore discriminatory.

In their acceptance that a wide range of beliefs can be covered by Title VII, and their acceptance of a subjective test of religious affiliation, the US courts provide a generous level of protection for religious freedom. However, acceptance that a set of beliefs is capable of protection by Title VII is not determinative of most discrimination cases. For example, claimants must also show that there was a failure to reasonably accommodate the religion, or the employer may show that there was a bona fide occupational qualification for the job which the claimant lacked. Thus it might be arguable, for jobs involving any contact with other colleagues or

---

[8] 955 F Supp 898, affirmed 134 F 3d 375 (1998).
[9] See, for example, *Wilson v US West Communications* 58 F 3d 1337 (1995).
[10] *Brown v Pena* 441 F Supp 1382 (SD Fla 1977), affirmed 589 F 2d 1113 (5th Cir 1979).
[11] *Slater v King Soopers Inc* 809 F Supp 809 (1992).
[12] 205 F Supp 2d 1014 (2002).

members of the public, that it is a requirement of the job that employees treat others with respect, and do not engage in political activity which demonstrates racial or religious hatred, or disrespect for others. Such a defence was not put forward in the *Peterson* case, which turned only on the question of whether 'Creativity' was a religion or not, but it is possible that, had it been argued, Peterson's case would have been unsuccessful. Alternatively, had the dismissal been for failing to accommodate his practice of declaring his faith through his newspaper column, it may have been arguable that the failure to accommodate would be reasonable because to accommodate the belief would cause undue hardship to the employer, who does not have to tolerate the upset caused to other colleagues by the behaviour.[13] Thus it is possible to have a generous and broad understanding of religion for the purposes of the discrimination protection, without having to provide broad and generous levels of accommodation for the practice of such beliefs when they are likely to cause offence to others.

One further matter which has arisen in relation to discrimination because of religion at work is the difference between religious observance or practice, and other behaviour motivated by religion. The protection against discrimination is based on religious practice and observance, and does not extend to behaviour motivated by religion. Thus, where a mother left work early without permission in order to be present to help set up and organise a children's play at her church, the dismissal did not amount to religious discrimination.[14]

## Direct and Indirect Discrimination

Title VII protects against intentional and unintentional discrimination, providing protection against direct and indirect discrimination as the terms are understood in the UK. Thus it is unlawful to discriminate against an individual 'because of such individual's . . . religion'.[15] Indirect discrimination, or disparate impact discrimination, was developed in *Griggs v Duke Power Company*,[16] and reflects the idea that some work requirements will be harder for some to comply with than for others, leading to inequality in practice. Although originally a common law development, amendments were made to the Civil Rights Act 1964 in 1991 to deal with disparate impact claims. Section 703(k) provides that it is for the claimant to establish a prima facie case that a job requirement has a disparate impact on those in the protected group. The employer must then show that the requirement is job-related and consistent with business necessity. This defence to indirect discrimination claims cannot be used in direct discrimination cases: it is not possible to justify direct discrimination.[17]

---

[13] See discussion of the duty of accommodation below.
[14] *Wessing v Kroger Co* 554 F Supp 548.
[15] S 703 (a)(1) Civil Rights Act 1964.
[16] 401 US 424 (1971).
[17] Sec 703(k)(2).

If the business necessity standard is met, the employee may still show that there is a less discriminatory alternative practice which would fulfil the business purpose. Where this can be shown, continued use of the employer's requirement will be unlawful discrimination. Unequal treatment does not have to be motivated by a desire to discriminate; if sex, race or religion plays a part in decision-making then there can be discrimination, even if there are mixed motives in play.

In the context of religion, the creation in 1972 of the duty of reasonable accommodation has displaced the use of indirect discrimination.[18] Where an employee fails to meet a requirement imposed by an employer, this is treated as a question of whether the employer should accommodate the employee, rather than as a matter of indirect discrimination. Thus most of the guidance from the USA on how to balance religious interests against other interests is found in the case law on the duty to accommodate considered below.

## Bona Fide Occupational Requirements

Section 703 (e)(1) provides a general BFOQ exception to the non-discrimination principle. This enables employers to make religion a requirement for a job where it is reasonably necessary for the normal operation of the business.

Where the job involves working as a religious minister the BFOQ exception is superceded by the 'free exercise' provisions of the Constitution, requiring that religious groups be free to choose their leaders.[19] This is justified on the basis that it is inappropriate for courts to interfere with the internal affairs of religious groups, so the protection of Title VII does not apply.[20] However, this broad exemption only applies to the appointment of those who are involved as ministers in religious observance. Where work is less directly linked to the religious mission of a religious organisation the BFOQ exception applies, and is more restricted. For example, in *Fike v United Methodist Children's Home Of Virginia, Inc*,[21] involving the appointment of a director for a care home which had been founded by the Methodist Church and which maintained close association with it, a requirement that the director be a Methodist minister was not allowed as a BFOQ, as the work was largely secular, despite the religious nature of the foundation.

Where a requirement imposed by an employer discriminates against others on other grounds, it will not be accepted as a BFOQ, except in the context of religious leaders as described above. Thus in *Bollenbach v Board of Education of Monroe-Woodbury Central School District*[22] a bus company assigned male drivers to a school bus route which transported boys to private religious schools. The boys would not board a bus driven by women. When men were assigned to the route in

[18] *EEOC v Sambo's of Georgia* 530 F Supp 86 (1981).

[19] *Kendroff v St Nicholas Cathedral of the Russian Orthodox Church of North America* 344 US 94 (1952).

[20] *McClure v Salvation Army* 460 F 2d 553 (5th Cir 1972).

[21] 547 F Supp 286 (1982). See W Stickman, 'An Exercise in Futility: Does the Inquiry Required to Apply the Ministerial Exception to Title VII Defeat its Purpose?' (2005) 43 *Duq LR* 285.

[22] 659 F Supp 1450 (1987).

breach of the usual seniority system for assigning routes, the female drivers complained. The employer was unsuccessful in its attempt to argue that women lacked a BFOQ for driving the route because the boys would not board the bus. The preference of clientele for a male driver could not make being male a BFOQ.

In addition to the general BFOQ exception, an additional exception is provided in section 702 for non-profit making religious organisations and societies. Where there is a clear religious dimension to the organisation's work, the section 702 BFOQ exception can apply even to secular activities of religious organisations, as long as the activity is non-profit making. Thus, for example, where a church operated a gymnasium which was open to the public, it was entitled to dismiss a caretaker for failing to comply with religious standards of behaviour, even though he had a secular role in a secular activity.[23] Where activity is for profit, however, religious discrimination will remain unlawful, as for any other employer.[24] The restriction to non-profit activity fits with the suggestion in chapter three that religious discrimination should be more limited where an organisation interacts with the public marketplace. The reason for the restriction of the exception to non-profit making work is that to allow religious organisations to discriminate with regard to their profit making work would be to breach the non-establishment clause of the US Constitution, as it would amount to giving privileged legal protection to religious organisations over those with a secular base.[25]

The position of religious employers contrasts with the position in the UK where religious employers can use the genuine occupational requirement exception for any part of the business where religion is relevant to the job, not just non-profit activity. Moreover, the genuine occupational requirement for religious ethos employers applies in Britain even where religion is not a determining aspect of the job.[26] This broader exception for religious ethos employers does not exist within the US framework of protection. For example, in *EEOC v Townley Engineering*[27] the employers were 'born again' Christians and wanted to run the engineering and manufacturing firm as a faith-operated business. To this end, it printed bible verses on invoices, donated money to churches, and held a weekly devotional service during working time, which all staff had to attend. One atheist employee left the organisation when required to attend the services.[28] The Court held that the BFOQ exception for religious organisations did not apply to Townley Engineering, as it was a for-profit organisation.[29]

---

[23] *Corporation of Presiding Bishop of Church of Jesus Christ of Latter-day Saints v Amos* 483 US 327 (1987).

[24] Unless the job is religious in nature, in which case the s 703(1)(e) exception will apply. See *Hishon v King & Spalding* 467 US 69 (1984).

[25] See *Lemon v Kurtzman* 403 US 602 (1971) and *Corporation of Presiding Bishop of Church of Jesus Christ of Latter-day Saints v Amos* above n 23.

[26] Religion must still be a genuine occupational requirement.

[27] 859 F 2d 610 (9th Cir 1988), discussed below.

[28] He had been given permission to read or sleep during the services, but attendance was mandatory.

[29] For an argument in favour of recognising 'quasi-religious' organisations see E Reuveni, 'On Boy Scouts and Anti-Discrimination Law: The Associational Rights Of Quasi-Religious Organizations' (2006) *Boston U LR* 109.

One further exception is provided in respect of schools, colleges and universities. Section 703(e)(2) provides an exception for religious educational establishments, where the establishment is owned, supported, controlled or managed by a religious association or society, or where the curriculum of the educational establishment is directed towards the propagation of a particular religion. The exception is fairly narrowly interpreted: where a school was set up under the terms of a will trust, with the terms of the will stating that teachers must be Protestant, the exception did not apply. The school was not actually owned, controlled or managed by a religious group, but by a trust which was secular in nature. The normal curriculum was taught, rather than a curriculum aimed towards the propagation of the faith, and so the second limb of the exception did not apply either.[30] Where the exception does apply, it only allows for discrimination on grounds of religion, and provides no defence to any claim of discrimination on other grounds such as gender.[31]

## Duty to Accommodate

As originally drafted in 1964, the Civil Rights Act did not contain a duty of reasonable accommodation. It is arguable that such a duty can be read in to the duty not to discriminate, as the barriers put up for religious practice by employers may act to discriminate, albeit indirectly, against religious observers. However, it was felt that amendment was required to make clearer that religious freedom requires the protection of religious practice or observance, as well as protection of belief itself, and that the Title VII protection should extend to the protection of religious practice[32]: if staff were to be protected in their rights to practise their religion, then a level of accommodation was required. As a result, Title VII was amended in 1972 to include a duty on the employer to accommodate the religious practices of employees, as long as to do so did not cause undue hardship to the employer. The amendment was made to the definition of religion:

> The term 'religion' includes all aspects of religious observance and practice, as well as belief, unless an employer demonstrates that he is unable to reasonably accommodate to an employee's or prospective employee's religious observance or practice without undue hardship on the conduct of the employer's business.[33]

The provisions are designed to cover matters such as requests for time off work for religious observance, and the Equal Employment Opportunities Commission (EEOC) provides guidelines on the types of accommodation that might be

---

[30]  *EEOC v Kamehameha Schools/Bishop Estate* 990 F 2d 458 (9th Cir 1993).

[31]  *Rayburn v General Conference of Seventh Day Adventists* 772 F 2d 1164 (4th Cir 1985).

[32]  See S Silbiger, 'Heaven Can Wait: Judicial Interpretation Of Title VII's Religious Accommodation Requirement Since *Trans World Airlines v Hardison*' (1985) *Fordham LR* 839.

[33]  42 USCA § 2000e j. As the Court of Appeals 3rd Circuit has pointed out 'Thus, perhaps counterintuitively, if an employer cannot accommodate a religious practice without undue hardship, the practice is not "religion" within the meaning of Title VII': *US v Board of Education for the School District of Philadelphia* 911 F 2d 882 (1990 CA 3rd Cir). Failure to offer reasonable accommodation can make the employer liable for punitive damages.

expected, for example, flexible scheduling, voluntary swaps, job reassignments and modification of grooming requirements. However, despite the suggestion from the wording of the duty and the EEOC's guidelines that religion should be accommodated unless there is undue hardship, the interpretation of the duty to accommodate has been somewhat restrictive, leaving employers with a most slender of duties to accommodate. Undue hardship has been interpreted to mean that, if accommodation is to be required, there must be no more than de minimis cost, either in terms of financial cost or in terms of disruption, or administrative inconvenience.[34]

The hardship must operate on the conduct of the employer's business.[35] It must create some form of economic hardship, and cannot be merely hardship of a spiritual nature. Thus in *Townley Engineering*[36] the employer sought to run the business as a Christian, faith-operated business. It held weekly mandatory devotional services during working time, sent out gospel tracts with outgoing mail and printed bible verses on invoices. The employers argued that accommodating an atheist employee by excusing him from attendance at the weekly service would cause 'spiritual' hardship to the company as it would 'chill' their religious purposes. The Court accepted that spiritual hardship could exist, but held that the restriction in section 701(j) to hardship in the conduct of the business ruled out the use of non-economic harm to justify a refusal to accommodate religion.

Excluding spiritual hardship may make it harder to override the duty to accommodate, but the low level of economic hardship required still means it is fairly easy to override the duty in practice. The main parameters of the duty of accommodation were set out in two cases before the Supreme Court, both involving members of the Worldwide Church of God. In *Trans World Airlines, Inc v Hardison*[37] a clerk in the stores department of TWA asked to change his hours after having joined the Church. The stores operated 24 hours a day, all year, and he wished to avoid working from sunset on Friday until sunset on Saturday. The shift system at TWA was operated on a seniority basis, agreed through a collective bargaining system. At first, Hardison's request was accommodated, as he had sufficient seniority to enable him to be given his requested shifts in accordance with the collectively agreed system. However, after having been moved to a new part of the business he lost seniority, and could no longer arrange shifts to suit his religious beliefs. The union was unwilling to agree a waiver of the seniority system to enable his beliefs to be accommodated, and TWA would not allow him to work a four-day week as that would mean incurring the additional expense of employing an extra worker for Saturdays. When he was dismissed, the court had to determine whether a reasonable accommodation had been available for Hardison. The Supreme Court ruled that the options available to the employer (overriding the seniority system that had been agreed with the union, or allowing Hardison to work a four-day

---

[34] *Ansonia Board of Education v Philbrook* 479 US 60 (1986).
[35] 42 USCA § 2000e j.
[36] Above n 27.
[37] 432 US 63 (1977).

week at extra cost to the employer) would have imposed undue hardship on the employer. The Court took the view that to override a seniority system would mean denying one member of staff's preference in favour of another's preference, and would not be reasonable. Overall, they ruled, the employer does not need to take on more than de minimis costs in order to offer reasonable accommodation.

The second case, *Ansonia Board of Education v Philbrook*,[38] involved a request to use 'personal business' leave to supplement leave for religious observance, so as to enable the applicant to take sufficient paid days off for religious observance. The employer would not allow the paid 'personal leave' days to be taken for this purpose. The employer was only prepared to accommodate the request for extra leave by allowing Philbrook to take unpaid leave. The question which arose was whether the employee has to accept a reasonable offer of accommodation once it is offered (here the unpaid leave) or whether he can claim that a failure to offer his preferred accommodation (here the paid 'personal business' leave) is unreasonable. The Supreme Court held that once the employer has shown that a reasonable accommodation has been offered, the employer's duty ends. The fact that an employee can identify an alternative accommodation which he or she would prefer does not change matters: the employer is under no obligation to offer the employee the least disadvantageous accommodation available.[39] There is a requirement on the employee to be flexible in accepting an accommodation if it is reasonable, even if he can identify less disadvantageous accommodations.

The combined effect of *Hardison* and *Philbrook* suggests that the duty of accommodation is more apparent than real. It would seem that what is given with one hand via the duty of accommodation is taken away with the other via the low level of hardship needed to defeat the duty. In effect, although a duty to accommodate exists it is so easily overridden that employees' religious interests are given very little practical protection. Once a countervailing interest is identified, the duty on the employer to accommodate religion tends to give way.[40]

However, it does require that an employer make some attempt at accommodation. Although only de minimis hardship is required, it must at least be real hardship, not merely hypothetical.[41] This means that the employer cannot rely, for example, on the fact that other staff might become unhappy, but must show that they will be. In effect, the duty of reasonable accommodation puts the onus on the employer to show that they have thought about trying to accommodate and have actual reasons why to do so would be difficult.

[38] Above n 34.

[39] In reaching this conclusion, the Supreme Court disregarded guidelines produced by the US Equal Employment Opportunity Commission (EEOC) that suggested that where there is an alternative accommodation which does not cause hardship, the employer should offer the one which least disadvantages the religious employee. See also *EEOC v Ilona of Hungary* 108 F 3d 1169 (7th Cir 1997).

[40] See, further, J D Prenkert and J M Magid, 'A Hobson's Choice Model for Religious Accommodation' (2006) 43:3 *American Business LJ* 467. The rationale for the de minimis test is that the courts do not want to overprotect one person's religion at the expense of another's.

[41] *EEOC v Alamo Rent-A-Car* 26 May 2006 and *Opuku-Boateng v California*, 95 F3d 1461, 1473–74 (9th Cir 1996). This is despite the fact that in *Hardison* the Supreme Court did allow TWA to rely on hypothetical hardship.

One matter which can give rise to hardship to the employer is a negative reaction to any accommodation by other staff. The cases are not always consistent on this issue. On the one hand, a refusal by other staff to accept a religious practice can give rise to undue hardship for the employer, and can give grounds to refuse to accommodate. Thus, in *Wilson v US West Communications*[42] a Catholic employee, who wore a badge with a picture of an aborted foetus on it as part of a vow to be a 'living witness' against abortion, was dismissed because her colleagues found the badge offensive. The court held that the duty to accommodate did not require an employer to allow an employee to impose her views on others. On the other hand, any hardship to the employer must be real, and cannot be purely hypothetical. Thus, in *Burns v Southern Pacific Transportation Co*[43] the employer argued that to accommodate a Seventh Day Adventist's refusal to pay union dues would cause dissention among workers, leading to inefficiency. This was rejected by the court, which stressed that undue hardship requires more than just proof that some employees would grumble. The employer would need to show that other employees were imposed upon, or that the work routine would be disrupted.[44]

Having set out the basic framework of the US duty to accommodate, it is worth considering how it has been applied to various common matters which can cause difficulties for employees in reconciling work and religious practice: working time, dress codes, work tasks and work cultures which conflict with religious beliefs.

*Working Time*   Many cases, including the seminal cases of *Hardison* and *Philbrook*, involve reconciling working time with religious observance. Difficulties involve requirements to work on religious days of rest and the need for leave from work to attend religious ceremonies. In most cases, where employers allow some flexibility, such as letting staff arrange shift swaps, they will be found to have met their obligation to accommodate religion. If the facility to swap shifts exists, the employer will have met the obligation to accommodate, even though such a facility may not work to accommodate the employee in all cases. Only if no attempt is made to accommodate will the employer be found to have failed in its duty.[45] The employee cannot require a specific accommodation, if what is offered by the employer is found to be reasonable. In cases involving the arrangement of shifts, the courts are clear that the duty of accommodation carries with it a responsibility on employees to attempt to accommodate their religious needs through the means offered by the employer.[46] Moreover, the fact that a religious accommodation will involve a reduction in pay or a demotion will not prevent a finding that it is reasonable.[47] In such cases, the employee cannot show a failure to offer reasonable accommodation just because he or she would prefer a different accommodation to be granted.

---

[42] 58 F 3d 1337 (1995).
[43] 589 F 2d 403 (9th Cir 1978).
[44] See also *Tooley v Martin-Marietta Corp* 648 F 2d 1239 (1981), and *Townley Engineering* above n 27.
[45] *EEOC v Ithaca Industries* 849 F 2d 116 (4th Cir 1988).
[46] See *Breech v Alabama Power* 962 F Supp 1447 (1997).
[47] *Matthewson v Florida Game and Freshwater Fish Comn* 6939 F Supp 1044 (1988).

Overall, the duty to accommodate does not impose very stringent demands on employers in terms of helping staff to reconcile religious observance with working time. The need of the employer to have an adequate workforce available to serve the business needs of the enterprise, and to balance the working time of all staff, takes precedence over the need to accommodate religious practice at work.

*Dress Codes*   Uniform and grooming codes are clearly capable of conflicting with religious dress codes, perhaps the most common being requirements to avoid head coverings which conflict with the religious practices of Sikhs and Muslims. As with other religious practices, the basic position is that dress code requests should be accommodated unless to do so would cause undue hardship. Where there was a statute banning religious garb in schools, a court held that the employer would suffer undue hardship if it were expected to contravene the statute, as the statute served the legitimate purpose of maintaining religious neutrality in schools.[48] However, in the absence of hardship, religious dress should be accommodated. For example, a general statement that deviating from the company's carefully cultivated image would amount to hardship is not sufficient to avoid the duty to accommodate. In *EEOC v Alamo Rent-A-Car*[49] the employee worked in a car rental office, and was involved in serving customers. She asked to wear a headscarf during Ramadan, but was refused. The employer required her to remove the headscarf while working with customers, and also refused to move her from her work involving meeting customers for the period of Ramadan. The court held that Alamo failed to show undue hardship.

However, the case law is not always consistent, and despite the finding in the *Alamo* case, in many more cases courts have accepted that the image or reputation of the employer can be damaged by religious or unorthodox dress, and that this can constitute undue hardship. For example, the continued employment of a shop assistant who refused to cover facial jewellery such as an eyebrow piercing (motivated by her membership of the 'Church of Body Modification') would cause undue hardship to the employer as it would prevent it from presenting to the public a workforce with a reasonably professional appearance.[50]

The cases illustrate the low level of protection afforded to religious practice as a result of the decision in *Hardison* that hardship need only be at a de minimis level. They also illustrate the difference in the standard of protection afforded to religious discrimination, in contrast to that for sex discrimination, where the preference of clients would not be accepted as a justification for discrimination.[51]

*Work Tasks*[52]   Religious members of staff may ask to be removed from certain tasks at work because they are incompatible with their beliefs. For example, staff

---

[48]   *US v Board of Education for the School District of Philadelphia* 911 F 2d 882 (1990).
[49]   Above n 41.
[50]   *Cloutier v Costco* 390 F 3d 126 (2004).
[51]   *Diaz v Pan American World Airways*, 442 F 2d 385 (5th Cir 1971).
[52]   Some states are currently considering legislation that will allow an employee to opt out of some tasks based on religious convictions.

may ask not to be involved in any work that is linked to abortion, or gambling, or other behaviour they believe is wrong. Here again, the hardship caused to employers in having to make special arrangements in the assignment of work will usually mean that such requests do not have to be accommodated. Moreover, the matching duty on religious employees to be flexible and to accommodate the employer[53] also means that they will find it difficult to claim that a failure to allocate tasks according to religious preference is unlawfully discriminatory. Accommodations such as allowing voluntary swaps of tasks, or offering to redeploy are reasonable,[54] although this will only be feasible where the employer is large enough and skills are transferable. Where the reallocation of work is not practical, dismissal can be lawful. Thus, where a counsellor refused, for religious reasons, to counsel clients who were homosexual or who were involved in extra-marital relationships, dismissal was not discriminatory: it would not be possible to determine in advance whether such an issue may arise in a counselling relationship, and to allow staff to opt out of some tasks would lead to an uneven distribution of work among colleagues.[55]

*Work Cultures*   Some employees have claimed that their religion prevents them from participating in training or complying with workplace diversity policies: employees have objected to 'diversity' training as they believe it requires them to condone homosexuality. Employers have not generally been required to accommodate such objections. The need to promote diversity and tolerance within the workplace has been seen as legitimate, and the hardship caused to an employer if he is prevented from promoting such a culture at work is seen to override any duty to accommodate religion. Thus in *Peterson v Hewlett Packard*[56] Peterson displayed bible verses denouncing homosexuality in response to posters celebrating the diversity of the Hewlett Packard workforce and the presence of female, ethnic minority and gay workers. Peterson's refusal to desist led to his dismissal, which was held not to be discriminatory. To require the employer to stop the diversity programme would have amounted to undue hardship.

Interestingly, the courts have allowed some accommodation of religious views which are critical of homosexuality, where to do so does not lead to any active discrimination against other workers. For example, *Buonanno v AT&T Broadband LLC*[57] involved an employee who was required to sign a diversity statement which stated that he 'valued' the differences among people. He claimed that this required him to make a statement which was supportive of homosexuality, even though this was incompatible with his religious view that homosexuality was sinful. He was prepared to sign an alternative statement agreeing to value the fact that there are differences between people (as opposed to valuing the differences themselves). Given that the employee in question had no intention of discriminating against or

---

[53] *Ansonia Board of Education v Philbrook* above n 34.
[54] *Shelton v University of Medicine and Dentistry of New Jersey* 223 F 3d 220 (2000).
[55] *Bruff v North Mississippi Health Services* 244 F 3d 495 (2001).
[56] 358 F 3d 599 (9th Cir 2004).
[57] 313 F Supp 2d 1069 (2004).

being disrespectful towards homosexual staff, and that a form of words which was compatible with the employer's diversity policy could have been found, the court determined that the employee's religious views should have been accommodated. The employer's refusal to investigate the possibility of an alternative wording amounted to a failure to accommodate; investigating a minor amendment to the wording of the statement would not cause undue hardship to the employer. It was significant to the decision that Buonanno was not asking to be exempt from the duty to respect others in the workplace. Indeed, he was prepared to sign a statement which involved a commitment to respect others. However, he was not prepared to sign a statement with which he disagreed, on religious grounds. In terms of balancing interests, it would seem that this is a correct balance: Buonanno's freedom of conscience could be accommodated as long as he was prepared to respect the diversity policy of the company in practice.

*Conclusion*   The cases illustrate that a range of fairly low level accommodations can be found to be reasonable by the courts. For example, using annual leave or unpaid leave is a common accommodation which courts will treat as reasonable, or moving staff to alternative duties, or requiring the employee to accept reductions in pay or status in order to reconcile work demands with religious conscience. These accommodations, if offered, cost the employer little, and leave the employee with no choice but to accept; there is no right to request a more advantageous accommodation if what is offered is deemed reasonable. The fact that such a low threshold of hardship is required to override the duty of accommodation may suggest that the protection offered by the duty is worthless. However, the duty does achieve some measure of protection for religious interests at work, albeit limited. The existence of the duty means that employers must make an attempt to accommodate. Although only de minimis hardship is required, it must be real and not merely hypothetical.

In effect, the onus is put on the employer to show that they have thought about trying to accommodate and have actual reasons why to do so would be difficult. Such a level of duty does not lead to a high level of protection for staff, but does mean that religious interests can be granted some degree of protection at work. The duty provides a mechanism whereby the employee's religious interests can be considered by the employer, who may only reject them where there are other interests that clash with the religious interests.[58]

## Harassment

Within the US context, harassment is viewed as an aspect of discrimination. Although not directly defined in Title VII of the Civil Rights Act 1964, it has developed via its case law on sex discrimination into a well recognised form of

---

[58] The question of whether a duty to accommodate could be useful in the domestic context is discussed in the concluding chapter.

discrimination.[59] The development stems from the recognition that the creation of a hostile environment at work, if severe enough, can alter the conditions of employment and so amount to discrimination.

The concept of harassment comprises quid pro quo harassment and hostile environment harassment. Quid pro quo sexual harassment arises where a supervisor uses the acceptance or rejection of sexual advances as a basis for employment decisions. Although quid pro quo religious harassment may be less common than its counterpart based on sex, courts do take into account any potential abuse of position in assessing whether religious harassment is actionable.[60] This is especially the case with regard to proselytism at work. Proselytism, or seeking to convert others to a religious view, can give rise to harassment claims if it is pervasive and the proselytiser knows that it is unwelcome. Where it occurs between those of a similar rank it is less likely to be found to be harassing than where a manager tries to convert an employee or appears to attach weight to matters such as church attendance when assessing work performance.[61]

The other form of harassment, hostile environment harassment, consists of unwanted conduct on the basis of religion. The conduct must be severe and pervasive before it becomes actionable, but does not need to be so bad that it causes psychological injury. There is no concrete test of when behaviour will be sufficiently pervasive to constitute harassment, but circumstances such as severity, frequency, its effect on job performance and whether it is threatening or humiliating or merely offensive will be taken into account.[62] In terms of whether the harassment is wanted, the test is both subjective and objective: conduct must be offensive to the victim, and a reasonable person must also find it offensive. For example, in *Venters v City of Delphi*[63] the manager tried to convert Venters; he threatened that if she was not saved he would need to replace her, but let her know that if she came to his church she would have a chance to be saved. Later the threat of dismissal for not attending church was made explicit. The manager also criticised Venters' lifestyle, and made it clear that he thought her immoral. The Court held this could be harassment as his remarks were clearly intrusive and offensive, they touched on intimate matters of personal life and were unrelenting.

Clearly, in the context of religious harassment, a number of rights can conflict, such as a right to religious freedom which may include a right to proselytise, and rights to be free from harassment at work. For example, a religious employee could attempt to convert a non-religious colleague, but may offend him in the process. Despite the fact that religious freedom may involve a right to proselytise, this does not extend to improper proselytism. Courts have suggested that where attempts to convert colleagues are unwelcome and continue after it is clear they are unwelcome, such behaviour can amount to harassment. For example, in *Brown*

[59] *Meritor Savings Bank v Vinson* 477 US 57 (1986).
[60] See, for example, *Brown Transport Corp v Commonwealth* 133 Pa Comm 545, A 2d 555 (1990).
[61] *Venters v City of Delphi* 123 F 3d 956 (1997).
[62] See *Harris v Forklift Systems* 114 S Ct 367 (1993).
[63] Above n 61.

*Transport Corp v Commonwealth*[64] a Jewish employee objected to bible verses appearing on pay slips, and religious articles appearing in a company newsletter. The employee complained, and was later sacked. He successfully claimed that he was subject to religious harassment.[65] However, it has also been suggested in other cases that occasional prayers and references to religious belief would not be sufficient to amount to harassment.[66]

Religious harassment can also occur where speech which is not religious in nature offends others because of their religious beliefs. For example, sexually explicit comments could offend a religious person.[67] Additionally, harassment can occur where speech is motivated by religion but offends others on non-religious grounds, for example, discussion of abortion.[68] The fact that religious rights may compete with rights to freedom of speech in such situations has led to a debate in the USA over the scope of religious freedom and freedom of speech in cases of harassment.[69] There is little consensus, but it seems clear that matters of religious freedom and freedom of speech do need to be taken into account in assessing whether there is actionable harassment in religious cases. It would seem that where speech is hostile and knowingly directed at a victim, then harassment will be made out. Where speech is not directed at a victim, it is less likely to be actionable.

The requirement that harassment must be severe and pervasive to amount to discrimination seems to set a fairly high threshold for the level of offence to be caused before harassment is shown.[70] For example, behaviour such as disparaging verbal remarks, graffiti, and the placing of proselytising material in a workmate's locker, have been found to be highly inappropriate and offensive, but insufficient to amount, even collectively, to 'threatening or humiliating' conduct sufficient to found a harassment claim, even though the series of incidents also included an

---

[64] Above n 60. The case was brought under the Pennsylvania Human Relations Act, rather than Title VII.

[65] See also *Chalmers v Tulon Co of Richmond* 101 F 3d 1012 (4th Cir 1996), where Chalmers sent letters to colleagues saying that they had done immoral things and needed to repent: the employers did not need to accommodate this behaviour as it would involve harassment of other staff; and *Wilson v US West Communications* 58 F 3d 1337 (1995), where colleagues brought claims of harassment when Wilson wore a badge to work with a picture on it of an aborted foetus. The presence of harassment claims by other staff meant that Wilson's behaviour did not have to be accommodated.

[66] *Brown v Polk County* 61 F 3d 650 (8th Cir 1995).

[67] *Finnemore v Bangor Hydro-Electric Co* 645 A 2d 15, where a colleague continued to make sexually explicit remarks with the plaintiff's wife as the target, even though he had objected on religious grounds to the comments.

[68] *Wilson v US West Communications* above n 65.

[69] E Volokh, 'Freedom of Speech and Workplace Harassment' (1992) 39 *UCLA L R* 1791; K R Browne 'Title VII as Censorship: Hostile Environment Harassment and the First Amendment' (1991) 52 *Ohio St LJ* 481; S Sangree, 'Title VII Prohibitions Against Hostile Environment Sexual Harassment and the First Amendment: No Collision in Sight' (1995) 47 *Rutgers LR* 461; J M Balkin, 'Free Speech and Hostile Environments' (1999) 99 *Columbia LR* 2295; D Epstein, 'Can a "Dumb Ass Woman" Achieve Equality in the Workplace? Running the Gauntlet of Hostile Work Environment Harassing Speech' (1996) 84 *Georgetown LJ* 339.

[70] See also cases cited in J G Grisham, 'Religion at Work' (2006) 42 *Tenn BJ* 4 such as *Lundy v GMC* where symbols displayed at work which the plaintiff found sacreligious were not sufficiently pervasive or severe to amount to harassment even though aimed directly at the 'victim'. See also Jamar, above n 1, who suggests that offensive jokes and teasing are not sufficient to amount to harassment.

attempt by co-workers to back over the plaintiff with a fork-lift truck.[71] It is arguable that the 'severe and pervasive' requirement means that the focus of enquiry in US cases on harassment is on the actions of the harasser, rather than on the impact on the employee.[72]

It would seem that the protection against harassment available in the USA is more limited than that available under the rules that have been introduced in Europe under the Employment Equality Directive.[73] Although also framed in terms of the creation of a hostile environment, the Directive also covers the violation of dignity, which may make it somewhat easier to claim harassment, particularly where there is no intention to harass, or where harassment is based on the causing of offence. However, the more restrictive approach of the US courts may in fact be appropriate in the context of religious harassment. The interaction of rights to freedom of speech and rights to religious freedom for religious and non-religious staff means that religious harassment cases are particularly complex, with the potential for conflict between the rights of religious staff to religious freedom and the rights of other staff to freedom of speech and freedom from religion as well as rights to equality. It may be that restricting the reach of religious harassment claims is necessary in order to safeguard the interests of others members of staff.[74]

## Conclusion

Although the protection of harassment may be somewhat more restrictive than that in Europe, in other respects the protection for religious interests appears fairly extensive, comprising non-discrimination principles and a duty of accommodation. Certainly, the first hurdle for gaining legal protection against discrimination is set reasonably low. In terms of how to determine the existence of a religion, tests are fairly subjective: if the set of beliefs holds a place equivalent to mainstream religion in the life of the employee, then courts will accept that it is eligible for protection. However, the later hurdles are set much higher, with the result that the protection could be said to be fairly elusive. The broad duty to accommodate is coupled with a low level of hardship needed to override the duty. However, this is not necessarily a shortcoming. In effect, the duty of accommodation merely requires employers to have real reasons for restricting religious freedom. But where the protection of religious freedom interferes with the rights of others, those other rights tend to prevail.[75] This reflects the fact that accommodation is not

[71] *Bourini v Bridgestone Firestone North American Tire LLC* 136 Fed Appx 747 (2005). Cited in Grisham, above n 70.

[72] C Williams, '*Peterson v Hewlett Packard*: Exposing Title VII Inconsistencies in its Protection of Employees from Workplace Harassment' (2005) 83 *NCL Rev* 776.

[73] Art 2(3) Directive 2000/78.

[74] See discussion of the British law on religious harassment above at pp 145–152 and L Vickers, 'Is All Harassment Equal? The Case of Religious Harassment' (2006) 65(3) *CLJ* 579 for the argument that religious harassment may warrant a different level of protection than other forms of harassment.

[75] See J A Sonne, 'The Perils of Universal Accommodation: The Workplace Religious Freedom Act of 2003 and the Affirmative Action of 147,096,000 Souls' (2004) 79 *Notre Dame LR* 1023 at 1079: 'the

'free' but imposes a price on the accommodator. The provision of a duty to accommodate where to do so does no harm to others does at least give recognition that there is a place for religious interests at work, but the level of protection afforded is very limited.

There is an additional sense in which the protection of religious interests at work is more limited in the USA than in the UK. In the USA there is little scope for the argument that religious ethos employers should be treated differently from other employers, unless the employer is a religious organisation engaged in non-profit making activities for the organisation. Thus the special protection available in the UK to religious ethos employers,[76] and which extends to secular businesses run along religious lines, is not available in the USA.[77]

The US framework for protection of religious interests at work meets many of the demands of the model for protection of religious interests set out in chapter three above, in particular because of the existence of the duty to accommodate. However, it is arguable that the low level of hardship that has been accepted in the case law to override the duty to accommodate leaves employees with less protection than was recommended in the proposed model. In contrast, in the domestic framework, the question of the extent to which religion should be accommodated is framed as a question of proportionality. This approach provides greater scope for religious interests to be given protection within the work sphere, as it allows for the necessity of restrictions on religious freedom to be assessed in a more detailed and nuanced way, taking into account all the circumstances, rather than being overridden as soon as a countervailing interest is identified.

## II  Canada

The legal protection against discrimination in Canada is provided within a federal legal system. Protection is provided by equality provisions contained in the legislation of the relevant province, with all provinces, municipal and federal governments also being subject to the Canadian Charter of Rights and Freedoms, and the Canadian Human Rights Act,[78] which contain general non-discrimination

status quo mixture of nondiscrimination and "de minimis" accommodation (with anything beyond that being entirely voluntary) . . . best suits the relevant balance between individual religious rights and the common good . . . Employees are protected from irrational decisions based on matters arguably beyond their control, employers are afforded discretion appropriate to the operation of a free and fair market, the rights of coworkers are safeguarded, and the interests of church and state are addressed in a spirit of neutrality and equal treatment'.

[76] Reg 7(3) Employment Equality (Religion and Belief) Regulations 2003. Such protection is also available across the EU where it is based on the Employment Directive 2000/78.

[77] See Jamar, above n 1, for the argument that religious employers involved in a secular business should be given more freedom to take religion into account in employment decisions, in order to uphold the freedom of religious groups.

[78] RSC 1985, c H-6. The Canadian Human Rights Act has less impact as it only applies to the few federally regulated industries such as banking, shipping, federal public service, post office, etc.

guarantees. This means that the discrimination decisions of provincial courts are subject to appeal to the Supreme Court of Canada. Although this creates a number of different religious equality provisions, most follow the same basic model, having non-discrimination as the general principle, but providing some form of occupational exception.[79]

The wording of the various provisions differs, but it is arguable that this makes little difference to the outcome of cases.[80] For example, most commonly, non-discrimination provisions contain an occupational exception where there is a bona fide occupational requirement.[81] Some codes additionally impose a duty on the employer to accommodate religious difference, up to the point of undue hardship to the employer. In those provinces which do not have this additional duty, however, the duty is imported through the question of whether the occupational requirement is bona fide: if no reasonable accommodation has been made, then an occupational requirement will not be bona fide, and so will not provide an exception to the non-discrimination rule. Similarly, where a general 'reasonable and justifiable' defence is used, the question of whether there was an attempt to accommodate can be relevant to the question of justification.[82]

## Determining a Person's Religion

Canadian courts have taken a fairly subjective approach when determining a person's religion, allowing self-determination to individuals and groups in terms of their religious identity. Where the employee has a religious view which does not fit in with the official teaching of the religion which he espouses, it is the employee's personal religious views which have counted, rather than the views of the faith to

---

[79] This chapter will not consider any individual province's code, but will look more generally at the approach of Canadian courts to cases of religious discrimination. More detail, particularly on the separate provincial laws, can be found in W Tarnopolsky and W Pentney, *Discrimination and the Law* (Toronto, Carswell, 2005).

[80] See A Esau, ' "Islands of Exclusivity": Religious Organizations and Employment Discrimination' (1993) 33 *Univ British Columbia LR* 719 for an overview of the provisions of the different provincial codes.

[81] For example, Alberta's Humans Rights, Citizenship and Multiculturalism Act, RSA 2000, c H-14 7:

(1) No employer shall

    (a) refuse to employ or refuse to continue to employ any person, or

    (b) discriminate against any person with regard to employment or any term or condition of employment, because of the race, religious beliefs, colour, gender, physical disability, mental disability, marital status, age, ancestry, place of origin, family status or source of income of that person or of any other person . . .

(3) Subsection (1) does not apply with respect to a refusal, limitation, specification or preference based on a bona fide occupational requirement.

[82] See, for example, s 11 of the Alberta Act:

A contravention of this Act shall be deemed not to have occurred if the person who is alleged to have contravened the Act shows that the alleged contravention was reasonable and justifiable in the circumstances.

which he officially belongs. Thus, in *Re Funk and Manitoba Labour Board*,[83] where a Mennonite employee sought exemption from the employer's closed shop union agreement, the Labour Board was criticised for considering the fact that the Mennonite church itself did not teach that it was unacceptable to join a trade union. The employee's Mennonite faith gave rise to his personal religious objection to joining the union, and this was sufficient, regardless of whether he shared this view with other members of the same faith. Similarly, in *Hutterian Brethren of Wilson Colony v Alberta*,[84] the Court of Appeal of Alberta accepted as genuine the beliefs of the particular Hutterite community that they could not have their photographs taken for drivers' licences, even though others of the same faith did allow photographs in the circumstances.[85]

However, although courts will not question the sincerity of an individual's belief, they do draw a distinction similar to that drawn under the ECHR between religiously motivated behaviour and religiously required behaviour.[86] For example, in *Spellman v University of Windsor*[87] a Hindu member of staff's refusal to strike for an increase in pay was not motivated by a proscription in Hinduism on striking, but by a more personal conviction of anti-materialism. Here the failure to accommodate his behaviour was not religiously discriminatory as his behaviour was not religiously motivated.[88]

## Bona Fide Occupational Requirements and the Duty to Accommodate

Discrimination on grounds of religion is unlawful. An exception exists where there is a bona fide occupational requirement to be of the particular religion. In some provinces there is an explicit requirement on employers to accommodate the religious employee up to the point of undue hardship. Other provinces do not have an explicit requirement, but the overall protection is very similar: as the Supreme Court case law discussed below has made clear, there is an overarching duty to accommodate up to the point of undue hardship, and so the duty can be understood to form part of the common law.

---

[83] (1976) 66 DLR (3d).

[84] (2007) ABCA 160.

[85] *Ibid* at 118. The requirement for photographic ID was held to be constitutional, despite the infringement of the Hutterite's religious freedom, as long as accommodations identified by the court, which would minimise the effect of the requirement, could be offered. The case could be of relevance in cases involving photographic ID at work.

[86] *Arrowsmith v UK* [1978] 3 EHRR 218.

[87] *Spellman and the University of Windsor v The University of Windsor* [1979] Ontario Labour Relations Board Reports 458.

[88] Of course, the approach of the court in the case of *Re Funk* means that it should have been possible for Spellman to argue that although Hinduism itself may not prohibit striking, his understanding of the Hindu faith did require such a stance. In such a case, it would seem that the subjective view of religious belief expounded in *Re Funk* should prevail, and that an employee with a (personal) religiously motivated conscientious objection should be able to claim that the objection is religious in nature.

In effect, a defence to a discrimination claim arises where an employer imposes a prima facie discriminatory rule or standard for a purpose rationally connected to the purpose of the job, in good faith, in the belief that it was necessary to a legitimate work-based purpose, and that the rule or standard is reasonably necessary to accomplish the work-based purpose. In order to show that the rule or standard is necessary, it must be shown that the employer cannot accommodate the employee without undue hardship.[89] As a result of this legal structure, matters such as dress codes, working time and days off, which are dealt with as matters of indirect discrimination in the UK, have been dealt with in Canada using the rules concerning bona fide occupational requirements and the duty to accommodate.

## The Duty to Accommodate and Undue Hardship

Early Canadian cases took a similar approach to the USA, with the view that requiring that an employer bear anything more than a de minimis cost was 'undue hardship' (and therefore not required of an employer).[90] However, more recently courts have required employers to go further to accommodate religious practice,[91] while still acknowledging that it can be acceptable for the employee to bear some of the costs of religious practice. Factors that can be taken into account in assessing whether there is undue hardship include financial cost, disruption of a collective agreement, problems of morale of other employees, interchangeability of workforce and facilities, size of employer and the ease with which the workforce can be adapted.[92] Although the list of factors which can justify failure to accommodate is extensive, the Canadian duty to accommodate is much stronger than that in the USA. It can impose some considerable hardship on the employer, as long as it is not 'undue' hardship.

*Working Time*   In relation to requests for time off for religious observance (commonly, requests not to work on Friday evenings or Saturdays) the employee has to show that her religion *requires* compliance which is only possible with time off work, rather than that the desire for time off is inspired by a religious view.[93] Once a requirement is established, there is a duty to accommodate the practice. In *Chambly (Commission Scolaire Regionale) v Bergevin*[94] the school's requirement that Jewish staff should use unpaid leave to celebrate Yom Kipppur amounted to

---

[89]  *British Columbia (Public Service Employee Relations Comm) v BCGEU* [1999] 3 SCR 3 ('Meiorin') and confirmed in *British Columbia (Superintendent of Motor Vehicles) v British Columbia (Council of Human Rights)* [1999] 3 SCR 868 ('Gismer'). In some provinces, the exception only applies to religious organisations operating in a not-for-profit environment.

[90]  *Froese v Pine Creek School Division No 30*, M Rothstein QC, 28 December 1978 (Man Bd Adjud) (unreported).

[91]  *Central Okanagan School District No 23 v Renaud* [1992] 2 SCR 970, a case involving dismissal for refusing to work days designated as holy by the employee's religion.

[92]  *Central Alberta Dairy Pool v Alberta (Human Rights Commission)* [1990] 2 SCR 489.

[93]  Again, a distinction is drawn between religiously motivated behaviour and religiously mandated behaviour. *Cf Arrowsmith v UK* [1978] 3 EHRR 218.

[94]  [1994] 2 SCR 525.

a failure to accommodate. The court pointed out that the effect of the calendar, which recognises Christian holidays but not others, involves religious discrimination, and so a duty to accommodate arises.

However, the duty to accommodate is mutual, and employees may need to accommodate employers as well. This point was made in *Renaud*,[95] which involved dismissal for refusing to work on days that were viewed by the employee as religious. The court referred to the fact that accommodation is a multi-party exercise: on the employer's part this may require flexibility. For example, the fact that the employer operates a standardised leave policy will not be sufficient to provide a defence in a discrimination case. Moreover, the court also commented that although considerations as to the effect on employee morale may be relevant, such considerations should be applied with caution. The fact that an accommodation may be unpopular with others in the workplace is not sufficient of itself to amount to undue hardship. The court pointed out that to decide otherwise would enable an employer to contract out of its human rights obligations as long as other employees are '*ad idem*' with the employer on the issue.

The courts recognise that equality is not achieved in the context of working time by treating all groups the same, especially in a context where most work calendars are supportive of Christian religious observance. In this respect the Canadian approach can be contrasted with that in the USA, with its de minimis standard of hardship which can override the duty of accommodation. In the US cases, failure to accommodate could be justified by the undue hardship caused by overturning established means of allocating shifts.

Although the Canadian approach requires much more in terms of accommodation than the US, the duty to accommodate does have clear limits. In *O'Malley*[96] the non-discrimination principle did not require that religious adherence be cost-free for the employee. The case involved a long-serving employee who had become a Seventh Day Adventist and who was therefore no longer able to work from sunset on Friday until sunset on Saturday, and had to move to part-time status. The Supreme Court took the view that the employer had not shown that it had taken reasonable steps to accommodate O'Malley's religious practices:

> The duty in a case of adverse effect discrimination on the basis of religion or creed is to take reasonable steps to accommodate the complainant, short of undue hardship: in other words, to take such steps as may be reasonable to accommodate without undue interference in the operation of the employer's business and without undue expense to the employer.[97]

In this case, there was no evidence of any attempt by the employer to accommodate save by offering part-time hours. At the same time the Court pointed out that where the employer has gone to sufficient effort to accommodate an employee, it

---

[95] *Central Okanagan School District No 23 v Renaud* above n 91.
[96] *Ontario Human Rights Commission and O'Malley v Simpsons-Sear* [1985] 2 SCR 536.
[97] *Ibid* para 23.

is not unreasonable for some cost to be put on the employee, who may be faced with the option of choosing employment or full religious observance.

*Work Tasks*    A number of specific exceptions allow staff to refuse to undertake certain work tasks. For example, professional bodies, such as physicians, make explicit allowance for their members to conscientiously object to performing abortions, and section 3 of the Civil Marriage Act recognises that officials of religious groups are free to refuse to perform marriages that are not in accordance with their religious beliefs.

In more general terms, the question will be dealt with as a matter of accommodation. The question of whether an employer must accommodate an employee's refusal to undertake certain tasks, on religious grounds, arose in *Moore v British Columbia (Ministry of Social Services)*.[98] The case involved the dismissal of a financial aid worker, Moore, for refusing to grant a client financial aid for an abortion, because of religious objections to abortion. The Human Rights Council decided that as the employer had taken no steps to accommodate her religious views, Moore had suffered religious discrimination. For example, requests of the type refused by Moore were relatively infrequent, and other workers could have been asked to deal with them. What is interesting about the case is that, although it was suggested that Moore should have removed herself from the client's case (rather than taking it on and then refusing assistance), it does not place much responsibility on the employee to avoid the problem of clashes between religious scruple and compliance with the employer's reasonable job requirements.[99] The issue was not discussed because it was clear that no attempt to accommodate had been made. However, it may well be that in some cases the onus will pass to the employee not to undertake work which he or she is unable fully to perform on religious grounds.

*Dress Codes*    As a general rule, the duty to accommodate should extend to dress codes, unless there is a clear job-related purpose for a restriction on religious dress. In *Bhinder v Canadian National Railway*[100] a Sikh maintenance technician who wore a turban refused to wear a hard hat at work. The employer's requirement that he should wear a hard hat was found to be a bona fide requirement, and there was no need for his religious dress code to be accommodated. Since *Bhinder*, the requirement for motorcyclists to wear a helmet has been modified to accommodate Sikhs, based in part on the fact that the cost involved (that is, the greater likelihood of severe injury in the event of a crash) is largely borne by the person accommodated.[101] Although the case did not arise in the employment context, it suggests a greater willingness on the part of courts to require accommodation of

---

    [98]  (1992) 17 CHRR D/426.
    [99]  See W Tarnopolsky and W Pentney, *Discrimination and the Law* (Toronto, Carswell, 2001) para 6.2(d).
    [100]  [1985] 2 SCR 561.
    [101]  *Dhillon v British Columbia (Ministry of Transportation and Highways)* (1999) 35 CHRR D/293.

dress codes. However, this obligation still only arises where there is no undue hardship. Where a no-beard rule had a legitimate health and safety explanation, involving the health and safety of others, the failure to adapt the rule to accommodate a Sikh employee was not discriminatory as health and safety concerns prevail over religious interests.[102]

## Religion: A Bona Fide Occupational Requirement?

In order for an employer to show that being of a particular religion or belief is a bona fide occupational requirement, the employer will need to show that there is a legitimate reason for imposing a religious requirement on the job, in terms of the effect of religion on the ability of a person to perform the job. The employer must then demonstrate that the religious requirement was imposed honestly and in good faith in the belief that it was necessary, and that it would impose undue hardship on the employer to be forced to employ those not meeting the religious requirement. Where the employer has no link to a religious group it will be very difficult to meet this standard, except in fairly distinct and restricted circumstances where the job is clearly of a religious nature, such as a role as a religious chaplain in a secular hospital. Where the employer is religious in ethos, either because the employer is a religious organisation, or because it is owned and run by a religious individual, different considerations apply.

### Religious Employers

In addition to the general bona fide occupational requirement exception, some provinces have additional exceptions that apply to religious employers, but practice differs across provinces. For example, Ontario provides an exception to the non-discrimination principle for religious bodies, as well as philanthropic, educational, fraternal or social institutions where there is a bona fide occupational qualification because of the nature of the job.[103] British Columbia, Nova Scotia, Newfoundland and Prince Edward Island all contain similar exceptions, but they are limited to the non-profit making activities of religious groups.[104]

The varied levels of protection available in different provinces for religious organisations illustrates that there is no uniform Canadian approach to the question of whether a religious group can impose religious requirements on staff. However, it is of significance that where provinces do allow religious bodies to impose religious requirements on staff, they have not been struck down by the

---

[102] *Pannu v Skeena Cellulose Inc* (2000) 38 CHRR D/494. The employee was responsible for shutting down a kiln in the event of a gas leak, and this job required him to wear a close-fitting mask, for which he needed to be clean shaven. It was agreed that exempting *Pannu* from the 'no beards' rule would put other workers at risk.

[103] eg, Ontario Human Rights Code 1990 s 24(1)(a).

[104] Nova Scotia Human Rights Act 1989 s 6(c)(iii) and s 6d; Newfoundland Human Rights Code 1990 s 9(6)(a); and Prince Edward Island Human Rights Act 1988 s 6(4)(c).

Supreme Court as incompatible with the Canadian Charter, regardless of whether they are limited to non-profit activity. This suggests that it is accepted under the Charter that exceptions of either type can be compatible with human rights norms.

Courts have upheld the use of religious requirements for jobs where religion is a defining aspect of the job. They have also upheld the imposition of requirements on 'non-defining' support jobs such as administrators and ancillary staff. For example, in *Schroen v Steinbach Bible College*,[105] which involved the dismissal of an accounts clerk in a Mennonite college, a religious requirement was upheld for a non-religious post. Schroen had applied for the job knowing that the requirement was for a Mennonite, and had not disclosed that although she was brought up as a Mennonite (and could relate to the students and their religious beliefs) she had become a Mormon. Not only did she not disclose her new faith, she even affirmed the College statement of faith when applying for the job. Even though Mrs Schroen was not teaching students at the college, her job involved interacting with them, making herself available to talk with them about her faith, participating in college functions, etc. Given the particular religious nature of the Bible college, the court decided that it was reasonable for all staff, teaching and support staff, to share the same faith.

## Religious Requirements that Discriminate on Other Grounds

Courts have had to consider cases where allowing religious occupational require-ments can lead to discrimination on other protected grounds. In *Caldwell v St Thomas Aquinas High School*[106] a Catholic school did not renew the contract of a Catholic teacher, Mrs Caldwell, after she had married a divorced Methodist man in a civil ceremony. Although the school employed non-Catholics, and would not have objected to non-Catholic staff entering such a marriage, Mrs Caldwell was dismissed because she was Catholic and her actions were incompatible with Catholic teaching on divorce. She claimed that this treatment was discriminatory on grounds of religion and marital status. The school argued that she was not rehired as she lacked a bona fide qualification for the job, that of being in good standing in the church. This requirement was imposed in good faith in the belief that it was necessary for upholding the special nature of the school where the teachers led the pupils by example. The Supreme Court of Canada held that the school was entitled to impose the faith requirement, and so could discriminate against her for her failure to comply with the requirement. The Court acknowl-edged that this case involved conflicting rights, but the decision contains little by way of discussion of the implications of the decision for her, and the impact of the discrimination on grounds of marital status.

Similar decisions have been made in other cases involving dismissal for failure to live up to moral standards set by the religious group. For example, in *Garrod v*

---

[105] (1999) 35 Canadian Human Rights Reports D/477 Ontario Board of Inquiry CHRR D/1.
[106] (1984) 2 SCR 603.

*Rhema Christian School*[107] a teacher in a Christian school was dismissed for having an extra-marital affair. The Board of Inquiry again acknowledged the clash of rights, but viewed the existence of a genuine occupational qualification as a 'tie-breaker', allowing the religious rights of the employer to require its staff to lead exemplary Christian lives to trump the rights of the employee not to be discriminated against on grounds of marital status. In this case, the employee had assented to the school's 'exemplary' life requirement, and this may have influenced the decision.

Despite these decisions allowing religious organisations to set standards of behaviour which discriminate against staff on other grounds, the courts have not always been ready to find such requirements necessary to the job. In *Parks v Christian Horizons*[108] a carer in a group home run by a Christian organisation was dismissed for being involved in an extra-marital relationship. The tribunal held that this was not justified. The religious requirement (not to live in a relationship outside marriage) had not been made plain to the assistant; it was not contained in the contract of employment; and the employing organisation had not acted consistently on the issue in the past. These factors suggested that the religious requirement was not so fundamental to the employer as to justify dismissal.[109]

In these cases, the context in which the dismissals took place means that the requirement to conform to a religious lifestyle is rationally connected to the performance of the job and arguably necessary to accomplish a legitimate work-based purpose[110]: teachers in a school and carers in a home perform jobs which are fundamental and defining to the organisation's purposes, and so a religious organisation may impose religious requirements on such staff. What is less clear from the cases is how to deal with clashes between non-discrimination rights. In these cases, such issues were not discussed explicitly.

One case, in which a clash, between the right to religious freedom and the right not to be discriminated against on grounds of sexual orientation, arose explicitly is worth considering as an illustration of how the clash was resolved by the Supreme Court of Canada, even though it does not involve employment discrimination. In *Trinity Western University v College of Teachers*[111] a college had a Statement of Community Standards to which all students signed up, including a commitment to refrain from 'biblically condemned' sins of pre-marital sexual activity, adultery and homosexual sex. The college sought accreditation for its teacher training course with the British Columbia College of Teachers, accreditation which would allow its graduates to teach in local schools. Accreditation was refused, as the British Columbia College of Teachers viewed Trinity Western University as institutionally discriminatory against homosexuals, and believed there was a real risk that

[107] (1991) 15 Canadian Human Rights Reports D/477 Ontario Board of Inquiry.
[108] *Ibid.*
[109] It may also be that the care context was treated differently from the education context, although this is not explicit in the case.
[110] ie, it complies with the test in *Meiorin*, above n 89.
[111] (2001) SCR 772.

teachers trained there would bring discriminatory attitudes into the classroom. The college appealed, and the Supreme Court found in its favour on the basis that there was no evidence that individual students had acted in a discriminatory manner. Signing up to a generalised statement in support of a position did not mean that the individual necessarily acted according to the statement. Without concrete evidence of a negative stance taken by individual students towards homosexuality, the students' freedom of religion should be respected. If an individual student held negative views which were communicated to students, then this may be treated differently, but a generalised refusal to accredit all students from the college was discriminatory on grounds of religion. If allowed, it could allow all members of denominations such as Baptists to be prevented from teaching, because of the stance of the denomination to homosexuality.

The Court pointed out that freedom of religion co-exists with freedom from discrimination on grounds of sexuality. Neither right trumps, and so individuals should be free to retain their views on sexuality, and even to denounce it, as long as a line was not crossed between belief and conduct. For example, it would be acceptable to restrain the denunciation of homosexuality if it amounted to hate speech. The students at Trinity Western University had not crossed this line, and should be able to enter the workplace, and retain their freedom to believe as they wished. In contrast, in *Ross v New Brunswick School District No 15*[112] the dismissal of a teacher with racist anti-semitic views was justified because his vehement anti-semitism was very public, involving many public and media appearances. He had caused a poisoned work atmosphere, and had crossed the line between belief and practice.

These cases indicate that the Canadian courts will contemplate upholding occupational requirements that discriminate on other grounds, as long as the requirement can be viewed as reasonably necessary to the religious ethos of the organisation.[113] *Caldwell*[114] and *Garrod*[115] are both cases where the courts allowed religious employers to introduce requirements which discriminated on the prohibited ground of marital status. Even though in Caldwell's case there were many other non-Catholic staff in the school, a factor that may have suggested that the requirement to be a fully observant Catholic was not necessary to the job, this did not prevent a finding that it was acceptable for the school to make that requirement of the Catholic staff. However, in both the cases the employers were able to demonstrate satisfactorily that the requirement was sufficiently important to them. In contrast, in *Parks*[116] the failure to emphasise the religious requirement

[112] (1996) 1 SCR 825.
[113] Note that in *Vriend v Alberta* [1998] 1 SCR 493 the Supreme Court was asked to consider whether the dismissal of a gay employee from a religious school offended the equality principle in the Canadian Charter of Rights and Freedoms. The decision related to the failure of the province of Alberta to protect against discrimination on grounds of sexual orientation. The question of whether the employer could have raised a bona fide occupational requirement defence was not considered by the Court.
[114] Above n 106.
[115] Above n 107.
[116] *Ibid.*

(of 'biblical living') at the time of hiring suggested that the requirement was not in fact viewed as essential by the employer.

## Conclusion

In terms of the amount of effort required of employers to accommodate religious practices at work, the Canadian courts put the onus on both parties to compromise. Employers are required to do more than merely state that there is some impact upon their business: they can be required to tolerate some level of inconvenience or expense. To this extent, the approach in Canada can be contrasted with that in the USA. The Canadian courts have recognised equally that it is acceptable to allow some cost on the employee's part, thus achieving a reasonable balance between the interests of the religiously observant employee and the needs of the employer.

The approach of the Canadian courts to religious employers can be contrasted with the approach elsewhere in the world. A fair amount of freedom is given to religious groups to act as employers and to impose religious requirements on their staff. The Canadian framework thus provides greater protection to religious employers than that available in the USA.[117] In Canada, the religious interests of employers appear to be given greater protection: discrimination on other grounds can be allowed in order to enable the religious needs of the employer to be met.[118] Moreover, the Canadian courts seem prepared to take an 'organic' view of the workplace,[119] allowing for the fact that groups of workers may view the workplace as a form of church where they worship together through the performance of their jobs, and so allowing bona fide occupational requirements to apply even where religion is not integral to the job function.[120] In the religious sphere, groups can operate in an exclusive manner, without offending against the human rights norms upheld by the Supreme Court.[121]

It is interesting to note that different levels of protection for religious employers are available in different provinces, with some limiting protection to non-profit activities of religious organisations. The fact that some protect only non-profit organisations, and others a broader range of religious employers, is striking, particularly as it was suggested above that the question of the extent to which religious discrimination by religious bodies should be tolerated should be determined to some extent by this criterion. In the discussion of proportionality in chapter three it was suggested that where groups wish to engage economically with the rest of society it was acceptable to require them to respect the dignity and equality interests of others. Where they had retreated from mainstream society,

[117] See discussion at pp 183–185 above.
[118] *Caldwell* (1984) above n 106.
[119] *Esau* above n 80. See discussion in ch 3 above.
[120] *Schroen* above n 105.
[121] *Esau* above n 80.

and were not engaging in such a way with the rest of society, then allowing discrimination against others might be acceptable in order to uphold the religious freedom of the group. This approach suggests that the question of whether or not a religious group is engaged in profit making activity may be of significance in determining where the balance may lie between religious freedom and freedom from discrimination. Yet, within the Canadian jurisprudence, provincial codes which restrict protection to non-profit activity are compatible with the Canadian Charter of Rights and Freedoms and the Canadian Human Rights Act, and so are those which allow protection to economic activity.

This suggests that according to the Canadian understanding of religious freedom the issue of economic interaction with society is not of defining importance: both approaches can be acceptable. Special protection for religious groups to act as employers and to maintain a religious ethos among staff is compatible with human rights norms; but equally, religious freedom does not demand such protection for religious groups, and codes that restrict protection to not-for-profit activity are also compatible with the provisions of the Human Rights Act and Charter.

# III  Europe

Non-discrimination in employment on grounds of religion is governed in the European Union by the Employment Equality Directive 2000/78. The main provisions of the Directive have been referred to in the discussion in the previous chapter of the implementation of its terms in the UK. Although all members of the EU are bound to comply with the terms of the Directive, implementation has not been uniform and a number of states have introduced exceptions to the protection provided in the Directive. The variance in state practice is perhaps not surprising given the very different historical contexts into which the religious non-discrimination principle has been introduced. For example, in Germany, religious bodies are long established in the provision of public services such as health care, whereas in France there is a long tradition of *laïcité* or secularism in the public sector.

In this section, the position in a number of EU states will be discussed, and the extent to which they accord with the requirements of the Directive highlighted.[122] In particular, there seems to be a common practice of exempting religious bodies from the need to comply with the provisions of the Directive. The ways in which this has been done vary, but it is arguable that where exceptions are too broad in their scope they will fail adequately to implement the Directive. Although a number of matters will be considered in what follows, particular attention will be given

---

[122] For more detail on the implementation of the Directive in the EU see L Vickers, *Religion and Belief in Employment—The EU Law* (European Commission, 2007).

to the question of whether religious ethos organisations are provided with additional protection, and whether they are excepted from the obligation to refrain from discrimination on other grounds. In addition, the varied approach of EU states to the question of dress codes and the wearing of religious symbols will be considered.

## Directive 2000/78[123]

Under the Employment Equality Directive, protection against religious discrimination is introduced as part of a single approach to equality. The Directive was introduced under the general non-discrimination provisions of Article 13 of the EC Treaty.[124] This provides authority for the EU to legislate on a number of grounds, religion forming part of a longer list. The list contains no hierarchy. Indeed, the early decisions of the ECJ interpreting legislation introduced under a different ground reinforce the idea of a common understanding of equality and the need for common standards to be introduced across the different equality grounds.[125] The difficulties that this may create were highlighted in the discussion of justification in the previous chapter.

The Directive prohibits direct discrimination, which is defined as less favourable treatment on grounds of religion or belief. Direct discrimination is not limited to less favourable treatment on the grounds of a victim's own religion or belief. It would therefore cover treatment based on a person's association with people of a particular religion (eg, discrimination against someone married to a member of a religious group). The definition of direct discrimination does not provide any general exceptions or justifications,[126] but some specific exceptions exist. First, under the Directive, where a measure is 'necessary for public security, for maintenance of public order . . . and for the protection of the rights and freedoms of others', a general exception to the non-discrimination principle can be made.[127] Second, an exception exists where, because of the particular occupational activities or the context in which they are carried out, a religious characteristic is a genuine and determining occupational requirement, provided that the objective is legitimate and the

---

[123] References are made in this section to the law and practice of Member States. Details have been drawn from the Country Reports produced by the European Network of Legal Experts in the non-discrimination field (on the grounds of Race or Ethnic origin, Age, Disability, Religion or belief and Sexual Orientation). The network is established and managed by Human European Consultancy, Netherlands and the Migration Policy Group, Belgium. Reports can be found at <http://ec.europa.eu/employment_social/fundamental_rights/policy/aneval/legnet_en.htm#coun> accessed 3 January 2008.

[124] Note that in *Mangold v Helm* C-144/04 [2005] ECR I-9981the ECJ held that non-discrimination is a principle of Community law, and that the Directive merely lays down a framework to combat discrimination. L Waddington, 'Recent Developments and the Non-Discrimination Directives: *Mangold and More*' (2006) 13 *Maastricht Journal of European and Comparative Law* 365.

[125] *Chacón Navas v Eurest Colectividades SA* (2006) C-13/05 at para 40. See ch 5 above.

[126] In relation to sex discrimination, the ECJ in *Dekker v Stichting Vormingscentrum voor Jong Volwassenen (VJV-Centrum) Plus* [1990] ECR I-3941 confirmed that direct discrimination cannot be justified.

[127] Art 2(5).

requirement is proportionate.[128] Third, a slightly wider exception exists where the employer is a church or an organisation the ethos of which is based on religion or belief. Under this exception religious foundations, such as hospitals run with a religious ethos, can require that members of staff are loyal to that ethos. This is the case even though sharing a religious belief may not be an essential requirement for carrying out the core duties of the job. For example, a religious medical practice might require all partners to share a particular religion, even though religious belief is not an essential requirement for carrying out medical duties. The Directive explicitly states that any religious requirement imposed by a religious ethos organisation must not entail discrimination on any other ground.[129]

The Directive also prohibits indirect discrimination, 'where an apparently neutral provision, criterion or practice would put persons of a particular religion or belief . . . at a particular disadvantage compared with other persons' unless it can be justified.[130] Indirect discrimination is capable of justification where the practice or criterion can be objectively justified by a legitimate aim and the means of achieving the aim are appropriate and necessary.[131] The question of justification is left to domestic courts, and it is not clear what types of factor will be accepted as justification. For example, the Danish Supreme Court[132] allowed an employer to justify clothing guidelines in order to create a religiously neutral workplace, but it is unclear whether such an interpretation is consistent with the Directive. It would be unlikely that such business-related reasoning would be acceptable in relation to sex discrimination,[133] and it is as yet unclear whether a uniform standard of justification is to be adopted across all strands of discrimination law in the EU.
The Directive also prohibits harassment, defined as unwanted conduct related to religion and belief with the purpose or effect of violating the dignity of a person and of creating an intimidating, hostile, degrading, humiliating or offensive environment.[134] Victimisation is also prohibited.[135]

## Definition of Religion

The Directive does not define the term 'religion or belief', and most Member States have also declined to define the term in their implementing legislation. However, some states have definitions for other specific purposes, such as constitutional protections and tax exemptions. Thus the Netherlands distinguishes in its case law between religion and belief, on the basis that for religion a 'high authority' ('God') is central. Thus Rastafarianism has been classified as a

---

[128] Art 4(1).
[129] Art 4(2). Any requirement as to religion or belief must constitute a genuine, legitimate and justified occupational requirement, having regard to the organisation's ethos. Note that, unlike for the general exception in Art 4(1), the requirement does not have to be 'determining'.
[130] Art 2(2).
[131] Art 2(2)(b).
[132] Decision 21 January 2005, 22/2004.
[133] *Bilka-Kaufhaus v Weber von Hartz* [1986] ECR 1607–1631 [1986] ECR 1607.
[134] Art 2(3).
[135] Art 11.

religion,[136] but not Bhagwan Shree Rajneesh philosophy, which is instead a 'philosophy of life'.[137] In German constitutional law religion is understood to mean any specific certainty as regards the whole of the world and the origin and purpose of mankind which gives sense to human life and the world, and which transcends the world.[138] The Federal Constitutional Court has also accepted some groups as self-evidently religious, such as the Bahá'í, relying on current trends in society, cultural tradition and the understanding of religion in general and in religious science.[139] In the law transposing the European Directives, approved in August 2006, protection extends to religion and other consciously held beliefs, but these terms are not further defined.

The Directive protects belief as well as religion, and this may help overcome some issues of definition, including the question of whether atheism is included.[140] However, it may just shift the location of any debate to the divide between religions and beliefs of sufficient seriousness to warrant protection, and those beliefs which are not, as beliefs are only likely to be protected if, in the words of the ECtHR, they 'attain a certain level of cogency, seriousness, cohesion and importance'.[141] Such restrictions are reflected in some implementing legislation in Member States. Thus, for example, in Austria the explanatory notes to the implementing legislation state that:

> the term 'belief' is tightly connected with the term 'religion' . . . Belief is a system of interpretation consisting of personal convictions concerning the basic structure, modality and functions of the world; it is not a scientific system. As far as beliefs claim completeness, they include perceptions of humanity, views of life, and morals.[142]

In the Netherlands the term 'philosophy of life' (*levensovertuiging*) is used in place of 'belief' (*overtuiging*), in order to place limitations on the type of belief that can be covered. The term 'philosophy of life' requires a coherent set of ideas about fundamental aspects of human existence. It includes broad philosophies such as humanism, but does not extend to more general views about society.

Political opinion does not seem to be covered by the Directive itself, but a variation in practice and expectation can be found on the protection of political beliefs across the EU.[143] The differences in treatment are likely to give rise to

---

[136] Equal Treatment Commission Opinion 2005–162.

[137] Equal Treatment Commission Opinion 2005–67.

[138] Definition from the Federal German Constitutional Court: BVerwGE (Decisions of the Federal Administrative Court) 90, 112 (115).

[139] BVerfGE 83, 341 (353). See Country Report, Germany, European Network of Legal Experts in the non-discrimination field (Human European Consultancy, Migration Policy Group, 2006).

[140] Atheism is included in the protection of the ECHR: *Angelini v Sweden* (1988) 10 EHRR 123 (Eur Comm HR).

[141] *X, Y and Z v UK* (1982) 31 DR 50, and *Campbell and Cosans v UK* (1982) 4 EHRR 293.

[142] Explanatory notes of the amended Equal Treatment Act, Country Report, Austria, European Network of Legal Experts in the non-discrimination field (Human European Consultancy, Migration Policy Group, 2006).

[143] Protection for political opinion can be found in Belgium, Cyprus, Czech Republic, Denmark, Estonia, Finland, France, Hungary, Italy, Latvia, Luxembourg, Malta, the Netherlands, Poland, Portugal, Slovenia, Spain and the UK (Northern Ireland only). The remaining Member States do not provide specific protection for political opinion.

several difficulties, not least inconsistency as between Member States.[144] Moreover, at times it may be difficult to determine the borders between beliefs and political beliefs as well as between religions and political beliefs. Some political beliefs, such as communism, might be capable of meeting the criteria for philosophies of life; others may be more clearly political, such as views on taxation. Beliefs on matters such as abortion could be classified as religious, or political or just general 'beliefs'.

## Determining an Individual's Religion or Belief

The Directive is drafted in general terms, and does not provide guidance on how to determine a person's religion, nor does it deal with questions such as whether there can be discrimination within one religious tradition. However, although not expressly addressed, it is likely that interpretation will accord with the case law of the ECtHR which recognises that the state does not have the power to assess the legitimacy of individual religious beliefs,[145] and requires states to ensure that conflicting groups tolerate each other, even where they originated in the same group.[146] Thus the fact that some groups identify themselves as being separate from others within the same religion should be recognised within the Directive. This approach is taken in the Netherlands, where case law from the Equal Treatment Commission suggests that individuals can still be counted as holding a religion or belief, even though they dissent from a majority religious view.[147]

## Potentially Indirectly Discriminatory Requirements

*Dress Codes*    The imposition of uniforms at work or other restrictions on dress can be potentially indirectly discriminatory, as they can put at a particular disadvantage those whose religions impose an alternative, incompatible, dress code. Although there is no duty to accommodate religious dress under the Directive, uniforms which are not compatible with religious practice may indirectly discriminate unless they can be justified by a legitimate aim, and the means of achieving the aim are appropriate and necessary.

The practice of allowing restrictions on what can be worn at work varies significantly between Member States. The country with perhaps the clearest approach is

---

[144] For example, recognition of scientology as a religion is not consistent across the EU. It is recognised in Italy (Country Report Italy, European Network of Legal Experts in the non-discrimination field (Human European Consultancy, Migration Policy Group, 2006)) but not in Germany (Federal Labour Court, *Bundesarbeitsgericht* 22 March 1995, *Neue Juristische Wochenschrift* 1996, 143, Country Report Germany, European Network of Legal Experts in the non-discrimination field (Human European Consultancy, Migration Policy Group, 2005)).

[145] However, see *Kosteski v The Former Yugoslav Republic of Macedonia* [2006] ECHR 403, where the ECtHR accepted that investigations as to whether an employee in fact held a particular belief were not inappropriate in the context of an employment dispute.

[146] *Metropolitan Church of Bessarabia v Moldova* Application No 45701/99, 13 December 2001.

[147] Opinion 2004/148, 2004/129. Country Report Netherlands, European Network of Legal Experts in the non-discrimination field (Human European Consultancy, Migration Policy Group, 2006).

France,[148] where there is a strict policy of *laïcité*[149] in the state sector.[150] This applies to workers in the civil service[151] and to education. In relation to schools, the Law on the Application of the Principle of Secularity in Public Schools was adopted on 15 March 2004. Discreet signs are allowed, but ostensible manifestation of religion through clothing or other signs is prohibited, in particular those by which one is immediately identified by his or her religious beliefs such as the Islamic veil, the kippa or a cross of manifestly excessive dimension.[152] The restriction applies to all religions, but it causes particular difficulties for Jews and Muslims, as their symbols would appear always to be banned, whereas crosses are only banned when their size is 'manifestly excessive'. Beyond education, the principle of secularism also applies to public sector employment, on the basis that civil servants must be religiously neutral and be seen to be so. Although the formal ban on wearing the headscarf applies only in the public sector, headscarves are also banned at times in the private sector, and these bans can be upheld on the basis of business need.[153] It is doubtful whether these rules meet the requirements for justification included within the Directive, and it may be that the broad ban on wearing of headscarves in the public service in France could be challenged under the Directive.[154] Although there is a legitimate aim of *laïcité* behind the ban on religious dress, it may not meet the standard of proportionality required, in particular because it is so broad in its scope. The need for proportionality requires that any ban be objectively justified, and that the means used to achieve the legitimate aim be appropriate and necessary.[155] This in turn requires that any action taken is no more than is necessary to achieve the legitimate aim. It is arguable, for example, that a ban on religious dress among administrative staff who do not meet the public is unnecessarily restrictive of religious freedom, even though it may serve the legitimate aim of secularism, particularly given the fact that its effects are felt unequally as between religions.

Although the ban on religious dress in the French public sector may be difficult to justify under the Directive, it is interesting to note that headscarf bans have been

[148] See D McGoldrick, *Human Rights and Religion: The Islamic Headscarf Debate in Europe* (Oxford, Hart Publishing, 2006).

[149] There is no precise translation of the term, but the phrase 'secularism' is used as an approximate translation.

[150] The ban does not apply in the private sector: see CA Paris 19/06/2003, *Dallila Tahri v Téléperformance France*, appeal from the Conseil de Prud'hommes (Labour Court of Paris) 17 December 2002, RG No 0203547, where an employee dismissed for refusing to take off her headscarf obtained, on the basis of L122-45LC, the annulment of her dismissal and damages amounting to wages for the entire period and moral damages as well as reintegration in her employment (Country Report France, European Network of Legal Experts in the non-discrimination field (Human European Consultancy, Migration Policy Group, 2006)).

[151] Conseil d'Etat, 3 May 2000, Mlle Marteaux No 217017; Conseil d'Etat, 15 October 2003, No 244428. See also K Berthou, 'The Issue of the Voile in the Workplace in France: Unveiling Discrimination' (2005) 21 *IJCLLIR* 281.

[152] The administrative instruction of 18 May 2004, Circulaire No 2004-084.

[153] For examples, see Berthou, above n 151.

[154] *Ibid.*

[155] Art 2(2)(b).

imposed by various employers across Europe, and in most cases challenges in domestic courts and before the European Court of Human Rights have been unsuccessful. Those that have been successful have usually turned on procedural issues or matters of proof, rather than being decisions based on the principle that religious dress can be worn by right. The approach of the ECtHR suggests that bans on wearing religious dress will continue to be lawful under the Directive when imposed by individual employers, particularly where there is a justification, based on the particular circumstances of the employer. For example, in *Dahlab v Switzerland*[156] the ECtHR decided that a restriction on the headscarf was proportionate in relation to teaching young children, where the teacher had influence on the intellectual and emotional development of children. Similarly, in Belgium, a ban on wearing headscarves in a school was challenged as a breach of freedom of religion.[157] On the question of whether the ban complied with Article 9(2) ECHR the Antwerp Court noted that the ban was precise and accessible; that it pursued the legitimate aims of preserving order in the teaching institution and of protecting the rights of others, in particular against unwanted proselytism; and that the restriction to the freedom of religion of the applicants was narrowly tailored to achieve that objective, so that it met the requirement of necessity.[158] A similar ban was upheld by the Danish Supreme Court,[159] justified on the basis that the employer wished to create a religiously neutral workplace.

In Germany, prior to the transposition of the Directives,[160] the Federal Labour Court held that the dismissal of a salesperson based on the wearing of a headscarf was invalid[161]; and the Federal Constitutional Court held that a schoolteacher must not be denied employment on grounds of wearing a headscarf. However, the decisions are fact specific and do not suggest that the wearing of headscarves should generally be allowed. The Federal Labour Court case was influenced by the fact that the employer had not shown any actual financial loss caused by the wearing of the headscarf: if the employer had been able to show actual loss, the decision to ban the headscarf might have been upheld. The case in the Federal Constitutional Court was decided on procedural grounds: a ban could equally well be constitutional, as long as it was provided for in legislation.[162] In effect, the German case law suggests that proper procedural processes are necessary to impose a ban on religious clothing, and that where this has been done, such a ban will not necessarily infringe religious freedom.[163]

---

[156] App No 42393/98, decision 15 February 2001.

[157] A claim was also made that the ban breached the Directive, but the claim was not upheld on this basis as the Court found that education was outside the scope of Directive and the implementing legislation: judgment, 14 June 2005, delivered by the Antwerp Court of Appeals (Hof van Beroep te Antwerpen, AR/2004/2811).

[158] Country Report Belgium, European Network of Legal Experts in the non-discrimination field (Human European Consultancy, Migration Policy Group, 2006),

[159] Decision, 21 January 2005, 22/2004,

[160] Transposition was by a law approved on 10 August 2006.

[161] Federal Labour Court, 10 October 2002, 2 AZR 472/01,

[162] Federal Constitutional Court, 2 BvR 1436/02.

[163] See M Mahlmann, 'Religious Tolerance, Pluralist Society and the Neutrality of the State: The Federal Constitutional Court's Decision in the Headscarf Case' 4 (11) *German Law Journal*.

*Working Time*    Working time requirements may result in indirect discrimination against staff with religious objections to working on particular days. Although the Working Time Directive[164] does not make provision for a particular day off for staff, many states in Europe provide that the 24 hours uninterrupted rest should, in principle, be taken on a Sunday.[165] Under the Employment Equality Directive, requirements to work on particular days may be indirectly discriminatory if they cause particular difficulty for religious staff. However, such requirements may be justified.[166] It could be argued that if Sunday is recognised legally as a general day of rest, then other religious individuals should be given days off for religious observance. However, it is equally arguable that the giving of Sunday as a day off is now as much a cultural or social practice as a religious practice, even if its origin was religious.[167] Although the practice may disadvantage non-Christians, it may be that the desire to provide time off in accordance with cultural or social practices may give grounds for justification of any differential treatment of different religious groups. However, any justification must be proportionate, and where it is easy to accommodate requests to change working hours, for example where shift swaps can be made without detriment to others, it may not be proportionate to refuse a request for time off for religious observance.

## Genuine Occupational Requirments and Religious Ethos Employers

The Directive contains an exception in Article 4(1) where, because of the particular occupational activities or the context in which they are carried out, a religious characteristic is a genuine and determining occupational requirement, provided that the objective is legitimate and the requirement is proportionate. A slightly wider exception exists in Article 4(2) where the employer is a church or an organisation the ethos of which is based on religion or belief. Under this exception, religious foundations such as hospitals run with a religious ethos can require that members of staff are loyal to that ethos. This is the case even though sharing a religious belief may not be an essential requirement for carrying out the core duties of the job. Any such requirement must not entail discrimination on any other ground.

[164] Directive 2000/34 amended the original Working Time Directive (93/104/EC) to remove the requirement that the minimum rest requirement should in principle include Sunday. The original Working Time Directive was introduced as a measure to protect health and safety, and on the challenge by the UK government the ECJ held that the special protection for Sunday working could not be shown to be necessary on health and safety grounds: Case C-84/94.
[165] See the Report on the Implementation of Council Directive 93/104/EC 1 December 2000 COM (2000) 787. States requiring, in principle, Sunday as a day off include France, Germany, Spain, Luxembourg, Portugal, Finland and Italy.
[166] See discussion in the context of Great Britain at p 156 above.
[167] See the decision of the Spanish Constitutional Court (19/1985, 13 February 1985) that the consideration of Sunday as the general day of weekly rest (Art 37.1 of the Workers' Statute) is based not on a religious rule but on a secular tradition. Country Report Spain, European Network of Legal Experts in the non-discrimination field (Human European Consultancy, Migration Policy Group, 2006).

*Article 4(1)* The first level exception is not particularly controversial. It parallels the bona fide occupational requirement exceptions found in the USA and Canada, as well as in the non-discrimination provisions covering other grounds. It only applies where there is a very clear connection between the work to be done and the characteristics required: the occupational requirement must be genuine *and determining*, and it must be proportionate in the particular case involved. Under this provision religious discrimination is only really likely to be lawful in cases of those employed in religious service, whose job involves teaching or promoting the religion, or being involved in religious observance.

However, many Member States provide more extensive protection for religious employers than that provided by Article 4(1), because they exempt church bodies from the provisions of their equality legislation altogether. For example, the German Constitution separates church and state and establishes the principle of the neutrality of the state. Employers such as churches and institutions related to the church have been treated as autonomous, and so outside the protection of labour regulation; however, under the law transposing the Directives, sections 8 and 9 transpose Articles 4(1) and 4(2) directly, and so this may change. In Estonia, the Law on Employment Contracts does not apply to 'work in a religious organisation as a person conducting religious services'.[168] In the Netherlands the General Equal Treatment Act (GETA) does not apply to the internal affairs of churches, of other religious communities, or of associations of a spiritual nature. This is in order to respect the division between church and state, and to uphold the principle of freedom of religion. The restriction only concerns the internal affairs of churches. However, it means that the employment of clergy is outside the scope of the Directive's protection, and so any discrimination on grounds of sexual orientation or gender would not be subject to review.[169] Although these exemptions may have a legitimate aim, as they attempt to respect the autonomy of religious groups, the total exclusion of such cases from the consideration of the court leaves individuals unprotected, and may not be compatible with the protection provided by the Directive.

The exception under Article 4(1) does not allow for the total exemption of churches from the protection of the Directive, but instead requires that any exceptions be proportionate. This means that exceptions that apply to churches should be subject to review by courts to ensure that they are objective and reasonable. Clearly, in many cases involving the appointment of clergy or others who conduct religious services or who are involved in teaching the religion, discrimination on grounds of religion is likely to be proportionate. Courts will have regard to the clear case law of the ECtHR which protects the rights of religious groups to select their own leaders, as part of the protection due to religious groups.[170] However, it

---

[168] Art 7 Law on Employment Contracts 1992. The exception only applies if the founding document of the organisation does not require entry into an employment contract with the person.

[169] See discussion of the position in the UK at pp 139–142.

[170] '[T]he autonomous existence of religious communities is indispensable for pluralism in a democratic society and is thus an issue at the very heart of the protection which Article 9 affords': *Hasan and Chaush v Bulgaria* (2002) 34 EHRR 55 at para 62; see also *Serif v Greece* (2001) 31 EHRR 20.

is preferable to provide for review of exceptions by the Court using the standard of proportionality rather than exempting religious bodies all together, to ensure that any discrimination, particularly that based on other grounds such as gender, race, sexual orientation or disability is indeed proportionate to the legitimate aim of maintaining religious autonomy.

*Article 4(2)* Under Article 4(2) differential treatment may be allowed by religious ethos organisations, to require loyalty to the religious ethos. However, in order to comply with the Directive, such treatment must be guided by the requirements to be for a legitimate aim, and proportionate, as well as being linked to a genuine occupational requirement.

The exception contained in Article 4(2) has not been incorporated into implementing legislation in all Member States, including Belgium, France, Portugal and Sweden.[171] Although the provision of exceptions is optional under the Directive,[172] the failure to transpose Article 4(2) means that religious groups are unable to impose religious or loyalty requirements on other employees. In some cases, such as Belgium, exceptions based on Article 4(1) apply instead, where the requirements of proportionality and necessity are stricter. As a result, it may be that some degree of religious freedom is denied to religious groups, as they are unable to impose religious requirements on staff unless they are determining features of the job.

Other Member States have transposed Article 4(2) in terms that go beyond the Directive, so that religious ethos organisations are allowed to discriminate more than is allowed for under the Directive. For example, in Ireland section 37(1) of the Employment Equality Act 1998–2004 contains an exception to the non-discrimination principle for the purposes of maintaining the religious ethos of an institution. This is broader than is allowed for in the Directive, as it does not provide that religion or belief must be relevant to the particular job in question; nor does it limit the exception to discrimination based on the grounds of religion or belief so that it cannot be used to justify discrimination on another ground. As a result, the equality rights of others, particularly lesbian and gay people, are inadequately protected. Under the Directive requirements regarding sexual orientation must be genuine and determining occupational requirements, which can only be upheld where it is proportionate to do so.

In the Netherlands, Article 4(2) is transposed, but the equal treatment legislation does not apply at all to the internal affairs of churches, of other religious communities, or of associations of a spiritual nature. This restriction may accord with the Directive if the restriction to internal affairs limits discrimination to the appointment of religious staff for the purposes of teaching or practising the religion.[173] The Dutch legislation also provides an additional exception for churches and other organisations with an ethos based on religion or belief. This provides

---

[171] Also the Czech Republic, Estonia, Lithuania and Slovenia.

[172] Art 4(2) limits its exception to legislation in force at the date of adoption of the Directive, and future legislation incorporating national practices existing at the date of its adoption.

[173] See discussion of Reg 7(3) of the Sexual Orientation Regulations at pp 139–142 above.

that such organisations may discriminate where it is necessary, having regard to the institution's purpose, for the duties of the post to be fulfilled, so long as the discrimination does not lead to distinction on the sole grounds of political opinion, race, sex, nationality, heterosexual or homosexual orientation or civil status.[174] Although broadly in accordance with Article 4(2), the Dutch text does not seem to anticipate that discrimination may be on more than one ground simultaneously. For example, discrimination against an unmarried pregnant woman may be discrimination on grounds of sex, but also discrimination on grounds of religion (for example, a failure to live in accordance with the lifestyle requirements of the religion). It is, therefore, arguable that it is not on the 'sole ground' of sex, and so could be lawful under the Dutch legislation.[175] However, under the Directive such treatment would not be lawful, unless the employer can show that the sex discrimination involved is indirect and can be justified.

If the exception for religious ethos employers is to be used in accordance with the Directive, it is important that its use is limited to those cases where there is sufficient link between the religion and the job. Although religion does not have to be a defining characteristic of the job, it must still be a genuine, legitimate and justified requirement. In Denmark, where a young person was dismissed from a cleaning job in the Christian Cross Army, a Christian humanitarian organisation, it was accepted that, under Article 4, a requirement that all staff must be members of the National Lutheran Church was no longer permitted.[176] There was no genuine occupational need for cleaning work to be carried out by a member of the same religious group.

### Discrimination on Other Grounds

The effect of the genuine occupational requirements under Article 4(2) of the Directive is that religious employers may be able to create workplaces which are homogenous in religious terms, even where the work is not religious in nature. However, if discrimination on other grounds such as sex or sexual orientation results, such a practice will be in breach of the Directive, as it will amount to indirect discrimination on the other ground. An exception may be where the work itself is religious in nature. In such a case the religious requirement, which is indirectly discriminatory on other grounds, may be justified as proportionate, because of the need to uphold religious freedom.

---

[174] Art 5(2)a General Equal Treatment Act.

[175] See J Gerards, 'Implementation of the Article 13 Directives in Dutch Equal Treatment Legislation' (2006) 13 *Maastricht Journal of European and Comparative Law* 291.

[176] The case arose before the transposition of the Directive, but the Church did admit that under the Directive such discrimination against a cleaner would not be permitted. See Country Report, Denmark, European Network of Legal Experts in the non-discrimination field (Human European Consultancy, Migration Policy Group, 2006).

# IV  Conclusion

Religious interests are provided with a fairly high level of protection under the Employment Equality Directive, with protection against direct and indirect discrimination and harassment. Most of the expected exceptions are provided for religious job requirements which may be imposed by religious employers. However, none of these exceptions is absolute: there is no general exemption of religious bodies from the Directive, even in the case of clergy appointments. Of course, it is fairly inevitable that requirements for religious beliefs imposed on clergy or other religious leaders will meet the requirements of proportionality, given the strong protection for religious autonomy in Member States' legal traditions, as well as in international human rights law.

What is perhaps more significant is that the requirements of religious ethos employers more generally are protected. In contrast to the position in the USA, and some provinces of Canada, religious ethos employers can require loyalty to the religion in their staff, even where the employer is a for profit organisation, as well as where the employer is funded by the state.[177] However, the protection is not absolute, and does not amount to an exemption of religious organisation from the duty not to discriminate. In particular, the work has to have some religious element to it: religious discrimination is only lawful where there is some link between the work and the religious ethos of the organisation. It will be difficult for organisations to argue that all staff are covered by the exception, unless they are in some way involved in transmitting the ethos of the organisation. Moreover, it will be particularly difficult to argue that religious discrimination in these circumstances can justify any other form of discrimination such as discrimination on grounds of sexual orientation or gender.

Unlike the protection in North America, there is no duty to accommodate in the EU model. However, such a duty may be understood to form part of the protection provided through the concept of indirect discrimination. A failure to accommodate may be recast as the imposition of a requirement to conform, which must then be justified. As has been seen, any additional protection for religious interests provided by a duty to accommodate is only strong if that duty cannot be easily overridden. The ease with which the US 'undue hardship' standard can be met makes the protection fairly weak. The Canadian duty is stronger, as 'undue hardship' is harder to show. The level of protection provided does not necessarily depend on the legal framework: whether there is a duty to accommodate or a duty not to discriminate indirectly, the strength of the protection will be determined by the scope of the proportionality review.

---

[177] Where the employer is the state it may be difficult to say that it is a religious ethos organisation: *Glasgow City Council v McNab* UKEAT/0037/06. However, the position may not be the same where the employer is a religious organisation, but funding is received from the state (eg, a voluntary aided school, or a religious partnership running an NHS funded medical practice).

In its basic provisions, the protection provided in other jurisdictions is largely similar to that provided in the EU. However, the differences can be seen in the provisions protecting religious employers. In Canada the protection is broader, with religious employers protected in some provinces even where they discriminate on other grounds. In the USA religious employers cannot discriminate on grounds of religion, let alone on other grounds, where they are operating in the ordinary commercial marketplace. In the EU religious employers can discriminate on grounds of religion in order to maintain their ethos, but not when to do so discriminates on others grounds. The provision of protection for religious ethos employers in the EU reflects the practice across large numbers of Member States of providing public services through religious bodies, in particular in the provision of health care and education. While the protection of the interests of religious employers under the Directive may reflect this social and political context, the Directive also imposes an important restriction against discrimination by requiring that any religious discrimination practised by such organisations be proportionate. This provides a good balance between the religious interests of employers and employees, and the economic and equality interests of others.

These different approaches to the protection of religious employers' interests may reflect slightly different views of how a plural society should take shape. Canada's system has been termed a 'mosaic', with separate groups making up a whole. Groups can retreat from mainstream society to create 'islands of exclusivity' from which they can exclude those with different views. This pluralist vision involves space for all, including those who do not tolerate others. In the religious sphere, groups can operate in an exclusive manner, without being required to provide employment for those of other religions or lifestyles.[178] In contrast, the USA has been termed a 'melting pot' with groups being encouraged to mix. Those who choose to run a business along religious lines cannot discriminate against others on grounds of religion.[179] The EU approach seems to take something of a middle course: groups can remain separate, but only so far as they do not infringe the other equality rights. By allowing religious ethos employers to use religion as a criterion in employment decisions, but subjecting its use to scrutiny using the proportionality equation, the protection provided by the Directive largely meets the requirements recommended in chapter three's model for protection of religious interests at work.

---

[178] Esau, above n 80.
[179] *Townley Engineering* above n 27.

# 7

## Conclusion:
## Religious Freedom at Work

The right to freedom of religion is clearly recognised as a fundamental human right in European and international law. Its protection is based on the idea that freedom of thought, conscience and belief are necessary for the upholding of human autonomy and dignity. It is viewed as one of the foundations of a 'democratic society', and as one of the 'most vital elements that go to make up the identity of believers and their conception of life'.[1] The purpose of this book has been to explore the practical scope of that right in the particular context of the workplace, and in the light of the Regulations protecting against work-based discrimination on grounds of religion or belief. It has been suggested that despite the importance of religious freedom as a fundamental human right, its protection in the work context should be limited, because of its complex and contested interaction with the rights of others, whether they be employers, or those outside the religious group.

Formulating a response to the inherent conflicts arising between religious interests and other interests with which religion may conflict presents singular challenges. The suggestion has been made that a model for the accommodation of religious interests at work be developed, with a view to establishing some form of equilibrium between conflicting rights, based on the notion of proportionality. Thus in assessing whether the right to religious freedom should prevail over competing interests, the religious interest should be weighed against other interests such as the need to uphold equality, to protect freedom from religion, and to protect other human rights such as privacy and freedom of speech. The assessment of proportionality should also take into account matters such as the equality interests of service users, the freedom of religion of other members of staff, the right to freedom from religion for customers and colleagues, and an interest in religious neutrality for the employer. Where the balance lies may depend in part on the status of the employer, for example, whether it has a religious ethos, whether it is part of the public or the private sector, and whether it is has a monopoly on providing particular types of employment.

This proportionality-based model for the protection of religious interests at work is effectively a procedural mechanism which should enable courts and

[1] *Kokkinakis v Greece* [1993] 17 EHRR 397 para 31.

tribunals to reach reasoned decisions on where the balance should lie in cases involving conflicting rights. Its flexibility allows it to be responsive to the seemingly infinite range of interests at stake: the interests of religious and secular employers and employees, customers and service users; and the interests of the state in upholding equality and promoting social inclusion as well as religious pluralism and tolerance. The interests of all groups can be taken into account in assessing proportionality, enabling a careful and responsive standard to develop for creating an equilibrium between competing and conflicting interests.

The proportionality model is also compatible with the legal approaches taken to the protection of religious interests at work in the UK as well as in the USA and Canada. Although the legal framework for protection differs, all three jurisdictions ultimately engage in an assessment of the proportionality of restrictions on religious freedom and exceptions to the right not to be discriminated against on grounds of religion. It is suggested that in assessing proportionality the range of factual and contextual issues identified in chapter three should be taken into account.

Although they are all compatible with the proportionality model, the North American models do differ from the European model in that they impose on employers a duty to accommodate religion.[2] The question therefore arises of whether the imposition on employers of an explicit duty to accommodate religion is a preferable model for protection, in contrast to the European approach.

# I A Duty of Reasonable Accommodation?

The Religion and Belief Regulations are limited to protection against direct and indirect discrimination,[3] and they do not impose a specific duty on employers to make reasonable accommodation for the needs of religious employees. The concept of reasonable accommodation is one that is used in other jurisdictions to protect against religious discrimination, as well as forming part of the protection against disability discrimination in the UK. The main difference between a reasonable accommodation duty and non-discrimination is that with reasonable accommodation the onus is on the employer to accommodate the individual employment needs of religious individuals. Such a duty has the potential to create greater protection for religious interests at work, as well as being able to overcome the difficulties caused by the focus in indirect discrimination on group disadvantage.[4] It also reflects the fact that full protection of religious interests requires both religious identity and religious manifestation to be protected.[5]

---

[2] This is explicit in the USA and in some provinces of Canada. In other Canadian provinces, the duty of accommodation forms part of the assessment of whether there is a bona fide occupational exception to the non-discrimination principle. See discussion in ch 6 above.

[3] As well as victimisation and harassment.

[4] See discussion at p 129ff above.

[5] See discussion at p 41 above.

A duty to accommodate religion was developed in the USA after it was recognised that protection was needed for religious practice or observance, as well as belief. In order to protect religious practice, a level of accommodation is required. The Civil Rights Act of 1964 was amended in 1972 to include a duty on the employer to accommodate the religious practices of employees, as long as to do so would not cause undue hardship to the employer.[6] Common accommodations are rescheduling work to allow for time off for religious observance, and amendments to uniform or grooming rules to allow for religious dress codes.

Development of the duty of reasonable accommodation in Britain would be consistent with the concept of equality recognised by the ECtHR in *Thlimmenos v Greece.*[7] Here it was accepted that treatment can be unequal because those in the same situation are treated differently, or because those who are different are treated the same. Failure to accommodate difference therefore amounts to unequal treatment, because it amounts to a refusal to treat different people differently.

The concept of accommodation is already part of domestic disability discrimination law, with its duty on employers to make reasonable adjustments to the workplace. This recognises the fact that changes to the workplace to allow full participation by disabled people will be very individualised. The focus therefore needs to be on adapting workplaces to the individual needs of disabled people. As with the variety of experiences of disability, religious practices can vary widely, and so a personalised duty of reasonable accommodation for religious needs may well be thought an appropriate way forward to improve the protection of religious interests at work.

Although introducing a duty of reasonable accommodation in the UK was suggested by the Independent Review of the Enforcement of UK Anti-Discrimination Legislation,[8] there are some problems with the model as an alternative to the current indirect discrimination model of protection. The first is an argument that has been levelled at the disability discrimination model, namely, that a focus on accommodating the individual disabled person enables employers to be reactive in their response to disability, rather than addressing structural causes of discrimination. Employers can wait until they have a disabled employee and then look for adjustments. Stronger protection is provided if employers have to ensure in advance that practices are not causing disadvantage. In the context of religious

---

[6] 'The term "religion" includes all aspects of religious observance and practice, as well as belief, unless an employer demonstrates that he is unable to reasonably accommodate to an employee's or prospective employee's religious observance or practice without undue hardship on the conduct of the employer's business.' 42 USCA § 2000e j.

[7] (2001) 31 EHRR 15. Note, however, that the case law of Art 9 ECHR does not impose a duty to accommodate religion at work. See *Ahmad v UK* (1981) 4 EHRR 126 and *Stedman v UK* (1997) 23 EHRR CD168, both confirmed in *Kosteski v 'The Former Yugoslav Republic of Macedonia'* 55170/00 [2006] ECHR 403, discussed in ch 4.

[8] B Hepple, M Coussey and T Choudhury, *Equality: A New Framework—The Report of the Independent Review of the Enforcement of UK Anti-Discrimination Legislation* (Oxford, Hart Publishing, 2000).

discrimination, a focus on accommodating individual religious needs can mean that underlying causes of religious disadvantage can be left unaddressed.

An alternative set of objections can be found from a totally different standpoint, based on the concern that a duty of reasonable accommodation may provide too much protection for religious interests.[9] Accommodating religious personnel may involve a level of positive action in favour of religious individuals, and this could amount to a detriment to others, especially if other staff are required to change their working practices. This may cause particularly complex problems given that those who lack a particular belief are protected by the Regulations equally with those who hold the belief. In effect, any accommodation of one religious view-point has the potential to be interpreted as discrimination against those of another.[10] Imposing a duty to accommodate religious interests may involve the immediate creation of a corresponding disadvantage for others. Thus, for example, accommodating one person's need to have leave on a Sunday imposes on others the disadvantage of restricted availability of leave.

One way to reduce the potentially onerous nature of a duty of accommodation is to impose a low threshold for justifying any failure to accommodate. In the USA[11] the standard is indeed low. The duty is to accommodate religion unless to do so will cause 'undue hardship'. This has been interpreted as anything more than de mimimis hardship, and has meant that matters such as economic cost, inconvenience and even complaints from other workers[12] can be used to show that accommodation would cause 'undue hardship'. Such 'costs' would be unlikely to justify indirect sex discrimination. The standard of justification in sex discrimination cases can be contrasted with the justification of disability discrimination, where financial and other costs can be taken into account in considering whether the burden of accommodation is proportionate.

At first sight a duty to accommodate religion which is overridden as soon as there is any hardship caused may not seem to be very satisfactory as a form of protection for religious interests at work, and certainly may not appear to provide any advantages over protection based on indirect discrimination. However, such a duty is not entirely empty even if the level of hardship to be shown before it is overridden is low. In effect, such a duty requires that an employer makes an attempt to accommodate. Hardship must be actual hardship, even if set at a de minimis level,

---

[9]  R Allen and G Moon, 'Substantive Rights and Equal Treatment in Respect of Religion and Belief: Towards a Better Understanding of the Rights, and their Implications' (2000) *EHRLR* 580, 601. Such concerns could mean that courts are more conservative in other interpretations, such as of the meaning of religion, in order to protect employers from onerous duties of accommodation.

[10]  This argument arose in Ireland in case law on the constitutional protection of religion. In *Quinn's Supermarket v Attorney General* [1972] IR 1 it was argued that special exemption for Jewish kosher butchers from the Sunday trading laws was discriminatory against non-Jewish shop keepers. The argument was not accepted, and the exception was upheld on the basis that it was necessary adequately to protect the freedom of religion of the Jewish community.

[11]  See ch 6 for more detailed discussion of the US position.

[12]  *Trans World Airlines v Hardison* 432 US 63; (1976) *Turpen v Mo-Kan-Tex RR Co* 736 F 2d 1022, 1027.

not merely hypothetical.[13] This means that the employer cannot rely, for example, on the fact that other staff might become unhappy, leading to deteriorating morale, if a particular accommodation is made, but must show that they will in fact be unhappy. In effect, the duty of reasonable accommodation puts the onus on employers to show that they have thought about trying to accommodate and have real reasons why to do so would be difficult. Such a duty does not lead to extensive protection for religious staff, and thus does not cause too many clashes with the rights of others. If another's rights are infringed this probably provides grounds not to accommodate. If, however, another's rights might only hypothetically be infringed, it does not.

The protection of religious interests at work through the creation of a duty to accommodate where to do so does not cause undue hardship could therefore create an adequate level of protection for religious interests, whilst giving space to employers to find an appropriate and proportionate balance between the competing rights at work. Had the Regulations and their parent Employment Equality Directive used a model of 'reasonable accommodation', this might have been a useful vehicle for protecting against religious discrimination. As with disability discrimination, it allows for an individualised approach to providing protection, and ensures that religious staff can only be disadvantaged where there is a real reason to do so. However, it also provides the potential for a fair balance to be struck between the interests of all staff, some of which are not capable of reconciliation, and for the range of interests and contextual issues identified in chapter three above to be taken into account in assessing whether an accommodation can be required as reasonable.

It may well be that the indirect discrimination provisions of the Regulations amount in practice to a duty of reasonable accommodation: a failure to accommodate a request for different treatment by religious employees may amount to indirect discrimination, unless the refusal to accommodate can be justified. For example, employees whose requests that a work uniform be adapted to accommodate religious practice are refused would suffer indirect discrimination. The employer's requirement that staff wear the uniform would put religious members of staff at a particular disadvantage, and the requirement would need to be justified.

It may thus be possible to interpret indirect discrimination to impose a duty on employers to make reasonable accommodation for religion. Given the structure of protection that was created by the Religion and Belief Regulations and the Employment Equality Directive, the most appropriate level of protection for religious interests at work is likely to be achieved by developing indirect discrimination to include a duty of reasonable accommodation, on the basis that a failure to accommodate will amount to the imposition of a requirement which disadvantages the applicant, and which the employer must show to be justified. It remains

---

[13]   *EEOC v Alamo Rent-A-Car* 26 May 2006; *Opuku-Boateng v California* 95 F 3d 1461, 1473–74 (9th Cir 1996).

open to the employee to show that the general justification does not apply to her case. This interpretation of indirect discrimination enables the concept of discrimination, created with the aim of gaining equality for groups, to be adapted to provide an individualised level of protection. The test of proportionality would then need to be interpreted in a nuanced way, taking into account the various contextual issues and competing interests detailed in chapter three. In effect, the Regulations could be interpreted in a similar way to the protection in some Canadian provinces where a failure to accommodate means that there is no bona fide occupational requirement to provide an exception to the non-discrimination rule. In the context of the Regulations, the effect would be that indirect discrimination would not be justifiable where the employer has failed to make a reasonable accommodation. The assessment of whether a failure to accommodate was reasonable would be determined by considering whether it was proportionate.

Although the Regulations may be capable of interpretation to create an implicit duty of accommodation, the fact that this is the creation of statutory interpretation rather then being an explicit duty has two disadvantages. The first relates to the burden of proof. The employee's burden of proof may be easier to fulfil in relation to a duty to accommodate than in relation to indirect discrimination. In the case of *Cadman*[14] the issue of the burden of proof in sex discrimination cases was discussed in detail and, given the desire of the ECJ to have a unified approach to the treatment of equality concerns,[15] the same approach is likely to apply in cases of religious discrimination. The question for consideration in *Cadman* was essentially: if an employee can show a disparate impact, but the employer can justify the practice in general, is that the end of the case, or is it open to the employee to argue that the justification does not apply in her individual case? The ECJ ruled that even where there is a general justification, it remains open to the employee to show that the justification does not apply to the particular case. In effect, if the individual can show that particular personal hardship has been caused by a rule which, in general terms, can be justified, it may be possible to argue that there is indirect discrimination on the basis that the general justification does not apply to the particular case. However, there is a heavy burden of proof on the employee, who must first show disparate impact. Although the burden then shifts to the employer to justify, it returns to the employee to show that the general justification does not apply to her case.

In contrast, with a duty of reasonable accommodation, the burden is instead on the employer to show that any accommodation would create unreasonable hardship. Thus the burden on the employee to prove the case would be easier. However, the ease of proof which the duty of reasonable accommodation could provide for the employee will be counter-balanced by the fact that the standard of justification for reasonable accommodation is far lower than that available for indirect discrimination.

---

[14] [2006] IRLR 969.
[15] See *Chacón Navas v Eurest Colectividades SA* (2006) C-13/05 discussed at p 133 above.

A second disadvantage to relying on interpretation of indirect discrimination, rather than the creation of a separate duty to accommodate religion and belief, is that it makes it more difficult to develop different standards of protection for religion than for some other grounds. Although the creation of different standards of protection for different strands of equality offends against the view that there should be no hierarchy as between grounds of discrimination, this view becomes less sustainable the more one considers the contested nature of many of the interests at stake. Moreover, the danger of keeping one set of provisions for the protection of sex and race discrimination alongside religious discrimination is that any restrictions placed on the scope of religious discrimination provisions may work to 'level down' the protection from discrimination on other grounds. It would be unfortunate if a decision that economic cost can justify religious discrimination were to result in a finding that the same were true of sex or race discrimination. The fact that cost can also justify disability discrimination does not run the same danger, because of the different framework of the protection: reasonable adjustment rather than indirect discrimination. Hence the creation of a special framework to protect the religious interests of employees based on a duty of accommodation might be a preferable way to protect religious interests at work.

## II  Protecting Religious Work

Apart from the challenge of protecting the interests of religious employees at work, the other dimension to the interaction of religious freedom and the workplace involves religious employers, or to use the terminology of the Directive, organisations with a religious ethos. The problem here is that the collective aspect of the right to freedom of religion may be engaged when religious ethos organisations wish to use the employment relationship to regulate their relationships. Where the relationship being regulated is that of an individual who officiates at religious ceremonies, it is fairly clear that the religious interests of the group are served by allowing it significant freedom of choice. To require a religious group to employ anyone other than a co-religionist in any teaching or leadership position would offend the right to religious freedom enjoyed by the group.

Moreover, it is also clear that for jobs with a religious nature it may be proportionate to allow some level of religious discrimination to enable a religious employer to create a religiously homogenous workplace.[16] Things become more complex when the religious beliefs of the group mean that employing someone who shares the beliefs may involve discriminating on other grounds. In most cases, discrimination against others, motivated by religion, will not be proportionate. However, a case has been made for allowing some limited space for religious

---

[16] See discussion at pp 135–138.

groups to discriminate, where the impact on others is limited.[17] In effect, it has been suggested that where religious individuals wish to retreat from mainstream society, and work in a religious ethos organisation, they may be able to exclude those with different views.[18] This allows for the protection of the religious freedom of individuals, who retain the freedom to regulate the provision of services within the group through the employment relationship. In effect, this will allow groups to operate in an exclusive manner, without being required to provide employment for those of other religions or lifestyles. Any exception to the general non-discrimination principle must be proportionate and, given the strength of the general principle, it is unlikely to be proportionate in many cases. However, in the context of, for example, the appointment of a church administrator, caterer or children's work co-ordinator, it may be proportionate to allow religious discrimination by the organisation even though this results in indirect discrimination against others, because of the self-serving or inward-looking nature of the employment.[19] Where the group interacts with the rest of society, such as by providing services to the public, they can be expected to conform to the norms of the rest of society in terms of respect for the dignity and autonomy of others. Whether or not a particular case of discrimination is proportionate will depend on all the factors identified in chapter three, but the fact that at times some level of discrimination may be proportionate illustrates the importance of considering the religious rights of the individual and the group alongside the deliberation on the scope of non-discrimination rights. The relationship between the two concepts, freedom of religion and non-discrimination, was discussed in detail in chapter three; both were said to be based fundamentally on the same concepts, a respect for individuals' essential autonomy, dignity and equality. Interpreting the legal duty not to discriminate in the employment area on grounds of religion and belief, taking due account of the right of all people to freedom of religion and belief, in both its positive and negative aspects, is possible, but only if a detailed proportionality review is undertaken. Again, the concept of proportionality is the tool by which a reconciliation of conflicting interests is sought to be achieved.

## III  Remaining Difficulties

It has been suggested that protection of religious interests at work can best be achieved by a two-fold approach: the creation of a duty on employers to make reasonable accommodation of religion unless to do so causes undue hardship; together with some limited protection for religious employers who wish to create

---

[17] See discussion at pp 138–139.

[18] A Esau, ' "Islands of Exclusivity": Religious Organizations and Employment Discrimination' (1993) 33 *Univ British Columbia LR* 719.

[19] See S Wessels, 'The Collision of Religious Exercise and Governmental Nondiscrimination Policies' (1989) 41 *Stanford LR* 1201.

religiously homogenous workplaces. However, further underlying difficulties remain with this approach to reconciling religious and other interests at work. The continuing presence of difficulty is inherent in the subject matter, not least because of the coexistence of a positive and a negative aspect to religious interests. In effect, the right to freedom of religion encompasses a corresponding right to be free to have no religion or to be free from religion. This means that an equilibrium or 'practical concordancy'[20] needs to be found between the rights of those who wish to practise their faith, and those who wish to be free from such practices. It is suggested here that the way to deal with this inherent conflict is though the procedural mechanism of proportionality, and certainly this is the standard legal response to this type of difficulty. However, its use leaves in place at least two remaining difficulties. First is the problem of consistency as between different strands of equality law, and as between different states relying on the same protective framework. The second is that the use of proportionality lends a false objectivity to the judgments made, and masks the fact that ultimately the decisions are based on the subjective opinion of the decision-maker. These difficulties will be considered in turn.

## False Consistency?

In practical terms, the benefit of an approach based on proportionality is that it allows for contextual interpretation which can take into account all the circumstances, including, for example, the socio-political context in which the discrimination occurs. However, this leaves the problem of consistency as between different strands of discrimination or equality law. In effect, having such a flexible concept at the heart of the protection for religious interests allows a hierarchy to develop as between grounds of discrimination. For example, as has been noted above, sex discrimination can rarely be justified on the basis of economic cost, and yet using the proportionality model advocated here might allow economic cost to justify indirect religious discrimination.

The creation of a 'hierarchy' of equality rights is something which was warned against in the Commission's 'Explanatory Memorandum' to the Directives.[21] It has also been suggested in case law from the ECJ that a unified approach to the treatment of equality concerns is desirable.[22] Hierarchies between different strands of discrimination can be difficult to justify, not least because they create particular difficulties in relation to multiple discrimination.

However, although hierarchies may develop as between different grounds, this may in fact not be too problematic. In fact, McCrudden has argued that the search

---

[20] The phrase comes from German constitutional law: classroom crucifix case, BVerfGE 93, 1, 1 BvR 1087/91.

[21] *Proposal for a Council Directive: Establishing a General Framework for Equal Treatment in Employment and Occupation* COM (1999) 565 final, 6

[22] See *Chacón Navas v Eurest Colectividades SA* (2006) C-13/05.

for consistency and the removal of hierarchy may hinder the proper development of equality law. He argues that there is a danger in attempting to create 'false consistency'[23] as between grounds, as this can mask a range of differences between the different grounds. The theoretical justification for protecting against discrimination may differ, as well as the socio-political context in which the discrimination occurs. Levels of historical and current disadvantage, and levels of social exclusion experienced by the different groups, will also differ. To seek consistency and to rule out hierarchy would be to ignore these fundamental differences, and may lead to alternative disadvantages to replace those removed.

A number of suggestions have been made about ways in which the grounds of discrimination are inherently different, which may justify the development of a degree of hierarchy as between them. For example, it is arguable that some grounds (gender, race, sexual orientation) are truly irrelevant to a person's ability to undertake work, while other grounds are relevant some of the time, because they may either limit availability to do a job (pregnancy, religion) or may limit ability to perform a job (disability, age). Thus treating different strands differently may be acceptable.[24] Other differences exist between the grounds in terms of whether the characteristics are biological differences (sex, age), ascriptive differences (ethnicity), or chosen characteristics (arguably sexual orientation and religion,[25] although the question of whether these latter characteristics are chosen is clearly contentious).[26] The fact that distinctions can be drawn between the different grounds does suggest that discrimination is not all equal, and that hierarchies may not only be inevitable but may also be acceptable.

Hierarchies are also likely to be inevitable given the variety which exists in the understanding of what is meant by equality. Equality has been understood to have a variety of meanings, including the individual justice model, the group justice model, equality as recognition of individual dignity, and equality as a means of addressing social exclusion.[27] The regulatory framework of the Directive does not reflect a single coherent approach. For example, as a framework for achieving individual justice it fails on a number of fronts, such as its lack of a mechanism to deal with intersectional or multiple discrimination. In terms of group justice, the positive discrimination provisions may be useful, but the symmetrical model of protection created may reduce its potential to act as a strong tool in achieving group justice. However, it may be that no single understanding of equality can be complete, given the range of meanings it can have, and so different grounds of discrimination may fit better with different understandings of equality. Again, hierarchy may be both an inevitable and an acceptable response.

---

[23] C McCrudden, 'Thinking about the Discrimination Directives' (2005) 1 *European Anti-Discrimination Law Review* 17.

[24] M Bell and L Waddingon, 'Reflecting on inequalities in European equality law' (2003) 28 *EL Rev* 349.

[25] For example, D Schiek, 'European Union: A new framework on equal treatment of persons in EC law?' (2002) 8 *European LJ* 290.

[26] See the discussion at pp 30–31 above.

[27] See C Barnard and B Hepple, 'Substantive Equality' (2000) 59 *CLJ* 562, and H Collins, 'Discrimination, Equality and Social Inclusion' (2003) 66 *MLR* 16.

Assuming that it is acceptable to treat different grounds of discrimination differently, then it is unnecessary to provide for interchangeable interpretation of similar terms used in relation to the different grounds of discrimination. For example, indirect discrimination on any ground is acceptable where it is justified as proportionate in pursuit of a legitimate aim. If consistency is not required as between grounds, then an aim which is potentially justifiable for religious discrimination does not have to be similarly justifiable for sex discrimination. Thus, economic cost could justify indirect religious discrimination but not indirect sex or race discrimination.

Similarly, the proportionality concept is flexible enough to take into account the different contexts in which religious discrimination may occur across Europe. The development of the interpretation of the Regulations will to a certain extent be driven by the case law which develops in the European Court of Justice, to which appeals under the parent Directive can be taken. Consistency in approach can be achieved by using the concept of proportionality, even though the factual outcome may not be uniform across the EU. For example, a decision to allow workers to wear a headscarf at work may be proportionate in one country, but not in another, if the full national political, social and historical context is taken into account. Thus courts can consistently require employers to act proportionately, without dictating the factual outcome of cases. The model of protection based on proportionality is flexible enough to take these issues into account, and it should be allowed to do so.

## False Objectivity?

It has been suggested throughout this book that the answer to the complexities involved in gauging the proper protection for religious interests is to be found in the concept of proportionality. Thus, where equilibrium is sought between a right to manifest religion at work and the rights of the employer to run the business as he or she thinks fit, the answer has been to determine whether it is proportionate to restrict religion given full examination of all the relevant factors. Or where a balance is to be found between the rights of colleagues to be free from religion at work, and the rights of a member of staff to proselytise, the answer has been to determine the proportionality of any restriction on religious expression taking into account a wide range of contextual issues. In effect, the concept of proportionality is made to do all the work in determining the proper outcome.

One difficulty with this approach is that it is open to the charge that it is too vague and uncertain a concept to be useful. Certainly the approach is fact-dependent, and therefore cannot lead to the development of clear and simple precedent. The answer to a simple question such as 'do employees have a right to refuse to work on Saturdays?' is, in effect, the stereotypical lawyer's answer of 'it depends'. Of course, it depends on a huge variety of factors, and it may be that those with legal training will be able to make a good prediction as to how proportionality would be determined. However, it remains difficult for an employer or employee to determine in advance, and without legal advice, whether it is acceptable to refuse a request to miss work on a particular day, for example.

An even more serious charge can be levelled at the reliance on proportionality to do the work of determining the proper parameters of legal protection for religious interests at work. This is that the test is ultimately a subjective one: in effect, 'it depends' becomes 'it depends on the personal view of the individuals who make up the court hearing the case'. The fact that many and varied factors can be identified to feed in to the consideration of proportionality may only work to create a false sense of objectivity, and may mask the fact that the judgment is ultimately personal and subjective. The danger here is more serious than merely a lack of predictability, serious as that is. A false sense of objectivity runs the danger of perpetuating precisely the disadvantage which the creation of legal protection for religious interests was designed to prevent. For example, it may be proportionate, depending on the circumstances, to restrict the wearing of a headscarf at work, even though this perpetuates the social exclusion of Muslim women. In some circumstances it will be proportionate to uphold a Christian's request not to work on Sunday, and then to reject the Muslim's request to work reduced hours on a Friday.[28] The fact that these decisions are so fact-sensitive, and dependent on the context in which the requests are made, can leave the law open to the charge that the decisions merely reflect the personal views and political opinions of those who judge them, even though they are dressed up in the objective language of proportionality.

These are powerful arguments, and it may well be that the determination of proportionality can never be fully objective.[29] The model of proportionality advocated here takes into account so many interests that it is becomes difficult to determine the 'right' answer; outcomes will always be open to the charge that they reflect the personal agendas of those who determine them. However, it may be that in the absence of anything better, a reliance on proportionality provides the best answer, even if it cannot be proved, objectively, to be the 'right' answer.[30]

Yet it is arguable that a reliance on proportionality to do the work of setting the parameters for the protection of religious interests is more than a flawed option taken in the absence of anything better. Although not perfectly objective, it is also far from totally subjective. The range of factors suggested to be used to determine proportionality is not a random choice, but the result of careful consideration of the range of competing interests at stake and the theoretical reasons for protecting the interests at all. Not every interest was said to be relevant: for example, the inter-

---

[28] For example, it may be that in a particular workplace shift swaps are possible for a reduced Sunday workforce, but that a full complement of staff is required on a Friday.

[29] See D Beatty, *The Ultimate Rule of Law* (Oxford, OUP, 2004) for a sustained argument that proportionality can enable impartial and objective methods of judicial review to occur. However, powerful though his arguments are, they ultimately seem to rely on his own assessment that where proportionality is used the 'right' answer has been found.

[30] See J E Fulcher, 'Using a Contextual Methodology to Accommodate Equality Protections along with the Other Objectives of Government (with Particular Reference to the Income Tax Act): "Not the Right Answer, Stupid. The Best Answer" ' (1996) 34 *Alta LR* 416.

est in not being subject to bare offence was said not to be suitable for inclusion.[31] Thus the proportionality model does more than just create a list of every factor which might possibly be relevant: it relies instead on reasoned and principled analysis to determine which factors are relevant.

Moreover, a purely subjective test would not be open to challenge, whereas the creation of a range of interests and contextual factors to take into account in determining proportionality does allow scope for decisions to be tested. Requiring any limits on the equality principle to be subject to the test of proportionality means that the decisions must be open, and the factors which were relevant subject to review. Although ultimately courts may allow for an area of discretion in the final outcome, this does allow for challenge to be made if an important factor has been left out of the proportionality equation. Thus a determination that an individual cannot take time off work for prayer must be proportionate taking into account not only the needs of the business but also the individual's interest in religious freedom. Failure to take into account the religious interests of the employee may mean that a disproportionate decision is made. This does not mean that the employer must explicitly go through the criteria for the decision to be proportionate. Instead, the focus should be on the proportionality of the outcome. Thus a tribunal hearing a religious discrimination case will need to determine whether the employer has reached a proportionate decision, taking into account the various relevant factors, not necessarily whether the employer itself has taken the factors into account explicitly.[32]

Finally, although this may seem a somewhat negative reason for advocating the proportionality approach, it may well be that to argue for more certainty, instead of relying on the elusive proportionality test, would result in inferior protection for religious interests. Certainly, more clarity would be achieved if decisions could be made in more definite terms as to which employment rights individuals should have, either by legislation or by guidelines established by courts when interpreting the legislation. For example, there could be a right to wear the headscarf, together with a right to a given time off for prayer, an agreed number of days off work for religious observance, and a right to conscientious objection to undertaking particular tasks which conflict with religious beliefs. Of course, such rights would have some exceptions, so that reasonable notice of the need for time off would need to be given, and health and safety exceptions to changes in dress codes could be allowed. However, the approach would be based on enumerating clear entitlements to particular accommodations of religion which are relevant to the workplace. The obvious benefit is the clarity which is created: employers and employees would know their entitlement.

The main disadvantage to such an approach is that, almost certainly, the range of rights created by such a process would be very restricted. Certainty could only be achieved if there were no 'depending on the circumstances' or 'proportionality'

---

[31] See discussion at p 62ff.
[32] This was the approach of the House of Lords in *R (on the application of Begum (Shabina)) v Denbigh High School Governors* [2006] UKHL 15.

limitation, and this would mean that any court or legislature would be very wary of creating such rights. For example, faced with deciding whether or not employees have a 'right' to wear a headscarf, courts are likely to decide that there is no such right. They may be happy to protect the right for some employees to wear a headscarf, in some circumstances, but faced with a choice of a right in all circumstances or no right they are likely to make a more conservative decision that there is no such right. The factors which are relevant to the question have been considered in detail elsewhere, but their range makes very clear that the matter is complex, and it may be that in some cases or contexts such a right should not be given.[33] Creating certainty does have some benefits, but it is likely to result in more limited protection, as courts or legislatures will be wary of creating concrete rights on such a contested and challenging issue. It is one thing to say that it is proportionate as a matter of employment law to allow a female Muslim employee to wear the headscarf to work in a particular case. It is another to say that all employees have a legal right to wear the headscarf.

The unwillingness to create concrete rights in relation to religious freedom can be seen in the approach of the ECHR to cases involving Article 9. Where the right to religious freedom is absolute, with regard to the right to believe,[34] the ECtHR and the Commission have been very restrictive in their interpretations, invariably deciding that religious rights are not applicable to the workplace. The cases in which rights have been found to apply in the work context have been those where the rights are not absolute, such as cases involving Article 8 and Article 10. It is perhaps unsurprising that courts are wary of creating absolute rights, because of the need to balance rights where they conflict with each other. Where courts are considering rights to privacy and free speech, the rights as protected by the ECHR include a proportionality limit. In contrast, religion in the pure form of a right to hold beliefs is enjoyed absolutely. To enable an absolute right to be exercised in the workplace would put in jeopardy a number of other interests—not only the rights of non-believers, but also the ability of employers to take positive action aimed at redressing disadvantage suffered by religious groups.[35] Thus the absolute nature of the *forum internum* rights under Article 9, where no balancing can be undertaken with competing rights, have led to very restrictive interpretations of the right.

It seems, then, that if certainty is required in relation to religious rights in the workplace, any rights created will be likely to be extremely limited and restrictive. The best chance for religious interests to be given protection is if the rights are flexible and can be interpreted to take into account the interests of others. In effect, an approach based on proportionality provides clear procedural safeguards, to ensure that restrictions on religious freedom, and exceptions to the non-discrimination principle, are only imposed after proper consideration of the varied interests at stake.

---

[33] Discussed at pp 158–164.

[34] It is only the right to manifest religious belief that is limited in Art 9(2).

[35] See discussion of *Re Parsons*, above at pp 95–96.

Although an approach based on proportionality may be open to the charge that it masks an inherent subjectivity, and fails to give sufficient certainty to employers and employees, it remains the best way to protect religious interests in the work context. The alternative, more certain, approach based on the creation of specific enumerated rights would almost inevitably result in more limited protection.

# IV  Conclusion

Examples given in the opening chapter demonstrated that religious discrimination in the workplace is a reality for many people. The search for an appropriate way to address the injustice which results has included an examination of the philosophical underpinnings of the right to freedom of religion, and the relationship between that right and the right not to be discriminated against on grounds of religion. The conclusion reached was that there are strong reasons for protecting religious freedom, based on equality, autonomy and human dignity, and that a right not to be discriminated co-exists with and supports the right to freedom of religion and belief.

The fact that religious freedom and non-discrimination can be shown to be necessary to protect equality, autonomy and dignity does not lead inevitably to the conclusion that religion should be protected at work. This is because religious interests can, alternatively, be protected through the freedom to resign or abstain from work: individuals may have a right to freedom of religion, but they do not necessarily have a right to a given job. In effect, any assessment of the level of protection that should be afforded to religious interests in the work sphere must be carried out in the light of the 'right to resign'. However, to limit protection of religion to the world outside work would be to severely limit the protection of religious interests in practice, and would mean that the religious inequalities identified in chapter one will persist. If freedom of religion and belief is to be given meaningful protection in practice, resignation should remain the residual protection, to be used where accommodation of the religious interest at work is inappropriate, rather than the starting (and swift ending) point for the provision of protection.

The difficulty in determining the proper parameters for protection arises from the conflict which can arise between religious interests and other interests, conflict which may stem from the positive and negative nature of religious rights. These conflicts present significant challenges, and interact with broader debates on equality, multiculturalism, and religious, political and social identity. Yet while the wider legal, political and philosophical debates continue, the Religion and Belief Regulations are in force and need to be applied. What is offered here is a methodology to mediate and resolve disputes in the employment sphere, based on a reasoned and reflexive notion of proportionality. The aim has been to find some form of equilibrium whereby religious individuals can enjoy a meaningful level of protection at work, without unduly interfering with the rights of others. Protection based on proportionality offers the best chance of developing a culture of 'respectful pluralism'[36] in the modern workplace, where religious interests are accommodated as part of a broader protection for equality, autonomy and dignity at work.

[36] D A Hicks, (Cambridge/New York, CUP, 2003).

# Index